T0184262

Lecture Notes in Computer Science 12609

Founding Editors

Gerhard Goos
Karlsruhe Institute of Technology, Karlsruhe, Germany
Juris Hartmanis
Cornell University, Ithaca, NY, USA

Editorial Board Members

Elisa Bertino
Purdue University, West Lafayette, IN, USA
Wen Gao
Peking University, Beijing, China
Bernhard Steffen
TU Dortmund University, Dortmund, Germany
Gerhard Woeginger
RWTH Aachen, Aachen, Germany
Moti Yung
Columbia University, New York, NY, USA

More information about this subseries at http://www.springer.com/series/7410

Pierre-Yvan Liardet · Nele Mentens (Eds.)

Smart Card Research and Advanced Applications

19th International Conference, CARDIS 2020
Virtual Event, November 18–19, 2020
Revised Selected Papers

Editors
Pierre-Yvan Liardet
eShard
Pesaac, France

Nele Mentens 🆔
Leiden University and KU Leuven
Leiden, The Netherlands

ISSN 0302-9743   ISSN 1611-3349   (electronic)
Lecture Notes in Computer Science
ISBN 978-3-030-68486-0   ISBN 978-3-030-68487-7   (eBook)
https://doi.org/10.1007/978-3-030-68487-7

LNCS Sublibrary: SL4 – Security and Cryptology

© Springer Nature Switzerland AG 2021
This work is subject to copyright. All rights are reserved by the Publisher, whether the whole or part of the material is concerned, specifically the rights of translation, reprinting, reuse of illustrations, recitation, broadcasting, reproduction on microfilms or in any other physical way, and transmission or information storage and retrieval, electronic adaptation, computer software, or by similar or dissimilar methodology now known or hereafter developed.
The use of general descriptive names, registered names, trademarks, service marks, etc. in this publication does not imply, even in the absence of a specific statement, that such names are exempt from the relevant protective laws and regulations and therefore free for general use.
The publisher, the authors and the editors are safe to assume that the advice and information in this book are believed to be true and accurate at the date of publication. Neither the publisher nor the authors or the editors give a warranty, expressed or implied, with respect to the material contained herein or for any errors or omissions that may have been made. The publisher remains neutral with regard to jurisdictional claims in published maps and institutional affiliations.

This Springer imprint is published by the registered company Springer Nature Switzerland AG
The registered company address is: Gewerbestrasse 11, 6330 Cham, Switzerland

Preface

These are the proceedings of the 19th International Conference on Smart Card Research and Advanced Applications (CARDIS 2020), which was originally planned to be held in Lübeck, Germany. Unfortunately, due to the COVID-19 pandemic, CARDIS 2020 was forced to be organized virtually by the Institute for IT Security of the Universität zu Lübeck, Germany on November 18–19, 2020.

CARDIS has been the venue for security experts from industry and academia to exchange ideas on the security of smart cards and related applications since 1994. For a long time already, smart cards have played an important role in our daily lives in applications such as payments, mobile communication, and identification. Over the years, the role of smart cards has extended to many more applications, in which the smart card serves as a root of trust in a larger system. But the increased applicability of smart cards also comes with an increased attack surface, both physical and theoretical attacks on the one hand, and both local and remote attacks on the other hand. Nowadays, System on Chip (SoC) devices have joined smart cards on the security market and CARDIS has naturally extended the discussions to these objects. Therefore, the goal of CARDIS is to offer a forum for experts from industry, academia, and standardization bodies to discuss research topics in the field of smart card security, IoT security, and embedded security.

This year, CARDIS received 26 submissions from different countries all over the world. Each paper was reviewed by four independent reviewers, resulting in 104 reviews. A total of 12 papers were accepted for presentation at the conference. In addition, the program featured three invited talks. The first invited speaker, Jörn Eichler, from Volkswagen and Freie Universität Berlin (Germany), presented "Automotive security - a focal point for security challenges". The second invited speaker, Nadia Heninger, from University of California, San Diego (United States), presented "Partial key recovery algorithms for side-channel cryptanalysis: results and open problems". The third invited speaker, Hannes Molsen, from Dräger (Germany), presented "Use Secure Boot, they said. It'll be fun, they said."

We would like to thank the general chair, Thomas Eisenbarth, for the smooth organization of the conference. We are also grateful to the Program Committee, consisting of 32 members, and the 19 external reviewers, for their thorough work. We also thank the Steering Committee for giving us the honour to serve as program chairs at CARDIS 2020. Furthermore, the financial support of the sponsors was highly appreciated: NewAE, NXP, Rambus, Riscure, and Thales. Last but not least, we would like to thank the authors who submitted their work to CARDIS 2020. Without them the conference would not have been possible.

December 2020

Pierre-Yvan Liardet
Nele Mentens

Organization

General Chair

Thomas Eisenbarth   Universität zu Lübeck, Germany

Program Committee Chairs

Pierre-Yvan Liardet   eShard, France
Nele Mentens   Leiden University, The Netherlands, and KU Leuven,
                                    Belgium

Steering Committee

François-Xavier Standaert   Université Catholique de Louvain la Neuve, Belgium
Sonia Belaïd   CryptoExperts, France
Begül Bilgin   Rambus-Cryptography Research, The Netherlands
Thomas Eisenbarth   Universität zu Lübeck, Germany
Jean-Bernard Fischer   Nagravision, Switzerland
Aurélien Francillon   Eurecom, France
Tim Güneysu   Ruhr-Universität Bochum, Germany
Marc Joye   Zama, France
Konstantinos   Royal Holloway, University of London, UK
   Markantonakis
Amir Moradi   Ruhr-Universität Bochum, Germany
Svetla Nikova   KU Leuven, Belgium
Jean-Jacques Quisquater   Université Catholique de Louvain la Neuve, Belgium
Francesco Regazzoni   University of Amsterdam, The Netherlands,
                                    and ALaRI, Switzerland
Yannick Teglia   Thales, France

Program Committee

Diego Aranha   Aarhus University, Denmark
Josep Balasch   KU Leuven, Belgium
Alessandro Barenghi   Politecnico Di Milano, Italy
Sonia Belaïd   CryptoExperts, France
Begül Bilgin   Rambus-Cryptography Research, The Netherlands
Billy Bob Brumley   Tampere University, Finland
Ileana Buhan   Radboud University, The Netherlands
Jeroen Delvaux   Open Security Research, China
Jean-Bernard Fischer   Nagravision, Switzerland
Domenic Forte   University of Florida, USA

Dahmun Goudarzi	PQShield, UK
Vincent Grosso	LHC Université Jean Monnet, France
Daniel Gruss	TU Graz, Austria
Tim Güneysu	Ruhr-University Bochum, Germany
Annelie Heuser	CNRS/IRISA, France
Kerstin Lemke-Rust	Bonn-Rhein-Sieg University of Applied Sciences, Germany
Roel Maes	Intrinsic ID, The Netherlands
Amir Moradi	Ruhr- Universität Bochum, Germany
Debdeep Mukhopadhyay	IIT Kharagpur, India
Colin O'Flynn	NewAE Technology Inc., Canada
Stjepan Picek	TU Delft, The Netherlands
Thomas Pöppelmann	Infineon, Germany
Francesco Regazzoni	University of Amsterdam, The Netherlands, and ALaRI, Switzerland
Thomas Roche	NinjaLab, France
Kazuo Sakiyama	University of Electro-Communications, Japan
Fareena Saqib	University of N. Carolina at Charlotte, USA
Erkay Savaş	Sabancı University, Turkey
Tobias Schneider	NXP Semiconductors, Austria
Peter Schwabe	Radboud University, The Netherlands
Yannick Teglia	Thales, France
Aurélien Vasselle	eShard, France
Yuval Yarom	University of Adelaide and Data61, Australia

Additional Reviewers

Abhijit Ambekar
Florian Bache
Arnab Bag
Debapriya Basu Roy
Olivier Bronchain
Jesús-Javier Chi-Domínguez
Lauren De Meyer
Thomas Decru
Lukas Giner
Julius Hermelink

Georg Land
Moritz Lipp
Victor Lomné
Erdinç Öztürk
Cesar Pereida García
Jan Richter-Brockmann
Luis Rivera-Zamarripa
Sayandeep Saha
Eloi Sanfelix

Contents

Post-Quantum Cryptography

A Constant Time Full Hardware Implementation of Streamlined NTRU Prime

Adrian Marotzke[1,2]([⊠]) [iD]

[1] TUHH, Hamburg, Germany
`adrian.marotzke@tuhh.de`
[2] NXP, Eindhoven, The Netherlands
`adrian.marotzke@nxp.com`

Abstract. This paper presents a constant time hardware implementation of the NIST round 2 post-quantum cryptographic algorithm Streamlined NTRU Prime. We implement the entire KEM algorithm, including all steps for key generation, encapsulation and decapsulation, and all en- and decoding. We focus on optimizing the resources used, as well as applying optimization and parallelism available due to the hardware design. We show the core en- and decapsulation requires only a fraction of the total FPGA fabric resource cost, which is dominated by that of the hash function, and the en- and decoding algorithm. For the NIST Security Level 3, our implementation uses a total of 1841 slices on a Xilinx Zynq Ultrascale+ FPGA, together with 14 BRAMs and 19 DSPs. The maximum achieved frequency is 271 MHz, at which the key generation, encapsulation and decapsulation take 4808 µs, 524 µs and 958 µs respectively. To our knowledge, this work is the first full hardware implementation where the entire algorithm is implemented.

Keywords: NTRU Prime · Post-quantum cryptography · FPGA · Hardware · VHDL · Key encapsulation mechanism · Lattice-based cryptography

1 Introduction

The NIST Post-Quantum-Cryptography standardization project has resulted in numerous new schemes designed to resist cryptanalysis by quantum computers [18]. Lattice based key encapsulation mechanism (KEM) schemes are the largest group, with nine submissions proceeding to round two. One common feature of all schemes is their complete dissimilarity to traditional public key cryptographic algorithms such as RSA and ECC. This makes existing hardware accelerators often sub optimal, though there has been some research on their use [1]. In addition, key sizes are significantly increased. This calls for fast and efficient hardware implementations, especially for embedded devices. NIST has addressed this by asking for performance benchmarks of the schemes on FPGA platforms. To our

© Springer Nature Switzerland AG 2021
P.-Y. Liardet and N. Mentens (Eds.): CARDIS 2020, LNCS 12609, pp. 3–17, 2021.
https://doi.org/10.1007/978-3-030-68487-7_1

knowledge, this paper presents the first full constant time hardware implementation of round 2 Streamlined NTRU Prime. A software/hardware co-design, where parts of the en- and decapsulation were implemented in hardware, was published recently [9]. However, the co-design did not include the key generation. Our implementation, while slower during en- and decapsulation, uses significantly less FPGA fabric resources, even though we implement more functions in hardware.

2 Preliminary

NTRU Prime is a Ring Learning with Rounding based scheme [6,8]. It has two KEM instantiations: Streamlined NTRU Prime (SNTRUP), and NTRU LPrime. The design goal behind NTRU Prime was to build a robust CCA secure public key scheme based on the original NTRU scheme [12], while minimizing the attack surface by removing the structures of cyclotomic rings. We focus on the Streamlined NTRU Prime variant. The Streamlined variant was the initial instantiation of NTRU Prime [5], has a smaller ciphertext, and faster en- and decapsulation. However, this comes at the cost of slower key generation and a larger public key [8]. However, both use the polynomial ring $\mathcal{R}/q = (\mathbb{Z}/q)[x]/(x^p - x - 1)$, with p and q being prime numbers, together with the ring $\mathcal{R}/3 = (\mathbb{Z}/3)[x]/(x^p - x - 1)$. A polynomial is *small* if all coefficients are in $-1, 0, 1$, e.g. elements of $\mathbb{Z}/3$. A polynomial has *weight* w if exactly w of its coefficients are non-zero. A polynomial is *short* if it is both *small* and of *weight* w. The values for p, q and w are part of the parameter set for SNTRUP, and are shown in Table 1. SHA-512 is used as a hash function internally, though only the first 256 bits of the output hash are used. Since all coefficients are either small or taken modulo a prime q, SNTRUP packs the coefficients together to reduce space. This is done with a decoding and encoding algorithm [6,8].

   Key generation, encapsulation and decapsulation are explained below. We use (a, b) to denote the concatenation of element a and b. Hash(a) denotes the hashing of a using SHA-512. Encode(a) and Decode(b) are the encoding and decoding functions respectively (see Sect. 4.5 for more details).

Key Generation: Generate a uniform random small element g which is invertible in $\mathcal{R}/3$. Calculate $1/g \in \mathcal{R}/3$. Generate a random short f. Calculate $h = g/(3f) \in \mathcal{R}/q$. Output Encode($h$) as the public key. Generate a random $\rho \in (0, \ldots, 255)^{(p+3)/4}$ and $k = $ (Encode(f), Encode($1/g$)). Output (k, Encode(h), ρ, hash(4, Encode(h))) as the secret key.

Encapsulation: Input is the encoded public key, Encode(h). Generate a random short r. Decode the public key h. Compute $hr \in \mathcal{R}/q$. Compute $c = $ Round(hr), where each element is rounded to the nearest multiple of 3. Compute $Confirm = $ hash(2, hash(3, r), hash(4, Encode(h))). Output ciphertext C = (Encode(c), $Confirm$), and hash(1, hash(3, r), C) as the shared secret.

Decapsulation: Input is the encoded secret key $(k, \text{Encode}(h), \rho, \text{hash}(4, \text{Encode}(h)))$ from the key generation step, and the encoded ciphertext $C = (\text{Encode}(c), Confirm)$ from the encapsulation. Decode polynomials f and $v \in \mathcal{R}/3$ from k (note that $v = 1/g$). Decode public key h. Decode ciphertext C and store as polynomial $c \in \mathcal{R}/q$. Compute $3fc \in \mathcal{R}/q$. While viewing each coefficient x of $3fc \in \mathcal{R}/q$ as an integer $-(q-1)/2 < x < (q-1)/2$, calculate each element modulo 3, and store as the new polynomial $e \in \mathcal{R}/3$. Calculate $r' = ev \in \mathcal{R}/3$. If r' does not have weight w, then set r' to $(1, 1, ..., 1, 0, 0..., 0)$, with the first w elements being 1. Redo the encapsulation for the Fujisaki-Okamoto transformation [10], setting $r = r'$, obtaining the ciphertext C'. If $C = C'$ then output hash(1,hash(3, r), C) as the shared secret, otherwise output hash(0, hash(3, ρ), C).

Table 1. Streamlined NTRU Prime parameters for the NIST round 2 standardization process, as well as the corresponding public key, secret key and cipher text sizes [8]. Note that the public key is contained in the secret key and does not have to be stored separately. Additional, non-standardized parameter sets can be found in [6].

Security level	p	q	w	Ciphertext bytes	Public key bytes	Secret key bytes
NIST level 1	653	4621	250	897	994	1518
NIST level 3	761	4591	286	1039	1158	1763
NIST level 5	857	5167	322	1184	1322	1999

3 Design Goals

Our primary goals was to develop a resource optimized Streamlined NTRU Prime implementation, while staying as *generic* as possible. Our implementation, except for the decoding module, is indeed fully generic, with parameters p, q, and w freely customizable, as long as they comply to the SNTRUP specifications. An expanded list of valid parameter sets can be found in [6]. This is useful, as any future parameter changes can be adopted with minimal changes. The encoding and decoding module do currently require some pre-calculated tables based on p and q. In addition, the design currently cannot process different values of p, q, and w at the same time, but needs to be resynthesized for any parameter changes. Though this also means that there is no performance and resource impact of being generic, as all modules and memories are synthesized to exactly match the requirements of the chosen parameter set. In addition, our design is written in platform agnostic VHDL.

4 Core Modules

4.1 $\mathcal{R}/q$ Multiplication

The multiplication in $\mathcal{R}/q$ is the core operation of both the en- and decapsulation. Due to the design of Streamlined NTRU Prime, the method of using the

NTT for multiplication is not naturally possible [6]. Instead, conventional means of multiplying polynomials are used.

During a multiplication, a polynomial in $\mathcal{R}/q$ is multiplied with a $\mathcal{R}/3$ polynomial. This means that $\mathcal{R}/q$ polynomial has signed 13 bit coefficients, whereas the $\mathcal{R}/3$ polynomial has signed two bit coefficients. However, these two bit coefficients can only have the values -1, 0 and 1. This results in the multiplier being almost trivial to implement. Using a pure product scanning schoolbook multiplication [14], our multiplier consumes only a small area (see Table 4). However, to improve performance, we use a combination of Karatsuba multiplication [15] and product scanning schoolbook multiplication. A single layer of Karatsuba multiplication is performed. This splits the multiplication of degree p into three multiplications of degree $\lceil p/2 \rceil$. The three partial multiplications are then done in parallel with schoolbook product scanning multiplication. This speeds up the multiplication by almost a factor of 4. During the schoolbook multiplication, we also make use of the dual port BRAM to read and write two words per clock cycle, doubling the speed of the multiplication. The use of Karatsuba does make the partial multiplication slightly more complicated, as one of the partial multiplications involves the addition of the lower and upper part of the $\mathcal{R}/3$ polynomial. This leads to a polynomial in $\mathcal{R}/q$ with 3 bit coefficients, with values between -2 and $+2$. The $\mathcal{R}/q$ multiplier also performs the multiplication of two polynomials in $\mathcal{R}/3$ during decapsulation. The single difference is that as a final step, all coefficients are reduced to $\mathbb{Z}/3$.

4.2   Reciprocal in $\mathcal{R}/q$ and $\mathcal{R}/3$

During key generation, two polynomial inversions must be performed, one in $\mathcal{R}/q$ and one in $\mathcal{R}/3$. We implement the constant time extended GCD algorithm from CHES 2019 [4]. For hardware accelerators for servers and other heavy-duty systems, batch inversion using Montgomery's trick [17] may be beneficial, but we did not consider this for our implementation. During key generation, the two inversions are done in parallel. Even so, the inversion is by far the single slowest operation (see Table 2).

In addition, we follow the reference implementation of SNTRUP by always calculating the inverse of g, rather than checking beforehand if g is invertible. Instead, we check the validity after the inversion has been completed. Should g not have been invertible, then we repeat the inversion with a new random small polynomial. In those cases, the key generation time is almost doubled.

4.3   Generating Short Polynomials and Constant Time Sorting

For the generation of the random short f during key generation and the random short r during encapsulation, a *constant time* sorting algorithm is used to sort a total of p 32 bit random values. In this context, *constant time* refers to being timing independent of the values sorted. Before sorting, the lowest 2 bits from first w 32 bit numbers are set so that they are always even. The lowest 2 bits from the rest are set so that they are odd. After sorting, the upper 30 bits are discarded, and the result is subtracted by 1. As a result, exactly w elements are either 1 or -1, and the rest are all zero, thus the polynomial is short. For the sorting itself, we implement a VHDL version of the algorithm suggested by [6]. The C-code of the sorting algorithm can be found in Listing 1.1.

```
void minmax(uint32 *x,uint32 *y) {
  uint32 xi = *x; uint32 yi = *y;
  uint32 xy = xi ^ yi;
  uint32 c = yi - xi;
  c ^= xy & (c ^ yi ^ 0x80000000);
  c >>= 31;
  c = -c;
  c &= xy;
  *x = xi ^ c; *y = yi ^ c;
}
void uint32_sort(uint32 *x,int n) {
  int top,p,q,i;
  top = 1;
  while (top < n - top) top += top;
  for (p = top;p > 0;p >>= 1) {
    for (i = 0;i < n - p;++i)
      minmax(x + i,x + i + p);
    for (q = top;q > p;q >>= 1)
      for (i = 0;i < n - q;++i)
        minmax(x + i + p,x + i + q);
  }
}
```

Listing 1.1. The C code of the sorting algorithm. The minmax function compares and swaps the two inputs [6].

4.4   Modulo Reduction in $\mathbb{Z}/q$ and $\mathbb{Z}/3$

In many parts during the KEM, we must reduce integers to $\mathbb{Z}/3$ and $\mathbb{Z}/q$, e.g. during the inversion, or after the $\mathcal{R}/3$ multiplication. To quickly reduce coefficients, we used pipelined Barrett reductions [3]. This is different from the reference implementation, which uses a constant time division algorithm [8]. Barrett reduction allows a modulo operation to be replaced with a multiplication and a bit shift. This can be implemented efficiently in the DSP units of the FGPA. For the reduction to $\mathbb{Z}/3$, we slightly modify the constants than those from Barrett's original paper. The modified constants are needed as we need to reduce values from a larger interval than normally allowed: Barrett reduction for a modulus n is only correct for the interval $[0, n^2]$. This obviously does not work if we wish to reduce values from $\mathbb{Z}/q$ to $\mathbb{Z}/3$ if $q > 9$. In addition, the modifications allows us to reuse the reduction during encapsulation to round coefficients to the nearest multiple of three. A Python version of our reduction algorithm with the constants is found in Listing 1.2. To verify the correctness of the modified constants, we mechanically verify in a simulator that all possible elements from $\mathbb{Z}/q$ are both rounded correctly and reduced to the correct values in $\mathbb{Z}/3$. This would mean that for elements outside of $\mathbb{Z}/q$, one would first have to reduce to $\mathbb{Z}/q$, and then again to $\mathbb{Z}/3$. However, this situation does not occur in our design.

```
import math
q=4591; q_half = math.floor(q/2); p=761
k=16; r=math.floor((2**k) / 3)
def reduce_and_round(input):
    rounded_output = 3*(((input+q_half) * r + 2**(k - 1)) >> k)-q_half
    mod_3_result = input - rounded_output
    return [rounded_output, mod_3_result]
```

Listing 1.2. A python version of our combined Barrett reduction to $\mathbb{Z}/3$ and rounding algorithm.

4.5 En- and Decoder for Polynomials $\mathcal{R}/q$ and $\mathcal{R}/3$

In order to save bytes during transmission, Streamlined NTRU Prime has specified an encoding for public and private keys and the ciphertext. The polynomials of the secret key f and $1/g$ are both in $\mathcal{R}/3$, and each polynomial coefficient is in $\mathbb{Z}/3$ and can be represented with 2 bits. Four of these coefficients are simply packed into a byte using a shift register. The encoder for the ciphertext and public key is more complicated, as both polynomials are in $\mathcal{R}/q$, with coefficients in $\mathbb{Z}/q$. Here, the coefficients are all have 13-bit size. However, since values in the interval between q and 2^{13} do not occur, packing can save space by "overlapping" the coefficients. There is a slightly different encoding for the ciphertext, as each coefficient of the ciphertext is rounded to the nearest multiple of 3. This allows us to save further space. See Appendix A for the Python code of the encoder.

Decoding elements in $\mathcal{R}/3$ is similar to the encoding, with a simple shift register. Decoding the elements from $\mathcal{R}/q$ however, is again more complex. In fact, the $\mathcal{R}/q$ decoder is one of the most expensive modules when it comes to resource consumption. One reason for this is that the decoder requires a 32 by 16 bit division. In order to avoid the need to implement a full division circuit, we precalculate all divisors, which are not dependent on any secrets, and store these in a table. For $p = 761$ and $q = 4591$, there are in total 42 different divisors, each fitting in 16 bits. Half of these are for the decoding the rounded coefficients of the ciphertext, the other half are for the public key. Due to the precalculation, we can then use integer division by a constant, allowing us to replace the division with a multiplication and a bit shift [16]. See Appendix A for the Python code of the decoder.

Before decapsulation and encapsulation can begin, the secret key and public key respectively must be decoded first. However, for subsequent en- and decapsulations, the decoding does not have to be repeated. Instead, the decoded public and secret keys are stored in internal memory. This can save time whenever a key is reused for multiple KEM runs.

4.6 SHA-512

Streamlined NTRU Prime uses SHA-512 as a hash function. This is used on the one hand to generate the shared secret after the en- and decapsulation, but also for the ciphertext confirmation hash. The confirmation hash is the hash of the short polynomial r and the public key, and is appended to the ciphertext during encapsulation. We did not write our own SHA-512 implementation, but instead used an open source one [20], with some slight modifications to improve performance and reduce resource consumption. The SHA-512 module consumes nearly half of all LUTs and over half of the flip-flops of the entire implementation (see Table 4), making it by the far the single most expensive component. A note to remember is that only the first 256 bits of the hash output are actually used. As such, usage of other hash functions such as SHA-256 or SHA3-256 could be worth a consideration in order to save resources. On the other hand, one could argue that in many systems, SHA-512 accelerators are already available, so using SHA-512 does not add any resource cost. From a speed perspective, the time spent on hashing is negligible (see Table 2 and 3).

Table 2. A summary of the cycle count of the core modules of our implementation for the parameter set $p = 761$, $q = 4591$ and $w = 246$. Note that the times for sub-modules are included (sometime multiple times) in upper modules. The cycle counts for key generation, encapsulation and decapsulation are all using the Karatsuba $\mathcal{R}/q$ multiplication.

Module	Clock cycles
Key generation	1 304 738
Key encapsulation	134 844
Key encapsulation inc. key load	142 229
Key decapsulation	251 425
Key decapsulation inc. key load	259 899
$\mathcal{R}/q$ Schoolbook multiplication	292 232
$\mathcal{R}/q$ Karatsuba multiplication	78 132
Reciprocal in $\mathcal{R}/q$	1 168 960
Reciprocal in $\mathcal{R}/3$	1 168 899
Generating short polynomials	50 927
Sorting algorithm	49 400
SHA-512 (per 1024 bit block)	325
Encode $\mathcal{R}/q$ (public key)	5 348
Encode $\mathcal{R}/q$ (ciphertext)	5 197
Decode $\mathcal{R}/q$ (public key)	7 380
Decode $\mathcal{R}/q$ (ciphertext)	6 721
Encode $\mathcal{R}/3$	761
Decode $\mathcal{R}/3$	761

Table 3. A summary of how the clock cycles of key generation, encapsulation and decapsulation are distributed among the sub modules for the parameter set $p = 761$, $q = 4591$ and $w = 246$. For en- and decapsulation, both times included the decoding of the public and/or secret key.

Operation	Function	Relative share of clock cycles (%)
Key generation	$\mathcal{R}/q$ and $\mathcal{R}/3$ reciprocal	89.6%
	$\mathcal{R}/q$ multiplication	6%
	Generating short polynomials	3.9%
	Other	0.5%
Encapsulation	$\mathcal{R}/q$ multiplication	54.9%
	Generating short polynomials	35.8%
	Decoding public key	5.2%
	Encoding cipher text	3.6%
	Other	0.5%
Decapsulation	$\mathcal{R}/q$ and $\mathcal{R}/3$ multiplication	60.3%
	Re-encapsulation	32.4%
	Decoding cipher text	2.6%
	Decoding secret key	2.7%
	Other	2%

5   Architecture

The architecture of our implementation is tailored to Streamlined NTRU Prime. After synthesis, the design is specific to a single parameter set. The design has the following inputs:

- **Start Encap.** Begin the encapsulation
- **Start Decap.** Begin the decapsulation
- **Start Key Gen.** Begin the key generation
- **Public Key.** Input a new encoded public key for encapsulation
- **Secret Key.** Input a new encoded secret key for decapsulation
- **Ciphertext.** Input a new encoded ciphertext for encapsulation
- **Random.** Source of randomness

The design has the following outputs:

- **Public Key.** Output encoded public key after key generation
- **Secret Key.** Output encoded secret key after key generation
- **Ciphertext.** Output encoded ciphertext after encapsulation
- **Shared secret.** Output shared secret after en- and decapasulation

The design has a main finite state machine (FSM), which controls the access to the different shared modules, as well as starting the separate main operations such as key generation. The design can only process a single key generation, encapsulation or decapsulation at a time. The shared modules are operations that are needed across key generation, de- and encapsulation. This includes the $\mathcal{R}/q$ multiplication, the en- and decoding, hashing, the reduction to $\mathbb{Z}/3$, the generation of short polynomials, as well as the parts of the encapsulation that are needed for the Fujisaki-Okamoto transformation [10] during decapsulation.

6 Implementation Results on an FPGA

We implemented the design on a Xilinx Zynq Ultrascale+ ZCU102 FPGA, using the parameter set for level 3 as an example. This means $p = 761$, $q = 4591$ and $w = 246$. We achieve a maximum clock frequency of 271 MHz. In total, the design uses 9538 LUT, 7802 flip-flops, 14 BRAMs, and 19 DSP units. An encapsulation takes 142 229 clock cycles. A decapsulation takes 251 425 clock cycles, excluding the time it takes to load and decode the secret key, and 259 899 clock cycles if it is included. A key generation takes 1 304 738 clock cycles. We did not implement any kind of RNG into our design, instead it simply has an input where cryptographically secure random bits are expected. During both encapsulation and key generation, 24 352 random bits are needed for the generation of the short polynomials, for which 761 (i.e. p) random 32 bit values are needed. During key generation, a further 24 352 bits are needed for the random g, and 1528 bits for

Table 4. A summary of the resources used for the parameter set $p = 761$, $q = 4591$ and $w = 246$. We also included a subset of non-shared sub-modules that are of special interest. Note that the resources for non-shared sub-modules are included (sometime multiple times) in upper modules. The row "total" is using the Karatsuba $\mathcal{R}/q$ multiplication. The numbers for the schoolbook multiplication are for comparison and are not included in the total.

	Module	Logic slices	LUT	Flip-flops	BRAM	DSP
Main operations	Key generation	458	2499	1082	3	11
	Key encapsulation	77	157	94	0.5	0
	Key decapsulation	204	739	263	1.5	0
Shared modules	Key encapsulation shared core	25	113	22	0.5	1
	$\mathcal{R}/q$ schoolbook multiplication	94	418	281	1	0
	$\mathcal{R}/q$ Karatsuba multiplication	298	1463	817	4	0
	Generating short polynomials	45	231	87	1	0
	SHA-512	716	3174	4710	1	0
	Encode $\mathcal{R}/q$	47	215	131	0.5	1
	Decode $\mathcal{R}/q$	128	676	571	2	5
	Reduce to $\mathbb{Z}/3$ & rounding	10	23	19	0	1
	Top level leaf cells	0	248	6	0	0
	Total	1841	9538	7802	14	19
Non-shared sub-modules	Sorting algorithm	33	159	56	0	0
	Reciprocal in $\mathcal{R}/q$	278	1642	726	2	11
	Reciprocal in $\mathcal{R}/3$	92	518	216	0	0
	Reduce to $\mathbb{Z}/q$	54	304	107	0	1
	Encode $\mathcal{R}/3$	8	18	20	0	0
	Decode $\mathcal{R}/3$	7	24	22	0	0
	Constant integer division	50	232	188	0	5

the random value ρ, for a total of 50 232 bits. No randomness is needed during decapsulation. A detailed list of the runtimes of all core modules can be found in Table 2. A summary of the resources used can be found in Table 4.

Table 3 details the cycles count for key generation, en - and decapsulation as percentages. For the key generation, the cycle count is dominated by the polynomial inversion, which take 89.6% of the total time. Both the $\mathcal{R}/q$ multiplication and the generation of short polynomials only take 6% and 3.9% respectively. Encoding and hashing are minuscule in comparison, and are grouped together under other. For encapsulation, the time for $\mathcal{R}/q$ multiplication and the generation of short polynomials is 54.9% and 35.8% respectively. Encoding and decoding only take a small single digit percentage of the cycles. The hashing is again negligible, and is grouped under other. For decapsulation, the time is dominated by the $\mathcal{R}/q$ and $\mathcal{R}/3$ multiplication. One each is performed during the core decapsulation itself, and a further $\mathcal{R}/q$ multiplication is done during the re-encapsulation for the Fujisaki-Okamoto transformation [10]. The cycles spent for the re-encapsulation differ from a normal encapsulation in that no short polynomials have to be generated, and the decoding of the public key is not needed, as it was already decoded as part of the secret key. Once again, decoding, encoding and hashing are almost negligible. As such, improving the $\mathcal{R}/q$ multiplication speed can significantly improve decapsulation speed. Encapsulation can also be improved, but not to such an extent, as the time taken for the generation of the short polynomials will quickly dominate. The cycles for the generation of the short polynomials are almost entirely due to the sorting algorithm, which takes 97.7% of the cycles. Thus, a faster sorting method would also lead to a speed improvement of the encapsulation. Key generation cannot be meaningfully improved by either faster $\mathcal{R}/q$ multiplication or faster sorting, as both only take a small percentage of the total cycles.

In the Xilinx Zynq FPGA, each Block RAM is 36 kilobits. They can be split into two 18 kb BRAMs. The majority of the BRAM are used by the en- and decoding, the $\mathcal{R}/q$ polynomial inversion, and the $\mathcal{R}/q$ multiplication. In several instances, we explicitly use disturbed RAM instead, in order to save BRAM resources from being consumed for very small memories. Examples for this is the storage of small polynomials, which only require 1522 bits. Note that all memory is instantiated where needed, i.e. there is no central memory. This means that there is no sharing or overlapping of memory.

The Xilinx FPGA has numerous Digital Signal Processor (DSP) cells, which can be used for fast addition and multiplication. Of the 23 DSP cells, 11 are used for the $\mathcal{R}/q$ polynomial inversion during key generation. More specifically, they are used for the modular multiplication and modular addition during the inversion (see also Sect. 4.4 on Barrett reduction). A further five DSP cells are used for the constant integer division during decoding. Only two DSPs are used during the core en- and decapsulation.

To test our implementation for correctness we use the known answer test (KAT) also used by the reference code. In total, we run 50 KATs, for key generation, encapsulation and decapsulation. In all cases, the outputs of our design match that of the reference code. We used the default synthesis and implementation settings of Vivado (version 2018.3.1), with two exceptions: We turn on register retiming, and set the synthesis hierarchy parameter to full.

6.1 Side Channels

The implementation is fully constant time, i.e. all operations are timing independent with regards to secret input. The case during key generation where the inversion of g fails is not relevant here, as the polynomial is discarded, and a new one generated. That being said, we did not employ any protections against more advanced side channels, such as DPA, nor invasive attacks such as fault attacks. There have been side channel attacks on the polynomial multiplication part of lattice schemes [13,19]. Many of these attacks were applied on software implementations, some were also applied to hardware implementations [2]. There have also been side channel attacks that exploit decryption failures of lattice schemes [7]. As Streamlined NTRU Prime does not have any decryption failures, these attacks do not apply. The authors from [11] show an attack on the re-encapsulation (based on the Fujisaki-Okamoto transformation [10]) of the FrodoKEM scheme, due to the ciphertext comparison being non constant time. This attack also does not apply to our implementation, as the comparison is completely constant time. We plan on investigating further side channel resistance in future work.

6.2 Comparison with Other Implementations

To our knowledge, there are no other complete pure hardware implementations of Streamlined NTRU Prime. The authors of [9] have a hardware software co/design, where some parts of the algorithm are implemented in hardware. Specifically, they have not implemented the key generation and decoding. Overall, our design uses significantly fewer LUTs and flip-flops, even when considering that our design implements more functionality in hardware (see Table 5). [9] however does not use any DSP units. Our design has an initially noticeable higher usage of block RAMs, but this is due to the inclusion of the key generation and decoding. When these are counted separately, our design uses the same amount of BRAMs. Our design runs at a slightly faster clock speed, though the total encapsulation and decapsulation time of [9] is shorter, as can be seen in Table 5. The main reason for this difference is in the implementation of the $\mathcal{R}/q$ multiplication. Our design uses a combination of Karatsuba and schoolbook multiplication, whereas [9] uses an linear feedback shift register (LFSR). While using an LFSR is faster, the resource cost is significantly higher. In addition, our multiplication design has the additional advantage that it can be easily tweaked, as the numbers of Karatsuba layers can be modified. Using more Karatsuba layers would increase performance, though also increase resource cost. See Table 5 for a full comparison of all metrics.

Table 5. A comparison of our design (both the full version, and once without the key generation and decoding) and existing Streamlined NTRU Prime implementations for the parameter set $p = 761$, $q = 4591$ and $w = 246$. For the implementation from [9], we only consider the timing from the hardware design.

Design	Slices	LUT	Flip-flops	BRAM	DSP	Clock speed	Encap time	Decap time
Ours	1841	9538	7803	14	19	271 MHz	524 μs	958 μs
Ours, without key gen or decoding	1261	6240	6223	9	3	279 MHz	483 μs	901 μs
[9], no key gen or decoding	10 319	70 066	38 144	9	0	263 MHz	56.3 μs	53.3 μs

6.3   Potential Improvements

In this section, we describe a number of potential improvements that we have not yet implemented or tested. We plan on investigating these improvements in future work.

An option would be to use an LFSR polynomial multiplier for the $\mathcal{R}/3$ multiplier only. As polynomials in $\mathcal{R}/3$ only require 2 bits of storage per coefficient, the resource cost is not as high as with a full $\mathcal{R}/q$ multiplier. Doing so would speed up decapsulation. In a similar vein, the $\mathcal{R}/q$ Karatsuba multiplication currently uses only a single layer of Karatsuba. Implementing more layers would bring further speedups, though also increase resource cost. In particular, the amount of memory needed to store intermediate results would increase, leading to an increase of BRAMs usage. In addition, the partial multiplier would increase in complexity: As the partial factors are added together, previously small factors become more and more complex, requiring an increasingly complex modular multiplication circuit.

During the key generation, the reciprocal algorithms work on a single coefficient per clock cycle. However, there is no interdependence between the coefficients. As such, it would be possible to operate on batches of coefficients. On Xilinx FPGAs, the BRAMs can have word width of up to 72 bits. For the $\mathcal{R}/q$ inversion, this would be enough to read five coefficients per clock cycle. This would speed up the inversion by roughly a factor of five. However, this would also significantly increase the resource consumption of the inversion, as we would need to duplicate the modular multiplication circuits five times. Since the modular multiplication during the $\mathcal{R}/q$ inversion currently requires six DSP units, the duplication would increase this to 30 DSP units.

Currently, the design has a single global clock. However, not all parts are required to run at the same speed. Parts such as the hashing, en- and decoding, which take only a small duration of the overall time, could be clocked at a slower speed, saving power, as well as reducing the number of pipeline steps needed. This is especially true for the hash function. We believe that there is still a potential for resource saving there, though finding the optimal SHA-512 implementation was considered out of scope for this work.

As mentioned previously, there is no central memory, instead block and distributed RAMs are inferred where needed. This aids performance and simplicity, but causes a larger memory footprint, as memory reuse is not possible. However, as many functions are executed sequentially, and not parallelly, sharing memory could save significant resources. At a higher level, this includes the fact that key generation, encapsulation and decapsulation cannot happen at the same time, thus memory space could be shared. At a lower level, this includes functions like the de- and encoding, which also never occur at the same time.

Currently, the design is also fixed to a single parameter set after synthesis. For greater flexibility, it would be useful if the design could switch between parameter sets during runtime.

7   Conclusion

We present the first full constant-time hardware implementation of the round 2 scheme Streamlined NTRU Prime. We implement the entire KEM in VHDL, including key generation, and all en- and decoding. Compared to existing partial implementations of Streamlined NTRU Prime, our design is slower, but uses significantly less resources. The source code of our implementation is available at https://github.com/AdrianMarotzke/SNTRUP.

Acknowledgments. I would like to thank Joppe Bos, Christine Van Vredendal, Björn Fey, Thomas Wille, Dieter Gollmann for their help. This work was supported by the Federal Ministry of Education and Research (BMBF) of the Federal Republic of Germany (grant 16KIS0658K, SysKit HW). This work was labelled by the EUREKA cluster PENTA and funded by German authorities under grant agreement PENTA-2018e-17004-SunRISE.

A   Encode and Decode algorithm

```
limit = 16384
def Encode(R,M):
    if len(M) == 0: return []
    S = []
    if len(M) == 1:
        r,m = R[0],M[0]
        while m > 1:
            S += [r%256]
            r,m = r//256,(m+255)//256
        return S
    R2,M2 = [],[]
    for i in range(0,len(M)-1,2):
        m,r = M[i]*M[i+1],R[i]+M[i]*R[i+1]
        while m >= limit:
            S += [r%256]
            r,m = r//256,(m+255)//256
        R2 += [r]
        M2 += [m]
    if len(M)&1:
        R2 += [R[-1]]; M2 += [M[-1]]
    return S+Encode(R2,M2)
```

Listing 1.3. The Python code of the encoder [8]. The lists R and M must have the same length, and $\forall i : 0 \leq R[i] \leq M[i] \leq 2^{14}$. Then, $Decode(Encode(R; M); M) = R$.

```python
limit = 16384
def Decode(S,M):
    if len(M) == 0: return []
    if len(M) == 1: return [sum(S[i]*256**i for i in range(len(S)))%M[0]]
    k = 0; bottom,M2 = [],[]
    for i in range(0,len(M)-1,2):
        m,r,t = M[i]*M[i+1],0,1
        while m >= limit:
            r,t,k,m = r+S[k]*t,t*256,k+1,(m+255)//256
        bottom += [(r,t)]
        M2 += [m]
    if len(M)&1:
        M2 += [M[-1]]
    R2 = Decode(S[k:],M2)
    R = []
    for i in range(0,len(M)-1,2):
        r,t = bottom[i//2]; r += t*R2[i//2];
        R += [r%M[i]]; R += [(r//M[i])%M[i+1]]
    if len(M)&1:
        R += [R2[-1]]
    return R
```

Listing 1.4. The Python code of the decoder [8].

References

1. Albrecht, M.R., Hanser, C., Hoeller, A., Pöppelmann, T., Virdia, F., Wallner, A.: Implementing RLWE-based schemes using an RSA co-processor. IACR Trans. Crypt. Hardw. Embed. Syst. **2019**(1), 169–208 (2019)

2. Aysu, A., Tobah, Y., Tiwari, M., Gerstlauer, A., Orshansky, M.: Horizontal side-channel vulnerabilities of post-quantum key exchange protocols. In: 2018 IEEE International Symposium on Hardware Oriented Security and Trust (HOST), pp. 81–88. IEEE (2018)

3. Barrett, P.: Implementing the Rivest Shamir and Adleman public key encryption algorithm on a standard digital signal processor. In: Odlyzko, A.M. (ed.) CRYPTO 1986. LNCS, vol. 263, pp. 311–323. Springer, Heidelberg (1987). https://doi.org/10.1007/3-540-47721-7_24

4. Bernstein, D.J., Yang, B.-Y.: Fast constant-time GCD computation and modular inversion. IACR Trans. Crypt. Hardw. Embed. Syst. **2019**(3), 340–398 (2019)

5. Bernstein, D.J., Chuengsatiansup, C., Lange, T., van Vredendaal, C.: NTRU prime: reducing attack surface at low cost. Cryptology ePrint Archive, Report 2016/461 (2016). https://eprint.iacr.org/2016/461

6. Bernstein, D.J., Chuengsatiansup, C., Lange, T., van Vredendaal, C.: NTRU prime: reducing attack surface at low cost. In: Adams, C., Camenisch, J. (eds.) SAC 2017. LNCS, vol. 10719, pp. 235–260. Springer, Cham (2018). https://doi.org/10.1007/978-3-319-72565-9_12

7. Bernstein, D.J., Groot Bruinderink, L., Lange, T., Panny, L.: HILA5 Pindakaas: on the CCA security of lattice-based encryption with error correction. In: Joux, A., Nitaj, A., Rachidi, T. (eds.) AFRICACRYPT 2018. LNCS, vol. 10831, pp. 203–216. Springer, Cham (2018). https://doi.org/10.1007/978-3-319-89339-6_12

8. Bernstein, D.J., Chuengsatiansup, C., Lange, T., van Vredendaal, C.: NTRU prime: round 2. In: Post-Quantum Cryptography Standardization Project. NIST (2019)

9. Dang, V.B., et al.: Implementation and benchmarking of round 2 candidates in the NIST post-quantum cryptography standardization process using hardware and software/hardware co-design approaches. Cryptology ePrint Archive, Report 2020/795 (2020). https://eprint.iacr.org/2020/795

10. Fujisaki, E., Okamoto, T.: Secure integration of asymmetric and symmetric encryption schemes. In: Wiener, M. (ed.) CRYPTO 1999. LNCS, vol. 1666, pp. 537–554. Springer, Heidelberg (1999). https://doi.org/10.1007/3-540-48405-1_34

11. Guo, Q., Johansson, T., Nilsson, A.: A key-recovery timing attack on post-quantum primitives using the Fujisaki-Okamoto transformation and its application on FrodoKEM. Cryptology ePrint Archive, Report 2020/743 (2020). https://eprint.iacr.org/2020/743

12. Hoffstein, J., Pipher, J., Silverman, J.H.: NTRU: a ring-based public key cryptosystem. In: Buhler, J.P. (ed.) ANTS 1998. LNCS, vol. 1423, pp. 267–288. Springer, Heidelberg (1998). https://doi.org/10.1007/BFb0054868

13. Huang, W.-L., Chen, J.-P., Yang, B.-Y.: Power analysis on NTRU prime. IACR Trans. Crypt. Hardw. Embed. Syst. **2020**(1), 123–151 (2020)

14. Hutter, M., Wenger, E.: Fast multi-precision multiplication for public-key cryptography on embedded microprocessors. In: Preneel, B., Takagi, T. (eds.) CHES 2011. LNCS, vol. 6917, pp. 459–474. Springer, Heidelberg (2011). https://doi.org/10.1007/978-3-642-23951-9_30

15. Karatsuba, A.A., Ofman, Y.P.: Multiplication of many-digital numbers by automatic computers. Doklady Akademii Nauk **145**, 293–294 (1962). Russian Academy of Sciences

16. Lemire, D., Kaser, O., Kurz, N.: Faster remainder by direct computation: applications to compilers and software libraries. Softw. Pract. Exp. **49**(6), 953–970 (2019)

17. Mishra, P.K., Sarkar, P.: Application of montgomery's trick to scalar multiplication for elliptic and hyperelliptic curves using a fixed base point. In: Bao, F., Deng, R., Zhou, J. (eds.) PKC 2004. LNCS, vol. 2947, pp. 41–54. Springer, Heidelberg (2004). https://doi.org/10.1007/978-3-540-24632-9_4

18. NIST. Nist post-quantum cryptography standardization. https://csrc.nist.gov/Projects/Post-Quantum-Cryptography/Post-Quantum-Cryptography-Standardization. Accessed 11 June 2020

19. Primas, R., Pessl, P., Mangard, S.: Single-trace side-channel attacks on masked lattice-based encryption. In: Fischer, W., Homma, N. (eds.) CHES 2017. LNCS, vol. 10529, pp. 513–533. Springer, Cham (2017). https://doi.org/10.1007/978-3-319-66787-4_25

20. Savory, D.: SHA-512 hardware implementation in VHDL. Based on NIST FIPS 180-4. https://github.com/dsaves/SHA-512. Accessed 11 June 2020

Lightweight Post-quantum Key Encapsulation for 8-bit AVR Microcontrollers

Hao Cheng[✉], Johann Großschädl, Peter B. Rønne, and Peter Y. A. Ryan

DCS and SnT, University of Luxembourg, 6, Avenue de la Fonte,
4364 Esch-sur-Alzette, Luxembourg
{hao.cheng,johann.groszschaedl,peter.roenne,peter.ryan}@uni.lu

Abstract. Recent progress in quantum computing has increased interest in the question of how well the existing proposals for post-quantum cryptosystems are suited to replace RSA and ECC. While some aspects of this question have already been researched in detail (e.g. the relative computational cost of pre- and post-quantum algorithms), very little is known about the RAM footprint of the proposals and what execution time they can reach when low memory consumption rather than speed is the main optimization goal. This question is particularly important in the context of the Internet of Things (IoT) since many IoT devices are extremely constrained and possess only a few kB of RAM. We aim to contribute to answering this question by exploring the software design space of the lattice-based key-encapsulation scheme THREEBEARS on an 8-bit AVR microcontroller. More concretely, we provide new techniques for the optimization of the ring arithmetic of THREEBEARS (which is, in essence, a 3120-bit modular multiplication) to achieve either high speed or low RAM footprint, and we analyze in detail the trade-offs between these two metrics. A low-memory implementation of BABYBEAR that is secure against Chosen Plaintext Attacks (CPA) needs just about 1.7 kB RAM, which is significantly below the RAM footprint of other lattice-based cryptosystems reported in the literature. Yet, the encapsulation time of this RAM-optimized BABYBEAR version is below 12.5 million cycles, which is less than the execution time of scalar multiplication on Curve25519. The decapsulation is more than four times faster and takes roughly 3.4 million cycles on an ATmega1284 microcontroller.

Keywords: Post-quantum cryptography · Key encapsulation mechanism · AVR architecture · Efficient implementation · Low RAM footprint

1 Introduction

In 2016, the U.S. National Institute of Standards and Technology (NIST) initiated a process to evaluate and standardize quantum-resistant public-key cryptographic algorithms and published a call for proposals [14]. This call, whose

© Springer Nature Switzerland AG 2021
P.-Y. Liardet and N. Mentens (Eds.): CARDIS 2020, LNCS 12609, pp. 18–33, 2021.
https://doi.org/10.1007/978-3-030-68487-7_2

submission deadline passed at the end of November 2017, covered the complete spectrum of public-key functionalities: encryption, key agreement, and digital signatures. A total of 72 candidates were submitted, of which 69 satisfied the minimum requirements for acceptability and entered the first round of a multi-year evaluation process. In early 2019, the NIST selected 26 of the submissions as candidates for the second round; among these are 17 public-key encryption or key-encapsulation algorithms and nine signature schemes. The 17 algorithms for encryption (resp. key encapsulation) include nine that are based on certain hard problems in lattices, seven whose security rests upon classical problems in coding theory, and one that claims security from the presumed hardness of the (supersingular) isogeny walk problem on elliptic curves [15]. This second round focuses on evaluating the candidates' performance across a variety of systems and platforms, including "not only big computers and smart phones, but also devices that have limited processor power" [15].

Lattice-based cryptosystems are considered the most promising candidates for deployment in constrained devices due to their relatively low computational cost and reasonably small keys and ciphertexts (resp. signatures). Indeed, the benchmarking results collected in the course of the pqm4 project[1], which uses a 32-bit ARM Cortex-M4 as target device, show that most of the lattice-based Key-Encapsulation Mechanisms (KEMs) in the second round of the evaluation process are faster than ECDH key exchange based on Curve25519, and some candidates are even notably faster than Curve25519 [10]. However, the results of pqm4 also indicate that lattice-based cryptosystems generally require a large amount of run-time memory since most of the benchmarked lattice KEMs have a RAM footprint of between 5 kB and 30 kB. For comparison, a variable-base scalar multiplication on Curve25519 can have a RAM footprint of less than 500 bytes [4]. One could argue that the pqm4 implementations have been optimized to reach high speed rather than low memory consumption, but this argument is not convincing since even a conventional implementation of Curve25519 (i.e. an implementation without any specific measures for RAM reduction) still needs only little more than 500 bytes RAM. Therefore, the existing implementation results in the literature lead to the conclusion that lattice-based KEMs require an order of magnitude more RAM than ECDH key exchange.

The high RAM requirements of lattice-based cryptosystems (in relation to Curve25519) pose a serious problem for the emerging Internet of Things (IoT) since many IoT devices feature only a few kB of RAM. For example, a typical wireless sensor node like the MICAz mote [3] is equipped with an 8-bit micro-controller (e.g. ATmega128L) and comes with only 4 kB internal SRAM. These 4 kB are easily sufficient for Curve25519 (since there would still be 7/8 of the RAM available for system and application software), but not for lattice-based KEMs. Thus, there is a clear need to research how lattice-based cryptosystems can be optimized to reduce their memory consumption and what performance such low-memory implementations can reach. The present paper addresses this research need and introduces various software optimization techniques for the

---

[1] See https://www.github.com/mupq/pqm4.

THREEBEARS KEM [8], a lattice-based cryptosystem that was selected for the second round of NIST's standardization project. The security of THREEBEARS is based on a special version of the Learning With Errors (LWE) problem, the so-called Integer Module Learning with Errors (I-MLWE) problem [5]. THREE-BEARS is unique among the lattice-based second-round candidates since it uses an integer ring instead of a polynomial ring as algebraic structure. Hence, the major operation of THREEBEARS is integer arithmetic (namely multiplication modulo a 3120-bit prime) and not polynomial arithmetic.

The conventional way to speed up the polynomial multiplication that forms part of lattice-based cryptosystems like classical NTRU or NTRU Prime is to use a multiplication technique with sub-quadratic complexity, e.g. Karatsuba's method [11] or the so-called Toom-Cook algorithm. However, the performance gain due to these techniques comes at the expense of a massive increase of the RAM requirements. For integer multiplication, on the other hand, there exists a highly effective approach for performance optimization that does not increase the memory footprint, namely the so-called hybrid multiplication method from CHES 2004 [6] or one of its variants like the Reverse Product Scanning (RPS) method [13]. In essence, the hybrid technique can be viewed as a combination of classical operand scanning and product scanning with the goal to reduce the number of load instructions by processing several bytes of the two operands in each iteration of the inner loop. Even though the hybrid technique can also be applied to polynomial multiplication, it is, in general, less effective because the bit-length of the polynomial coefficients of most lattice-based cryptosystems is not a multiple of eight.

Contributions. This paper analyzes the performance of THREEBEARS on an 8-bit AVR microcontroller and studies its flexibility to achieve different trade-offs between execution time and RAM footprint. Furthermore, we describe (to the best of our knowledge) the first highly-optimized software implementations of BABYBEAR (an instance of THREEBEARS with parameters to reach NIST's security category 2) for the AVR platform. We developed four implementations of BABYBEAR, two of which are optimized for low RAM consumption, and the other two for fast execution times. Our two low-RAM BABYBEAR versions are the most memory-efficient software implementations of a NIST second-round candidate ever reported in the literature.

Our work is based on the optimized C code contained in the THREEBEARS submission package [8], which adopts a "reduced-radix" representation for the ring elements, i.e. the number of bits per limb is less than the word-size of the target architecture. On a 32-bit platform, a 3120-bit integer can be stored in an array of 120 limbs, each consisting of 26 bits. However, our AVR software uses a radix of 2^{32} (i.e. 32 bits of the operands are processed at a time) since this representation enables the RPS method to reach peak performance and it also reduces the RAM footprint. We present two optimizations for the performance-critical Multiply-ACcumulate (MAC) operation of THREEBEARS; one aims to minimize the RAM requirements, while the goal of the second is to maximize performance. Our low-memory implementation of the MAC combines one level of Karatsuba with the RPS method [13] to accelerate the so-called tripleMAC operation of the optimized C source code from [8], which is (relatively) light in terms of stack memory. On the other hand, the speed-optimized MAC consists of three recursive levels of Karatsuba multiplication and uses the RPS method underneath. We implemented both MAC variants in AVR Assembly language to ensure they have constant execution time and can resist timing attacks.

As already mentioned, our software contains four different implementations of the THREEBEARS family: two versions of CCA-secure BABYBEAR, and two versions of CPA-secure BABYBEAREPHEM. For both BABYBEAR and BABY-BEAREPHEM, we developed both a Memory-Efficient (ME) and a High-Speed (HS) implementation, which internally use the corresponding MAC variant. We abbreviate these four versions as ME-BBear, ME-BBear-Eph, HS-BBear, and HS-BBear-Eph. Our results show that THREEBEARS provides the flexibility to optimize for low memory footprint *and* still achieves very good execution times compared to the other second-round candidates. In particular, the CCA-secure BABYBEAR can be optimized to run with only 2.4 kB RAM on AVR, and the CPA-secure version requires even less memory, namely just 1.7 kB.

2   Preliminaries

2.1   8-bit AVR Microcontrollers

8-bit AVR microcontrollers continue to be widely used in the embedded realm (e.g. smart cards, wireless sensor nodes). The AVR architecture is based on the modified Harvard memory model and follows the RISC philosophy. It features 32 general-purpose working registers (i.e. R0 to R31) of 8-bit width, which are directly connected to the Arithmetic Logic Unit (ALU). The current revision of the AVR instruction set supports 129 instructions in total, and each of them has fixed latency. Examples of instructions that are frequently used in our software are addition and subtraction (ADD/ADC and SUB/SBC); they take a single cycle. On the other hand, the multiplication (MUL) and also the load and store (LD/ST) instructions are more expensive since they have a latency of two clock cycles. The specific AVR microcontroller on which we simulated the execution time of our software is the ATmega1284; it features 16 kB SRAM and 128 kB flash memory for storing program code.

2.2   Overview of ThreeBears

THREEBEARS has three parameter sets called BABYBEAR, MAMABEAR, and PAPABEAR, matching NIST security categories 2, 4, and 5, respectively. Each parameter set comes with two instances, one providing CPA security and the other CCA security. Taking BABYBEAR as example, the CPA-secure instance is named BABYBEAREPHEM (with the meaning of ephemeral BABYBEAR), while the CCA-secure one is simply called BABYBEAR. In the following, we only give a short summary of the CCA-secure instance of THREEBEARS. In contrast to encryption schemes with CCA-security, CPA-secure ones, roughly speaking, do not repeat and verify the key generation and encryption (i.e. encapsulation) as part of the decryption (i.e. decapsulation) procedure, see [8] for details.

Notation and Parameters. THREEBEARS operates in the field $\mathbb{Z}/N$, where the prime modulus $N = 2^{3120} - 2^{1560} - 1$ is a so-called "golden-ratio" Solinas trinomial prime [7]. N is commonly written as $N = \phi(x) = x^D - x^{D/2} - 1$. The addition and multiplication $(+, *)$ in $\mathbb{Z}/N$ will be explained in Subsect. 3.1. An additional parameter d determines the the module dimension; this dimension is 2 for BABYBEAR, 3 for MAMABEAR and 4 for PAPABEAR, respectively.

Key Generation. To generate a key pair for THREEBEARS, the following operations have to be performed:

1. Generate a uniform and random string sk with a fixed length.
2. Generate two noise vectors $(a_0, \ldots, a_{d-1})$ and $(b_0, \ldots, b_{d-1})$, where $a_i, b_i \in \mathbb{Z}/N$ is sampled from a noise sampler using sk.
3. Compute $r = \text{HASH}(sk)$.
4. Generate a $d \times d$ matrix $\boldsymbol{M}$, where each element $M_{i,j} \in \mathbb{Z}/N$ is sampled from a uniform sampler using r.
5. Obtain vector $\boldsymbol{z} = (z_0, \ldots, z_{d-1})$ by computing each $z_i = b_i + \Sigma_{j=0}^{d-1} M_{i,j} * a_j \mod N$
6. Output sk as *private key* and $(r, \boldsymbol{z})$ as *public key*.

Encapsulation. The encapsulation operation gets a public key $(r, \boldsymbol{z})$ as input and produces a ciphertext and shared secret as output:

1. Generate a uniform and random string *seed* with a fixed-length.
2. Generate two noise vectors $(\hat{a}_0, \ldots, \hat{a}_{d-1})$, $(\hat{b}_0, \ldots, \hat{b}_{d-1})$ and a noise c, where $\hat{a}_i, \hat{b}_i, c \in \mathbb{Z}/N$ is sampled from noise sampler by given r and *seed*.
3. Generate a $d \times d$ matrix $\boldsymbol{M}$, where each element $M_{i,j} \in \mathbb{Z}/N$ is sampled from uniform sampler by given r.
4. Obtain vector $\boldsymbol{y} = (y_0, \ldots, y_{d-1})$ by computing each $y_i = \hat{b}_i + \Sigma_{j=0}^{d-1} M_{j,i} * \hat{a}_j \mod N$, and compute $x = c + \Sigma_{j=0}^{d-1} z_j * \hat{a}_j \mod N$.
5. Use Melas FEC encoder to encode *seed*, and use this encoded output together with x to extract a fixed-length string f.
6. Compute $ss = \text{HASH}(r, seed)$.
7. Output ss as *shared secret* and $(f, \boldsymbol{y})$ as *ciphertext*.

Decapsulation. The decapsulation gets a private key sk and ciphertext $(f, \boldsymbol{y})$ as input and produces a shared secret as output:

1. Generate a noise vector $(a_0, \ldots, a_{d-1})$, where $a_i \in \mathbb{Z}/N$ is sampled from a noise sampler by given sk.
2. Compute $x = \Sigma_{j=0}^{d-1} y_j * a_j \bmod N$.
3. Derive a string from f together with x, and use Melas FEC decoder to decode this string to obtain the string $seed$.
4. Generate the public key $(r', \boldsymbol{z'})$ through Key Generation by given sk.
5. Repeat Encapsulation to get ss' and $(f', \boldsymbol{y'})$ by using the obtained $seed$ and key pair $(sk, (r', \boldsymbol{z'}))$.
6. Check whether $(f', \boldsymbol{y'})$ equals to $(f, \boldsymbol{y})$; if they are equal then output ss' as $shared\ secret$; if not then output $\text{HASH}(sk, f, \boldsymbol{y})$ as $shared\ secret$.

The three operations described above use a few auxiliary functions such as samplers (noise sampler and uniform sampler), hash functions, and a function for the correction of errors. Both the samplers and hash functions are based on cSHAKE256 [12], which uses the Keccak permutation [1] at the lowest layer. In addition, THREEBEARS adopts Melas BCH code for Forward Error Correction (FEC) since it is very fast, has low RAM consumption and small code size, and can also be easily implemented to have constant execution time.

We determined the execution time of several implementations contained in the THREEBEARS NIST submission package on an AVR microcontroller. Like is the case with other lattice-based cryptosystems, the arithmetic computations of THREEBEARS determine the memory footprint and have a big impact on the overall execution time. Hence, our work primarily focuses on the optimization of the costly MAC operation of the form $r = r + a * b \bmod N$. Concerning the auxiliary functions, we were able to significantly improve their performance (in relation to the C code of the submission package) thanks to a highly-optimized AVR assembler implementation of the permutation of Keccak[2]. Further details about the auxiliary functions are outside of the scope of this work; we refer the reader to the specification of THREEBEARS [8].

3   Optimizations for the MAC Operation

The multiply-accumulate (MAC) operation of THREEBEARS, in particular the 3120-bit multiplication that is part of it, is very costly on 8-bit microcontrollers and requires special attention. This section deals with optimization techniques for the MAC operation on the AVR platform. As already stated in Sect. 1, we follow two strategies to optimize the MAC, one whose goal is to minimize the RAM footprint, whereas the other aims to maximize performance. The result is a memory-optimized MAC and a speed-optimized MAC, which are described in Subsect. 3.3 and 3.4, respectively.

3.1   The MAC Operation of ThreeBears

THREEBEARS defines its field operations $(+, *)$ as

$$a + b := a + b \bmod N \quad \text{and} \quad a * b := a \cdot b \cdot x^{-D/2} \bmod N$$

---

[2] See https://github.com/XKCP/XKCP/tree/master/lib/low/KeccakP-1600/AVR8.

where $+$ and $\cdot$ are the conventional integer addition and multiplication, respectively. Note that a so-called clarifier $x^{-D/2}$ is multiplied with the factors in the field multiplication, which serves to reduce the distortion of the noise. As shown in [7], the Solinas prime N enables very fast Karatsuba multiplication [11]. We can write the field multiplication in the following way, where $\lambda = x^{D/2}$ and the subscripts H and L are used to denote the higher/lower half of an integer:

$$
\begin{aligned}
z = a * b = a \cdot b \cdot \lambda^{-1} &= (a_L + a_H \lambda)(b_L + b_H \lambda) \cdot \lambda^{-1} \\
&= a_L b_L \lambda^{-1} + (a_L b_H + a_H b_L) + a_H b_H \lambda \\
&= a_L b_L (\lambda - 1) + (a_L b_H + a_H b_L) + a_H b_H \lambda \\
&= (a_L b_H + a_H b_L - a_L b_L) + (a_L b_L + a_H b_H) \lambda \\
&= (a_H b_H - (a_L - a_H)(b_L - b_H)) + (a_L b_L + a_H b_H) \lambda \mod N \qquad (1)
\end{aligned}
$$

Compared to a conventional Karatsuba multiplication, which requires three half-size multiplications and six additions/subtractions, the Karatsuba method for multiplication in $\mathbb{Z}/N$ saves one addition or subtraction. Consequently, the MAC operation can be performed as specified by Eq. (2) and Eq. (3):

$$
\begin{aligned}
r = r + a * b \bmod N & \\
&= (r_L + a_H b_H - (a_L - a_H)(b_L - b_H)) + (r_H + a_L b_L + a_H b_H) \lambda \bmod N \qquad (2) \\
&= (r_L + a_H b_L - a_L(b_L - b_H)) + (r_H + (a_L + a_H) b_H + a_L(b_L - b_H)) \lambda \bmod N \qquad (3)
\end{aligned}
$$

3.2 Full-Radix Representation for Field Elements

The NIST submission package of THREEBEARS consists of different implementations, including a reference implementation, optimized implementations, and additional implementations (e.g. a low-memory implementation). As mentioned in Sect. 1, they all use a *reduced-radix* representation for the 3120-bit integers (e.g. on a 32-bit platform, each limb is 26 bits long, and an element of the field consists of 120 limbs). Since this representation implies that there are six free bits in a 32-bit word, it is possible to store the carry (or borrow) bits that are generated during a field operation instead of immediately propagating them to the next-higher word, which reduces dependencies and enables instruction-level parallelism. Modern super-scalar processors can execute several instructions in parallel and, in this way, improve the running time of THREEBEARS.

Our implementations of BABYBEAR for AVR use a *full-radix* representation for the field elements for a number of reasons. First, small 8-bit microcontrollers have a single-issue pipeline and can not execute instructions in parallel, even when there are no dependencies among instructions. Furthermore, leaving six bits of "headroom" in a 32-bit word increases the number of limbs (in relation to the full-radix case) and, hence, the number of (32×32)-bit multiplications to be carried out. This is a bigger problem on AVR than on high-end processors where multiplications are a lot faster. Finally, the reduced-radix representation requires more space for a field-element (i.e. larger memory footprint) and more load/store instructions. In our full-radix representation, an element of the field consists of 98 words of a length of 32 bits and consumes $98 \times 4 = 392$ bytes in RAM, while the original representation requires $120 \times 4 = 480$ bytes. The full-radix representation with 32-bit words has also arithmetic advantages since (as mentioned in Sect. 1) it allows one to accelerate the MAC operation using the RPS method [13]. Thus, we fix the number representation radix to 2^{32}, despite the fact that we are working on an 8-bit microcontroller.

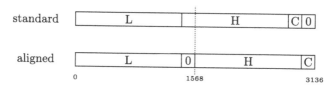

Fig. 1. Standard and aligned form of a field element (AVR uses little-endian)

We define two forms of storage for a full-radix field element: *standard* and *aligned*. Both forms are visually sketched in Fig. 1, where "L" and "H" stands respectively for the lower and higher 1560 bits of a 3120-bit field element. The standard form is basically the straightforward way of storing a multi-precision integer. Since a 3120-bit integer occupies 98 32-bit words, there are 16 unused bits (i.e. two empty bytes) in the most significant word. In our optimized MAC operations, the result is not always strictly in the range $[0, N)$ but can also be in $[0, 2N)$, which means the second most significant byte is either 0 or 1. We call this byte "carry byte" and mark it with a "C" in Fig. 1. Furthermore, we use "0" to indicate the most significant byte because it is 0 all the time.

The reason why we convert a standard integer into aligned form is because it allows us to perform the Karatsuba multiplication more efficiently. From an implementer's viewpoint, the standard form is suboptimal for Karatsuba since it does not place the lower ("L") and upper ("H") 1560 bits into the lower and upper half of the operand space (see Fig. 1). Concretely, the lowest byte of the upper 1560 bits is located at the most significant byte of the lower half in the space, which introduces some extra effort for alignment and addressing. The aligned form splits the lower and upper 1560 bits in such a way that they are ideally located for Karatsuba multiplication.

3.3 Memory-Optimized MAC Operation

The NIST submission package of THREEBEARS includes a low-memory implementation for each instance, which aims to minimize stack consumption. These low-memory variants are based on a special memory-efficient MAC operation that uses one level of Karatsuba's technique [11], which follows a modification of Eq. (3), namely Eq. (4) shown below:

$$(r_L + a_H b_L - 2a_L(b_L - b_H)) + (r_H + (a_L + a_H)b_H)\lambda + a_L(b_L - b_H)\lambda^2 \bmod N \quad (4)$$

This MAC implements the multiplications using the product-scanning method and operates on reduced-radix words. Our memory-optimized MAC operation was developed on basis of this original low-memory MAC, but performs all its computations on aligned full-radix words (after some alignment operations).

Algorithm 1. Memory-optimized MAC operation

Input: Aligned s-word integers $A = (A_{s-1}, \ldots, A_1, A_0)$, $B = (B_{s-1}, \ldots, B_1, B_0)$, and $R = (R_{s-1}, \ldots, R_1, R_0)$, each word contains ω bits; β is a parameter of alignment

Output: Aligned s-word product $R = R + A \cdot B \cdot x^{-D/2} \bmod N = (R_{s-1}, \ldots, R_1, R_0)$

1: $Z_0 \leftarrow 0, Z_1 \leftarrow 0$
2: $l \leftarrow s/2$
3: **for** i from 0 to $l-1$ by 1 **do**
4:    $Z_2 \leftarrow 0$
5:    $k \leftarrow i+1$
6:    **for** j from 0 to i by 1 **do**
7:       $k \leftarrow k-1$
8:       $Z_0 \leftarrow Z_0 + A_{j+l} \cdot B_k$
9:       $Z_1 \leftarrow Z_1 + (A_j + A_{j+l}) \cdot B_{k+l}$
10:      $Z_2 \leftarrow Z_2 + A_j \cdot (B_k - B_{k+l})$
11:   **end for**
12:   $Z_0 \leftarrow Z_0 - 2 \cdot Z_2$
13:   $k \leftarrow l$
14:   **for** j from $i+1$ to $l-1$ by 1 **do**
15:      $k \leftarrow k-1$
16:      $Z_1 \leftarrow Z_1 + 2^\beta \cdot A_{j+l} \cdot B_k$
17:      $Z_2 \leftarrow Z_2 + 2^\beta \cdot (A_j + A_{j+l}) \cdot B_{k+l}$
18:      $Z_0 \leftarrow Z_0 + 2^\beta \cdot A_j \cdot (B_k - B_{k+l})$
19:   **end for**
20:   $Z_0 \leftarrow Z_0 + Z_2 + R_i$
21:   $Z_1 \leftarrow Z_1 + Z_2 + R_{i+l}$
22:   $R_i \leftarrow Z_0 \bmod 2^\omega$

23:   $Z_0 \leftarrow Z_0/2^\omega$
24:   $R_{i+l} \leftarrow Z_1 \bmod 2^\omega$
25:   $Z_1 \leftarrow Z_1/2^\omega$
26: **end for**
27: $Z_0 \leftarrow 2^\beta \cdot Z_0 + R_{l-1}/2^{\omega-\beta}$
28: $Z_1 \leftarrow 2^\beta \cdot Z_1 + R_{s-1}/2^{\omega-\beta}$
29: $R_{l-1} \leftarrow R_{l-1} \bmod 2^{\omega-\beta}$
30: $R_{s-1} \leftarrow R_{s-1} \bmod 2^{\omega-\beta}$
31: $Z_0 \leftarrow Z_0 + Z_1$
32: **for** i from 0 to $l-1$ by 1 **do**
33:   $Z_1 \leftarrow Z_1 + R_i$
34:   $R_i \leftarrow Z_1 \bmod 2^\omega$
35:   $Z_1 \leftarrow Z_1/2^\omega$
36: **end for**
37: $Z_0 \leftarrow 2^\beta \cdot Z_0 + R_{l-1}/2^{\omega-\beta}$
38: $R_{l-1} \leftarrow R_{l-1} \bmod 2^{\omega-\beta}$
39: **for** i from l to $s-1$ by 1 **do**
40:   $Z_0 \leftarrow Z_0 + R_i$
41:   $R_i \leftarrow Z_0 \bmod 2^\omega$
42:   $Z_0 \leftarrow Z_0/2^\omega$
43: **end for**
44: **return** $(R_{s-1}, \ldots, R_1, R_0)$

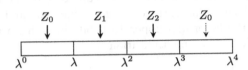

Fig. 2. Three accumulators for coefficients of $\lambda^0 = 1$, λ, and λ^2 of a product R

Algorithm 1 shows our low-RAM one-level Karatsuba MAC, which consists of two major parts: a main MAC loop interleaved with the modular reduction (from line 1 to 26) and a final reduction modulo N (from line 27 to 43). The designer of THREEBEARS coined the term "tripleMAC" to refer to the three word-level MACs in the inner loops (line 8 to 10 and 16 to 19). Certainly, this tripleMAC is the most frequent computation carried out by Algorithm 1 and dominates the overall execution time. In order to reach peak performance on AVR, we replace the conventional product-scanning technique by an optimized variant of the hybrid multiplication method [6], namely the so-called Reverse Product-Scanning (RPS) method [13], which processes four bytes (i.e. 32 bits) of the operands per loop-iteration. In addition, we split each of the inner loops containing a tripleMAC up into three separate loops, and each of these three loops computes one word-level MAC. Due to the relatively small register space of AVR, it is not possible to keep all three accumulators (i.e. Z_0, Z_1, and Z_2) in registers,which means executing three word-level MACs in the same inner loop would require a large number of LD and ST instructions to load and store the accumulators in each iteration. Thanks to our modification, an accumulator has to be loaded/stored only before/after the whole inner loop.

The three inputs and the output of Algorithm 1 are aligned integers, where s is 98 and ω is 32. The parameter β specifies the shift-distance (in bits) when converting an ordinary integer to aligned form ($\beta = 8$ in our case). Each of the three accumulators Z_0, Z_1, and Z_2 in Algorithm 1 is 80 bits long and occupies 10 registers. Figure 2 illustrates the relation between the accumulators and the coefficients of λ^0, λ, and λ^2 in an aligned output R. Referring to Eq. (4), we suppose each coefficient can be 3120 bits long, but Z_0, Z_1, and Z_2 accumulate only the lower 1560 bits of the coefficients of λ^0, λ, and λ^2, respectively, in the first tripleMAC (line 8 to 10). After the first inner loop, double of Z_2 must be subtracted from Z_0 (line 12), which corresponds to the operation of the form $a_H b_L - 2a_L(b_L - b_H)$ in Eq. (4). The second inner loop (beginning at line 14) computes the higher half of each coefficient, but this time the word-products are added to different accumulators compared to the first tripleMAC (e.g. the 64-bit word-products of the form $A_{j+l} \cdot B_k$ are added to Z_1 instead of Z_0). In the second tripleMAC, the factor 2^β needs to be considered in order to ensure proper alignment. The third word-level MAC (at line 18) can be regarded as computing (the lower half of) the coefficient of λ^3. Normally, we should use an additional accumulator Z_3 for this third MAC, but it is more efficient to re-use Z_0. This is possible since, after the second inner loop, we would normally have to compute $Z_1 \leftarrow Z_1 - 2 \cdot Z_3$, a similar operation as at line 12. But because

$$\lambda^3 = \lambda^2 \cdot \lambda = (\lambda + 1) \cdot \lambda = \lambda^2 + \lambda = (\lambda + 1) + \lambda = 2\lambda + 1 \bmod N,$$

we also have to compute $Z_0 \leftarrow Z_0 + Z_3$ and $Z_1 \leftarrow Z_1 + 2 \cdot Z_3$. Combining these two computations with $Z_1 \leftarrow Z_1 - 2 \cdot Z_3$ implies that Z_1 can simply keep its present value and only Z_0 accumulates the value of Z_3. Thus, Algorithm 1 does not compute $Z_1 \leftarrow Z_1 - 2 \cdot Z_3$, but instead directly accumulates the sum of the word-products $A_j \cdot (B_k - B_{k+l})$ into Z_0 (which also saves a few load and store instructions). This "shortcut" is indicated in Fig. 2 with a dashed arrow from Z_0 to the coefficient of λ^3. Lines 20 to 25 add the lower 32-bit words of Z_0 and Z_1 to the corresponding words of the result R and right-shift Z_0 and Z_1. The part from line 27 to 30 brings the output of the MAC into a properly aligned form. Thereafter (line 31 to 43), a modulo-N reduction (based on the relation $\lambda^2 \equiv \lambda + 1 \bmod N$) along with a conversion to 32-bit words is performed. The output of Algorithm 1 is an aligned integer in the range of $[0, 2N)$.

We implemented Algorithm 1 completely in AVR Assembly language. Even though each accumulator Z_i consists of 80 bits (ten bytes), we only load and store nine bytes of Z_i in each inner loop. A simple analysis shows that that the accumulator values in the first inner loop can never exceed 2^{72}, which allows us to only load and store the nine least-significant bytes. In the second tripleMAC loop, each word-product is multiplied by 2^β (i.e. shifted left by eight bits) and so it is not necessary to load/store the least-significant accumulator byte.

Algorithm 2. Speed-optimized MAC operation

Input: Aligned field elements $A = (A_H, A_L)$, $B = (B_H, B_L)$ and $R = (R_H, R_L)$
Output: Aligned product $R = R + A \cdot B \cdot x^{-D/2} \bmod N = (R_H, R_L)$

1: $(Z_H, Z_L) \leftarrow (0, 0)$, $(T_H, T_L) \leftarrow (0, 0)$	10: $R_H \leftarrow R_H + Z_H$
2: $T_L \leftarrow |A_L - A_H|$	11: $T_L \leftarrow Z_H + Z_L$
3: if $A_L - A_H < 0$ then $s_a \leftarrow 1$; else $s_a \leftarrow 0$	12: $R_L \leftarrow R_L + T_L$
4: $T_H \leftarrow |B_L - B_H|$	13: $R_H \leftarrow R_H + T_L$
5: if $B_L - B_H < 0$ then $s_b \leftarrow 1$; else $s_b \leftarrow 0$	14: $T_L \leftarrow A_L, T_H \leftarrow B_L$
	15: $(Z_H, Z_L) \leftarrow T_L \cdot T_H$
6: $(Z_H, Z_L) \leftarrow T_L \cdot T_H \cdot (-1)^{1-(s_a \oplus s_b)}$	16: $R_H \leftarrow R_H + Z_L$
7: $(R_H, R_L) \leftarrow (R_H, R_L) + (Z_H, Z_L)$	17: $R_L \leftarrow R_L + Z_H$
8: $T_L \leftarrow A_H, T_H \leftarrow B_H$	18: $R_H \leftarrow R_H + Z_H$
9: $(Z_H, Z_L) \leftarrow T_L \cdot T_H$	19: $(R_H, R_L) \leftarrow (R_H, R_L) \bmod N$
	20: **return** (R_H, R_L)

3.4 Speed-Optimized MAC Operation

The MAC operations of the implementations in the NIST submission package of THREEBEARS are not suitable to reach high speed on AVR. Therefore, we developed our speed-optimized MAC operation from scratch and implemented it according to a variant of Eq. (2), namely Eq. (5) specified below. We divide the three full-size 3120-bit products (e.g. $a_L b_L$) of Eq. (2) into two halves, and use l for representing $a_L b_L$, m for $-(a_L - a_H)(b_L - b_H)$ and h for $a_H b_H$:

$$
\begin{aligned}
r &= (r_L + h + m) + (r_H + l + h)\lambda \bmod N \\
&= (r_L + (h_L + h_H \lambda) + (m_L + m_H \lambda)) + (r_H + (l_L + l_H \lambda) + (h_L + h_H \lambda))\lambda \\
&= (r_L + h_L + m_L) + (r_H + l_L + h_L + m_H + h_H)\lambda + (l_H + h_H)\lambda^2 \\
&= (r_L + m_L + \underline{h_L + h_H + l_H}) + (r_H + m_H + h_H + l_L + \underline{h_L + h_H + l_H})\lambda \quad (5)
\end{aligned}
$$

The underlined parts in Eq. (5) are common parts of the coefficients of λ^0 and λ. Algorithm 2 specifies our speed-optimized MAC, which operates on half-size (i.e. 1560-bit) parts of the operands A, B and R. We omitted the details of the final step (line 19) in Algorithm 2, i.e. the modulo-N reduction, because it is very similar to lines 27 to 43 in Algorithm 1. Compared with Algorithm 1, the speed-efficient MAC operation is designed in a more straightforward way since it computes each entire half-size multiplication separately to obtain a full-size intermediate product (line 6, 9, and 15). However, it consumes more memory to store the intermediate products (e.g. Z_H, Z_L and T_H, T_L).

We still take advantage of RPS technique to speed up the inner-loop operation, but combine it Karatsuba's method. Our experiments with different levels of Karatsuba multiplication showed that the 2-level Karatsuba approach with the RPS technique underneath (i.e. 2-level KRPS) yields the best performance for a multiplication of 1560-bit operands. Consequently, we execute three levels of Karatsuba (i.e. 3-level KRPS) altogether for the MAC operation. Each level uses the so-called subtractive Karatsuba algorithm described in [9] to achieve fast and constant execution time. All half-size multiplications performed at the second and third level use space that was initially occupied by input operands to store intermediate values, i.e. we do not allocate additional RAM inside the half-size multiplications. This is also the reason for the two operations at line 8 and 14, where we move the operands to T_H and T_L before the multiplication so that we do not modify the inputs A and B.

4   Performance Evaluation and Comparison

Except of the MAC operations, all components of our ME and HS software are taken from the low-memory and speed-optimized implementation contained in the NIST package of THREEBEARS (with minor optimizations). Our software consists of a mix of C and AVR assembly language, i.e. the performance-critical MAC operation and Keccak permutation are written in AVR assembly, and all other functions in C. Atmel Studio v7.0, our development environment, comes with the 8-bit AVR GNU toolchain including avr-gcc version 5.4.0. We used the cycle-accurate instruction set simulator of Atmel Studio to precisely determine the execution times. The source codes were compiled with optimization option -O2 using the ATmega1284 microcontroller as target device.

Table 1. Execution time (in clock cycles) of our AVR implementations

Implementation	Security	MAC	KeyGen	Encaps	Decaps
ME-BBear	CCA-secure	1,033,728	8,746,418	12,289,744	18,578,335
ME-BBear-Eph	CPA-secure	1,033,728	8,746,418	12,435,165	3,444,154
HS-BBear	CCA-secure	604,703	6,123,527	7,901,873	12,476,447
HS-BBear-Eph	CPA-secure	604,703	6,123,527	8,047,835	2,586,202

Table 1 shows the execution time of a MAC operation, key generation, encapsulation, and decapsulation of our software. A speed-optimized MAC takes only 605 k clock cycles, while the memory-optimized version requires 70% more cycles.

The speed difference between these two types of MAC directly impacts the overall running time of ME-BBear(-Eph) versus HS-BBear(-Eph), because there are several MACs in KeyGen, Encaps and Decaps. Taking HS-BBear as example, KeyGen, Encaps, and Decaps needs 6.12 M, 7.90 M, and 12.48 M clock cycles, respectively. Their ME counterparts are roughly 1.5 times slower.

Table 2. RAM usage and code size (both in bytes) of our AVR implementations

Implementation	MAC		KeyGen		Encaps		Decaps		Total	
	RAM	Size	RAM	Size	RAM	Size	RAM	Size	RAM	Size
ME-BBear	82	2,760	1,715	6,432	1,735	7,554	2,368	10,110	2,368	12,264
ME-BBear-Eph	82	2,760	1,715	6,432	1,735	7,640	1,731	8,270	1,735	10,998
HS-BBear	934	3,332	2,733	7,000	2,752	8,140	4,559	10,684	4,559	11,568
HS-BBear-Eph	934	3,332	2,733	7,000	2,752	8,226	2,356	8,846	2,752	10,296

Table 2 specifies both the memory footprint and code size of the four basic operations (MAC, KeyGen, Encaps, and Decaps). The speed-optimized MAC consumes 934 bytes of memory, while the memory-optimized MAC requires as little as 82 bytes, which is just 9% of the former. Due to the memory-optimized MAC operation and full-radix representation of field elements, ME-BBear has a RAM footprint of 1.7 kB for each KeyGen and Encaps, while Decaps is more memory-demanding and needs 2.4 kB RAM. However, ME-BBear-Eph requires only 1.7 kB of RAM altogether. On the other hand, the HS implementations need over 1.5 times more RAM than their ME counterparts. In terms of code size, each of the four implementations requires roughly 11 kB.

Table 3. Comparison of our implementation with other key-establishment schemes (all of which target 128-bit security) on the 8-bit AVR platform (the execution times of Encaps and Decaps are in clock cycles; RAM and code size are in bytes).

Implementation	Algorithm	Encaps	Decaps	RAM	Size
This work (ME-CCA)	THREEBEARS	12,289,744	18,578,335	2,368	12,264
This work (ME-CPA)	THREEBEARS	12,435,165	3,444,154	1,735	10,998
This work (HS-CCA)	THREEBEARS	7,901,873	12,476,447	4,559	11,568
This work (HS-CPA)	THREEBEARS	8,047,835	2,586,202	2,752	10,296
Cheng et al. [2]	NTRU Prime	8,160,665	15,602,748	n/a	11,478
Düll et al. [4] (ME)	Curve25519	14,146,844	14,146,844	510	9,912
Düll et al. [4] (HS)	Curve25519	13,900,397	13,900,397	494	17,710

Table 3 compares implementations of both pre and post-quantum schemes (targeting 128-bit security) on 8-bit AVR microcontrollers. Compared to the CCA-secure version of the second-round NIST candidate NTRU Prime [2], HS-BBear is slightly faster for both Encaps and Decpas. On the other hand, when compared with the optimized implementation of Curve25519 in [4], the Encaps operation of each BABYBEAR variant in Table 3 is faster than a variable-base scalar multiplication, while the Decaps of ME-BBear is slower, but that of the HS variant still a bit faster. Notably, the Decaps operation of our CPA-secure implementations is respectively 4.0 times (ME) and 5.4 times (HS) faster than Curve25519.

Table 4. Comparison of RAM consumption (in bytes) of NIST PQC implementations (all of which target NIST security category 1 or 2) on 8-bit AVR and on 32-bit ARM Cortex-M4 microcontrollers.

Implementation	Algorithm	Platform	KeyGen	Encaps	Decaps
CCA-secure schemes					
This work (ME)	THREEBEARS	AVR	1,715	1,735	2,368
Hamburg [8]	THREEBEARS	Cortex-M4	2,288	2,352	3,024
pqm4 [10]	THREEBEARS	Cortex-M4	3,076	2,964	5,092
pqm4 [10]	NewHope	Cortex-M4	3,876	5,044	5,044
pqm4 [10]	Round5	Cortex-M4	4,148	4,596	5,220
pqm4 [10]	Kyber	Cortex-M4	2,388	2,476	2,492
pqm4 [10]	NTRU	Cortex-M4	11,848	6,864	5,144
pqm4 [10]	Saber	Cortex-M4	9,652	11,388	12,132
CPA-secure schemes					
This work (ME)	THREEBEARS	AVR	1,715	1,735	1,731
Hamburg [8]	THREEBEARS	Cortex-M4	2,288	2,352	2,080
pqm4 [10]	THREEBEARS	Cortex-M4	3,076	2,980	2,420
pqm4 [10]	NewHope	Cortex-M4	3,836	4,940	3,200
pqm4 [10]	Round5	Cortex-M4	4,052	4,500	2,308

One of the most significant advantages of the THREEBEARS cryptosystem is its relatively low RAM consumption, which is important for deployment on constrained devices. Table 4 compares the RAM footprint of implementations of THREEBEARS and a few other NIST candidates on microcontrollers. Due to the very small number of state-of-the-art implementations of NIST candidates for the 8-bit AVR platform, we include in Table 4 also some recent results from the pqm4 library, which targets 32-bit ARM Cortex-M4. In addition, we list the results of the original low-RAM implementations of BABYBEAR (for both the CCA and CPA variant) from the NIST package. Our memory-optimized BABY-BEAR is the most RAM-efficient implementation among all CCA-secure PQC schemes and needs 5% less RAM than the second most RAM-efficient scheme Kyber. Furthermore, ME-BBear-Eph requires the least amount of RAM of all (CPA-secure) second-round NIST PQC candidates, and improves the original low-memory implementation of the designer by roughly 26.2%.

5   Conclusions

We presented the first highly-optimized Assembler implementation of THREE-BEARS for the 8-bit AVR architecture. Our simulation results show that, even with a fixed parameter set like BABYBEAR, many trade-offs between execution time and RAM consumption are possible. The memory-optimized CPA-secure version of BABYBEAR requires only slightly more than 1.7 kB RAM, which sets a new record for memory efficiency among all known software implementations of second-round candidates. Due to this low memory footprint, BABYBEAR fits easily into the SRAM of 8-bit AVR ATmega microcontrollers and will even run on severely constrained devices like an ATmega128L with 4 kB SRAM. While a RAM footprint of 1.7 kB is still clearly above the 500 B of Curve25519, the execution times are in favor of BABYBEAR since a CPA-secure decapsulation is four times faster than a scalar multiplication. THREEBEARS is also very well suited to be part of a hybrid pre/post-quantum key agreement protocol since the multiple-precision integer arithmetic can (potentially) be shared with the low-level field arithmetic of Curve25519, thereby reducing the overall code size when implemented in software or the total silicon area in the case of hardware implementation. For all these reasons, THREEBEARS is an excellent candidate for a post-quantum cryptosystem to secure the IoT.

Acknowledgements. This work was supported by the European Union's Horizon 2020 research and innovation programme under grant agreement No. 779391 (FutureTPM).

References

1. Bertoni, G., Daemen, J., Peeters, M., Van Assche, G.: Keccak. In: Johansson, T., Nguyen, P.Q. (eds.) EUROCRYPT 2013. LNCS, vol. 7881, pp. 313–314. Springer, Heidelberg (2013). https://doi.org/10.1007/978-3-642-38348-9_19
2. Cheng, H., Dinu, D., Großschädl, J., Rønne, P.B., Ryan, P.Y.A.: A lightweight implementation of NTRU prime for the post-quantum internet of things. In: Laurent, M., Giannetsos, T. (eds.) WISTP 2019. LNCS, vol. 12024, pp. 103–119. Springer, Cham (2020). https://doi.org/10.1007/978-3-030-41702-4_7
3. Crossbow Technology, Inc.: MICAz Wireless Measurement System. Data sheet, January 2006. http://www.xbow.com/Products/Product_pdf_files/Wireless_pdf/MICAz_Datasheet.pdf
4. Düll, M., Haase, B., Hinterwälder, G., Hutter, M., Paar, C., Sánchez, A.H., Schwabe, P.: High-speed Curve25519 on 8-bit, 16-bit and 32-bit microcontrollers. Designs Codes Crypt. **77**(2–3), 493–514 (2015)
5. Gu, C.: Integer version of Ring-LWE and its applications. Cryptology ePrint Archive, Report 2017/641 (2017). http://eprint.iacr.org/2017/641
6. Gura, N., Patel, A., Wander, A., Eberle, H., Shantz, S.C.: Comparing elliptic curve cryptography and RSA on 8-bit CPUs. In: Joye, M., Quisquater, J.-J. (eds.) CHES 2004. LNCS, vol. 3156, pp. 119–132. Springer, Heidelberg (2004). https://doi.org/10.1007/978-3-540-28632-5_9
7. Hamburg, M.: Ed448-Goldilocks, a new elliptic curve. Cryptology ePrint Archive, Report 2015/625 (2015). https://eprint.iacr.org/2015/625

8. Hamburg, M.: ThreeBears: Round 2 specification (2019). http://csrc.nist.gov/projects/post-quantum-cryptography/round-2-submissions
9. Hutter, M., Schwabe, P.: Multiprecision multiplication on AVR revisited. J. Crypt. Eng. **5**(3), 201–214 (2015). https://doi.org/10.1007/s13389-015-0093-2
10. Kannwischer, M.J., Rijneveld, J., Schwabe, P., Stoffelen, K.: pqm4: testing and benchmarking NIST PQC on ARM Cortex-M4. Cryptology ePrint Archive, Report 2019/844 (2019). http://eprint.iacr.org
11. Karatsuba, A.A., Ofman, Y.P.: Multiplication of multidigit numbers on automata. Doklady Akademii Nauk SSSR **145**(2), 293–294 (1962)
12. Kelsey, J.M., Chang, S.-J.H., Perlner, R.A.: SHA-3 derived functions: cSHAKE, KMAC, TupleHash and ParallelHash. NIST Special Publication 800–185 (2016). http://doi.org/10.6028/NIST.SP.800-185
13. Liu, Z., Seo, H., Großschädl, J., Kim, H.: Reverse product-scanning multiplication and squaring on 8-Bit AVR processors. In: Hui, L.C.K., Qing, S.H., Shi, E., Yiu, S.M. (eds.) ICICS 2014. LNCS, vol. 8958, pp. 158–175. Springer, Cham (2015). https://doi.org/10.1007/978-3-319-21966-0_12
14. National Institute of Standards and Technology (NIST): Submission requirements and evaluation criteria for the post-quantum cryptography standardization process (2016). http://csrc.nist.gov/CSRC/media/Projects/Post-Quantum-Cryptography/documents/call-for-proposals-final-dec-2016.pdf
15. National Institute of Standards and Technology (NIST): NIST reveals 26 algorithms advancing to the post-quantum crypto 'semifinals'. Press release (2019). http://www.nist.gov/news-events/news/2019/01/nist-reveals-26-algorithms-advancing-post-quantum-crypto-semifinals

Classic McEliece Implementation
with Low Memory Footprint

Johannes Roth[1]([✉]), Evangelos Karatsiolis[1], and Juliane Krämer[2]

[1] MTG AG, Darmstadt, Germany
{jroth,ekaratsiolis}@mtg.de
[2] Technische Universität Darmstadt, Darmstadt, Germany
juliane@qpc.tu-darmstadt.de

Abstract. The Classic McEliece cryptosystem is one of the most trusted quantum-resistant cryptographic schemes. Deploying it in practical applications, however, is challenging due to the size of its public key. In this work, we bridge this gap. We present an implementation of Classic McEliece on an ARM Cortex-M4 processor, optimized to overcome memory constraints. To this end, we present an algorithm to retrieve the public key ad-hoc. This reduces memory and storage requirements and enables the generation of larger key pairs on the device. To further improve the implementation, we perform the public key operation by streaming the key to avoid storing it as a whole. This additionally reduces the risk of denial of service attacks. Finally, we use these results to implement and run TLS on the embedded device.

Keywords: Post-quantum cryptography · Classic McEliece · Low memory footprint · Embedded implementation · TLS

1 Introduction

Code-based cryptographic schemes are often named when researchers in the field of post-quantum cryptography are asked which cryptosystem they recommend until trusted standards exist, e.g., [1]. Since the code-based cryptosystem McEliece [16] and its variant, the Niederreiter cryptosystem [18], date back to the 1970s and 1980s, respectively, their security is widely trusted. The direct successor of these schemes is the key encapsulation mechanism Classic McEliece [4], which was selected as finalist in the ongoing PQC standardization process of the US-American National Institute of Standards and Technology (NIST)[1].

The prime reason that code-based cryptography - contrary to RSA and Diffie-Hellman, which are comparably old -, has not gained general acceptance so far, is the size of the public key. For instance, a McEliece public key of about one megabyte and an RSA key of few kilobytes achieve the same pre-quantum security level. Many works address this problem by replacing binary Goppa

---

[1] https://groups.google.com/a/list.nist.gov/forum/#!topic/pqc-forum/0ieuPB-b8eg.

© Springer Nature Switzerland AG 2021
P.-Y. Liardet and N. Mentens (Eds.): CARDIS 2020, LNCS 12609, pp. 34–49, 2021.
https://doi.org/10.1007/978-3-030-68487-7_3

codes with families of codes that lead to smaller public keys, e.g., [3,6,11,12,17]. That, however, is no option when working with Classic McEliece: Since other families of codes already led to security breaches, e.g., [2,8], or are not yet well-studied (which might lead to future security breaches), Classic McEliece focuses on binary Goppa codes since the scheme aims for conservative and well-studied cryptography.

When it comes to using cryptography in practical applications, a huge public key is especially problematic on memory-constrained devices, e.g., on embedded systems. On the other hand, there is a great demand for (post-quantum) cryptography for embedded devices, since on these devices, often sensitive data such as medical data and other personal information is processed. Hence, to obtain efficient and secure post-quantum cryptography for embedded devices by using Classic McEliece, we need to solve the problem that the public key is too big.

Contribution. In this work, we present memory-optimized algorithms for key generation and encapsulation of the Classic McEliece cryptosystem. We base our work on the Classic McEliece reference implementation. In accordance with NIST's request on recommended hardware[2], we use the ARM Cortex-M4 processor as our target platform. We emphasize that our goals are memory rather than speed optimizations. We demonstrate the practicability of our implementation by providing an operational instance of a Classic McEliece-based TLS on an embedded device.

Related Work. To the best of our knowledge, in the field of code-based cryptography there is not much related work addressing memory optimizations for handling the public key on embedded devices. In [7,10], a seed is used to generate the inverse of the scramble matrix that is multiplied by the public parity-check matrix. This considerably reduces the memory requirements for storing the private key. However, it does not address issues with storing the public key. The public key instead is stored on flash or external memory. In [20] it is demonstrated in the context of public key infrastructures that the McEliece encryption operation can be performed on a smart card, even though the public key is too large to be held in memory. We adapt this approach in Sect. 4. In Sect. 4.1 we briefly compare an aspect of our results with the McTiny protocol [5].

Organization. This paper is organized as follows: In Sect. 2 we provide basic background information on the notation and on the Classic McEliece cryptosystem. Sect. 3 presents a memory-efficient algorithm to retrieve the public key from the private key, thereby reducing storage requirements. Further, an adapted key generation algorithm, that in combination with the public key retrieval algorithm greatly reduces memory requirements, is presented. Section 4 describes

---

[2] https://groups.google.com/a/list.nist.gov/forum/#!topic/pqc-forum/cJxMq0_90 gU.

a memory-efficient variant of the encapsulation operation. In Sect. 5 we provide details on our implementation. Finally, Sect. 6 demonstrates the practical relevance of our results in a proof of concept TLS implementation.

2 Background

Notation. To be consistent with the Classic McEliece notation, elements of $\mathbb{F}_2^n$ are viewed as column vectors. All identity matrices in this work are of dimension $(n-k) \times (n-k)$, which is why we omit subscripts and denote the $(n-k) \times (n-k)$ identity matrix by I. The (Hamming) weight of a vector $v \in \mathbb{F}_2^n$ is denoted by $wt(v)$. To represent the ith row of a matrix A, we write A_i, while $A_{.i}$ refers to the ith column.

Classic McEliece. We do not detail the Classic McEliece algorithms here, but refer to the round-2 submission to NIST's PQC standardization process [4]. For readers not familiar with coding theory, we refer to [15].

We use symbols consistently with the Classic McEliece notation. Noteworthy symbols that are not explicitly introduced in this work are the Classic McEliece parameters $n, t, m, k = n - mt, q = 2^m$, the public key $T \in \mathbb{F}_2^{(n-k) \times k}$, the parity-check matrix $H \in \mathbb{F}_2^{(n-k) \times n}$, and its precursors $\hat{H} \in \mathbb{F}_2^{(n-k) \times n}$ and $\tilde{H} \in \mathbb{F}_q^{t \times n}$.

Note that we omit the *mceliece6960119* parameter set in this paper. These parameters produce bit sequences of length that are not multiples of 8. However, modern platforms operate on bytes. The trailing bits need an extra handling which our current implementation does not consider. This has no influence on the results.

3 Memory-Optimized Storing and Generation of the Key Pair

The public key of Classic McEliece is a parity-check matrix for the binary Goppa code that is chosen as private key. In McEliece and Niederreiter schemes, the public key is usually scrambled by multiplying suitable matrices. Instead of scrambling the rows by multiplying the parity-check matrix with a non-singular random matrix, Classic McEliece applies Gaussian elimination. This serves the same purpose and additionally transforms the parity-check matrix to systematic form, i.e., $H = (I \mid T)$. Choosing the systematic form has the benefit of reducing the public key size since the identity matrix I can be omitted.

For embedded devices, holding the parity-check matrix in memory and performing Gaussian elimination to obtain the resulting public key is challenging due to the size. To address this issue, we present an algorithm to generate a more compact form of the key pair (Sect. 3.1). We further present an algorithm to compute the public key ad-hoc in small chunks from the compact form (Sect. 3.2). The combination of both algorithms enables us to stream the public key to a peer without the need to hold it in memory in its entirety. This reduces both, memory and storage requirements for handling Classic McEliece key pairs.

3.1   Extended Private Key Generation

Classic McEliece defines the public key as $K_{pub} = T$ and the private key as $K_{priv} = (\Gamma, s)$. Here, $\Gamma = (g(x), (\alpha_1, ..., \alpha_n))$ where $g(x)$ is a polynomial in $\mathbb{F}_q[x]$, $(\alpha_1, ..., \alpha_n)$ are finite field elements in $\mathbb{F}_q$, and s is a uniformly random generated n-bit string. Our proposal is to omit the public key T altogether, and instead store a smaller matrix $S \in \mathbb{F}_2^{(n-k) \times (n-k)}$ in the private key. We call the new private key *extended private key* and define it as $K_{priv\_ext} = (\Gamma, s, S)$. We define S^{-1} as the leftmost $(n-k) \times (n-k)$ submatrix of $\hat{H}$, and S as its inverse, for which the relationship $S\hat{H} = H = (I \mid T)$ holds. The x86-optimized SSE and AVX code variants that have been submitted as additional implementations to NIST already make use of this relationship. The authors use it to speed-up the Gaussian elimination in the key generation operation, whereas we aim to reduce memory requirements instead.

With Algorithm 1, we present an algorithm to generate the extended private key. In comparison to the original Classic McEliece key generation [4, Section 2.4], no public key is computed. Further, Algorithm 1 does not operate on the complete matrix H and its precursors $\hat{H}$ and $\tilde{H}$. Instead, only the first $n - k$ columns are computed to produce S^{-1}, which in line 5 is inverted to obtain S.

Algorithm 1: Extended Private Key Generation

   Parameter: $n, t, m, q = 2^m, k = n - mt$

   Output: $K_{priv\_ext} = ((g(x), (\alpha_1, ..., \alpha_n), s, S)$

1   Generate a uniform random irreducible polynomial $g(x) \in \mathbb{F}_q[x]$ of degree t.

2   Select a uniform random sequence $(\alpha_1, \alpha_2, ..., \alpha_n)$ of n distinct elements of $\mathbb{F}_q$.

3   Compute the $t \times (n-k)$ matrix $\tilde{S}^{-1}$ over $\mathbb{F}_q$ by letting $(\tilde{S}^{-1})_{i,j} = h_{i,j}$, where
     $h_{i,j} = \alpha_j^{i-1}/g(\alpha_j)$ for $i = 1, ..., t$ and $j = 1, ..., n - k$.

4   Form an $(n-k) \times (n-k)$ matrix S^{-1} over $\mathbb{F}_2$ by replacing each entry
     $c_0 + c_1 z + ... + c_{m-1} z^{m-1}$ of $\tilde{S}^{-1}$ with a column of m bits $c_0, c_1, ..., c_{m-1}$.

5   Compute S as the inverse of S^{-1}.

6   **if** *the previous step fails (i.e., S^{-1} is singular)* **then**

7 | go back to line 1.

8   **end**

9   Generate a uniform random n-bit string s.

Note that entries of $\hat{H}$ (and $\hat{S}$) can be computed "on-the-fly" as the binary representation of entries of $\tilde{H}$: we obtain $\tilde{H}_{i,j}$ by $\tilde{H}_{i,j} = \alpha_j^{i-1}/g(\alpha_j)$. To efficiently access all entries of $\hat{H}$ and $\tilde{H}$, respectively, it is beneficial to produce the elements top-down. For $\tilde{H}_{i,j}$ with $i > 1$, it holds that $\tilde{H}_{i,j} = \alpha_j \tilde{H}_{i-1,j}$, i.e., computing $\tilde{H}_{i,j}$ from $\tilde{H}_{i-1,j}$ only encompasses one modular multiplication and preserves the previous work of computing the modular exponentiation and inversion.

3.2   Public Key Retrieval

In the following, we describe an algorithm that obtains chunks of the public key ad-hoc from the extended private key. We propose to call the process of obtaining the public key from the extended private key *retrieving the public key*[3].

The original Classic McEliece key generation algorithm already comprises a possibility to retrieve the public key. That is, for a valid private key, in lines 3–5 [4, Section 2.4], the corresponding public key is computed. This however entails holding the $(n-k) \times n$ matrix $\hat{H}$ in memory and subsequently performing Gaussian elimination. The matrix $\hat{H}$ is larger than the public key itself.

We therefore propose Algorithm 2 which operates on smaller matrices only. The algorithm has the additional property that it does not retrieve the complete public key in one large chunk, but instead can be used to retrieve single columns at a time. The public key column retrieval algorithm can therefore be used to stream the public key to a peer by ad-hoc retrieving single columns of it.

Algorithm 2: Public Key Column Retrieval

Input: $K_{priv\_ext} = (\Gamma, s, S)$, Column c (Integer)
Parameter: $n, t, m, q = 2^m, k = n - mt$
Output: cth column of the public key: $T_{\cdot c}$
1 Compute $\tilde{H}_{\cdot c}$ as the t-dimensional vector over $\mathbb{F}_q$ with $\tilde{H}_{j,c} = \alpha_c^{j-1}/g(\alpha_c)$ for $j = 1, 2, ..., t$.
2 Compute $\hat{H}_{\cdot c}$ as the mt-dimensional vector over $\mathbb{F}_2$ that results by replacing each entry $c_0 + c_1 z + ... + c_{m-1} z^{m-1}$ of $\tilde{H}_{\cdot c}$ with a column of m bits $c_0, c_1, ..., c_{m-1}$.
3 Compute $H_{\cdot c} = S\hat{H}_{\cdot c}$.

---

4   Streaming Encapsulation

In the previous Sect. 3 we specified the memory-efficient handling and the ad-hoc generation of the public key on a device that holds the (extended) private key. Now, we discuss the memory-efficient handling of the encapsulation operation [4, Section 2.7] that takes place on the device of a peer that, naturally, does not have access to the private key. The goal is to minimize the memory footprint of the operation. This is achieved by not processing the complete public key at once, but in smaller chunks. That is, we compute the encapsulation operation while the public key is streamed from a peer, without buffering it completely. A similar approach is already described for the McEliece PKE scheme in [20]. We adapt this approach for Classic McEliece.

---

[3] This wording avoids calling it *generating the public key* since the public key is already uniquely defined after the private key is chosen. The term "generate" might be misleading and imply that randomness is introduced into this process.

In Classic McEliece, the encapsulation operation calls the encoding subroutine that is used to compute the syndrome of a weight-t error vector. The computation of the syndrome is the only operation in the encapsulation algorithm that makes use of the public key. We therefore need to address the syndrome computation. The syndrome C_0 of e is computed as $C_0 = He$, where H is the parity check matrix that is formed by $H = (I \mid T)$.

A naive implementation will form a buffer that contains the complete parity-check matrix H and then perform the matrix-vector-multiplication. However, it is easy to see that for obtaining the matrix-vector-product all calculations are independent of each other and each entry of H is only used once. This means that it is not necessary to buffer more than a single byte of the public key at a time. Furthermore, it does not matter in which order the public key is processed as long as the order is defined.

With Algorithm 3 we introduce an encoding subroutine that operates on single columns of the public key, in accordance with the public key column retrieval algorithm (Algorithm 2). In lines 1 to 5, the implicit identity matrix that is part of the parity-check matrix is handled. In line 10 the syndrome computation is updated with the column that is received in line 9. Note that the ith column, i.e. $T_{\cdot i}$, can be discarded after each iteration of the while-loop.

Algorithm 3: Single-Column Encoding Subroutine

Input: weight-t Vector $e \in \mathbb{F}_2^n$
Parameter: $n, t, m, q = 2^m, k = n - mt$
Output: C_0

1 Initialize C_0 as an $n - k$-dimensional zero-vector.
2 Set $i := 1$.
3 **while** $i \leq n - k$ **do**
4   Set $C_{0i} := e_i$.
5   Set $i := i + 1$.
6 **end**
7 Set $i := 1$.
8 **while** $i \leq k$ **do**
9   Read the ith column of the public key T from some location into $T_{\cdot i}$.
10   Set $C_0 := C_0 + e_i \cdot T_{\cdot i}$.
11   Set $i := i + 1$.
12 **end**

4.1 Mitigation of the Risk of Denial-of-Service Attacks

In a scenario where clients connect to a server and send Classic McEliece public keys, a concern is that the server is vulnerable to denial-of-service attacks. If the server accepts multiple connections and buffers public keys of the size of a megabyte or more, an attacker can abuse this to exhaust the server's memory. This prevents any new connection to be made without dropping connections that currently are in progress. It might even cause the server to behave erratically if it does not properly handle the case of failed memory allocations.

Such concerns have already been addressed in [5] where the *McTiny protocol* is described. In the McTiny protocol the server does not need to keep any per-client state at all. The per-client state is instead stored encrypted (by the server) on the client-side, thereby preventing such attacks.

We argue that in protocols like TLS, there is already a per-client state of significant size. E.g. the TLS standard implies the use of input/output-buffers that can store record plaintext sizes of 2^{14} bytes. By using the streaming encapsulation approach, the additional per-client state that results from performing the streaming encapsulation is the size of the syndrome C_0. For the largest parameter set, *mceliece8192128*, this amounts to 208 bytes. The input buffer that temporarily holds public key data can be fully consumed each time data is received as outlined previously.

To clarify, we do not suggest that the streaming encapsulation replaces the McTiny protocol, as there is still a per-client state. However, with protocols such as TLS, the risk of such an attack is greatly reduced by using the streaming encapsulation as described in this paper.

5 Implementation

We implemented the algorithms presented in Sects. 3 and 4 on an STM32 Nucleo-144 development board with an STM32F429ZI MCU. It features an ARM Cortex-M4 with 256 KiB RAM and 2 MiB flash memory. The RAM is separated into two blocks: 192 KiB and 64 KiB of core coupled memory. The clock speed is set to 168 MHz. We use FreeRTOS v10.0.1 as operating system.

In the following, the network setup for the network-related measurements is detailed. We report our measurements for completeness, but we emphasize that we did not optimize the implementation for speed. This includes the Classic McEliece reference code, the SPHINCS$^+$ reference code, as well as the network stack. The lwIP library v2.0.3 is used to implement the TCP/IP stack. The development board is connected via ethernet to a PC that features an Intel i5-8400 CPU. The throughput of the TCP connection that we measured depends on the sending direction and the size of the packets that are sent. For receiving data on the board, we measured speeds between 3.04 MiB/s and 3.60 MiB/s. For sending data from the board, we measured speeds between 53.10 KiB/s and 2.07 MiB/s. The throughput for sending data from the board seems to drop to low speeds when exceeding the TCP MSS (Maximum Segment Size). This is the case when streaming the Classic McEliece public key in our current implementation. We further measured the average round-trip time of the connection as 0.39 ms. No package-loss has been observed. Measurements are generally rounded to two decimal places.

5.1 Memory-Efficient Matrix Inversion

The algorithms presented in Sect. 3 reduce the sizes of the involved matrices from $(n - k) \times n$ for H and $(n - k) \times k$ for T to $(n - k) \times (n - k)$ for S. Therefore, the total memory requirements now largely depend on the size of S as the dominating factor.[4] Furthermore, the temporary memory that is required to obtain S from S^{-1} determines how memory-efficiently Algorithm 1 can be implemented. For example, to obtain the inverse of S^{-1}, it suggests itself to use the Gaussian elimination algorithm. However, this induces the memory overhead of transforming an $(n - k) \times (n - k)$-identity matrix. We propose a variant that can be implemented more memory-efficiently, i.e. almost in-place with $2(n - k)$ bytes of non-constant overhead. We outline the steps in Algorithm 4.

Algorithm 4: LU-Decomposition-based Matrix Inversion

Input: $S^{-1} \in \mathbb{F}_2^{(n-k) \times (n-k)}$
Output: S
1 Find the LU decomposition of S^{-1}, i.e. $PS^{-1} = LU$ where
   $P, L, U \in \mathbb{F}_2^{(n-k) \times (n-k)}$ and P is a permutation matrix and L and U are lower and upper triangular matrices.
2 Invert L and U.
3 Compute the product $U^{-1}L^{-1}$.
4 Undo the permutation to obtain $S = U^{-1}L^{-1}P$.

The correctness of this approach follows by verifying $PS^{-1} = LU \iff S^{-1} = P^{-1}LU \iff S = U^{-1}L^{-1}P$. We now outline how these steps can be implemented almost-in-place.

Step 1 LU Decomposition. We implement the LU decomposition as in Algorithm 5. This is essentially the "kij-variant" of the outer-product formulation of Gaussian elimination [9, Section 3.2.9]. In the binary case, however, it becomes a bit simpler since there is no need to divide by the diagonal elements. The algorithm can be implemented to replace the buffer of S^{-1} by L as its lower triangular matrix and U as its upper triangular matrix in a straightforward manner. That is, the memory access pattern shown in line 10 of Algorithm 5 already leads to an in-place implementation. However, the permutation matrix P cannot be stored in-place. Thus, the algorithm does not entirely run in-place. Since P is a sparse matrix with exactly $n - k$ non-zero entries, we implement it as a $2(n - k)$-byte vector that keeps track of which rows are swapped. Two bytes per

---
[4] While there are other significant, temporary memory-overheads in the Classic McEliece code, none of them is as big as that for S. Furthermore, for the extended private key generation, temporary buffers can often be placed in the buffer where S is written into at the end of the key generation process. This results in a decreased overall memory consumption.

Algorithm 5: LU Decomposition

Input: $A \in \mathbb{F}_2^{(n-k) \times (n-k)}$

Output: $P, L, U \in \mathbb{F}_2^{(n-k) \times (n-k)}$, s.t. $PA = LU$. Return $\perp$ (error) if A is singular.

1 **for** $k := 1$ **to** $n - 1$ **do**
2   **for** $i := k + 1$ **to** n **do**
3   Swap row i with row k if the ith row has a non-zero entry at the kth column and update P accordingly (partial-pivoting).
4   **end**
5   **if** *Pivoting fails (i.e. A is singular)* **then**
6   return $\perp$
7   **end**
8   **for** $i := k + 1$ **to** n **do**
9   **for** $j := k + 1$ **to** n **do**
10         $A(i,j) := A(i,j) - A(i,k) \cdot A(k,j)$
11   **end**
12   **end**
13 **end**

---

entry are enough to handle the indices of matrices with up to $2^{16} = 65{,}536$ rows, enough to handle all Classic McEliece parameter sets. Additional care has to be taken to implement the pivoting in constant-time. For instance, this is achieved by not explicitly branching at the two distinct cases in line 3 of Algorithm 5, but masking the operations with all-zero or all-one masks, respectively. Further, the return command in line 6 can safely abort the key generation. Doing so possibly leaks at which step the key generation failed. However, as the Classic McEliece authors already argue, doing so does not leak any information on the actually generated key since separate random numbers are used for each attempt [4].

Step 2 Inversion of U and L. The inversion of U and L amounts to backwards and forwards substitution respectively. Implementing this in-place is straightforward as well as to achieve the constant-time property because no code path depends on secret values.

Step 3 Multiplication of $U^{-1}L^{-1}$. U^{-1} and L^{-1} are both stored in the memory where S^{-1} used to be – as upper and lower triangular matrix, respectively. To obtain an algorithm that multiplies both matrices in-place, we utilize the triangular structure of U^{-1} and L^{-1}. First, let us give a formula with which an element of the product can be computed. For convenience, we define $\bar{A}$ as the matrix that contains L^{-1} and U^{-1} as a lower and an upper triangular matrix and A as $A := U^{-1}L^{-1}$. Each entry $A(i,j)$ can then be written as $A(i,j) = \sum_{k=\max(i,j)+1}^{n} \bar{A}(k,j) \cdot \bar{A}(i,k)$. By appropriately ordering the computations of entries of A, we prevent overriding values that are needed for future computations. More precisely, our solution is to first compute the element in the top-left corner, i.e. the first diagonal element $A(1,1)$. Then, the three remaining elements in the top-left 2×2-matrix can be computed in any order. Continuing like this, i.e. computing the remaining five elements in the top-left 3×3-matrix in any order, and so on, all elements of A can be computed. Each evaluation of the given formula only depends on values of $\bar{A}$ that have not been overwritten by elements of A yet. Therefore, the outlined approach can be implemented in-place. Implementing this as constant-time is again straightforward since no computation path depends on secret values.

Step 4 Undo Permutation. Finally, the permutation needs to be undone. Since P is now multiplied from the right, this amounts to swapping the columns that are indicated by P.

5.2   Extended Private Key Generation

In Table 1 we list the performance of the extended private key generation (Algorithm 1) for the *mceliece348864* parameter set for different numbers of attempts that are made. Each time the key generation fails because S^{-1} is singular, the number of attempts is increased by one. One can see that the key generation is linear in the number of attempts. Each failed attempt roughly adds 1.77 s to the key generation time. On average, the key generation succeeds after 3.4 attempts [4]. We extrapolate the runtime for 3.4 attempts from our measurements as 1,938,512,183 cycles or 11.54 s.

Table 1. Timings for the private key generation for the *mceliece348864* parameter set on our development board. The key generation time depends on the number of attempts that have to be made until a non-singular matrix is found.

# Attempts	Algorithm 1	Algorithm 1
	Cycles	s
1	1,226,192,185	7.30
2	1,522,914,956	9.06
3	1,819,628,971	10.83
4	2,116,353,011	12.60
$\vdots$	$\vdots$	$\vdots$

In Table 2 we specify the size of the extended private key for different parameter sets and compare it to the size of the Classic McEliece key pair. We note that the private key size is implementation-dependent. In contrast to the reference implementation, we store the field elements $(\alpha_1, \alpha_2, ..., \alpha_n)$ as two-byte values. The reference implementation stores these elements by generating the control bits of a Beneš network. The benefits of the Beneš network are not utilized in the reference implementation, but only play a role in x86-optimized implementations that have been submitted as additional implementations.

Since the implementation that generates the control bits has a large memory footprint and our implementation does not benefit from it, we omit this step.

Table 2. Size of the extended private key compared to the Classic McEliece key pair. Note that for the extended private key, it is intended to omit storing the public key.

Parameter set	Key pair bytes	Extended private key bytes	Difference bytes	Ratio
mceliece348864	267,572	81,268	186,304	0.30
mceliece460896	537,728	204,672	333,056	0.38
mceliece6688128	1,058,884	360,580	698,304	0.34
mceliece8192128	1,371,904	363,776	1,008,128	0.27

Table 3 depicts the reduction of the memory footprint when performing the extended private key generation instead of the Classic McEliece key generation. For the Gaussian elimination we assume the required memory as the size of the matrix $\hat{H}$. For the inversion of S we assume that this is done in-place with the addition of storing $2(n - k)$ bytes for the pivoting (see Sect. 5.1). The reduction in the memory footprint is considerable, since the explicit representation of the public key is not stored. This amounts to over a megabyte of memory that is saved for the largest parameter set.

Table 3. Comparison of the memory footprint (in bytes) for producing the public key T or S^{-1}, respectively, from Γ. The original Classic McEliece algorithm applies Gaussian elimination to the $(n - k) \times n$ matrix $\hat{H}$. We propose to (almost) in-place invert the $(n - k) \times (n - k)$ matrix S^{-1} instead (Algorithm 1 and Sect. 5.1).

Parameter set	m	n	t	Gaussian elimination of $\hat{H}$	Matrix inversion of S^{-1}	Difference	Ratio
mceliece348864	12	3488	64	334,848	75,264	259,584	0.22
mceliece460896	13	4608	96	718,848	197,184	521,664	0.27
mceliece6688128	13	6688	128	1,391,104	349,440	1,041,664	0.25
mceliece8192128	13	8192	128	1,703,936	349,440	1,354,496	0.21

5.3   Public Key Column Retrieval

In Table 4 we list the timings for the public key column retrieval algorithm (Algorithm 2) for consecutively retrieving the complete public key. The numbers are the raw computation time, i.e. the cycle count does not include sending the resulting columns over a network to a peer. As an implementation detail, we do not operate on chunks of single columns but on eight columns at a time. This is easier to implement and also faster since bytes (i.e. eight bits) usually are the smallest addressable memory unit. Working on eight columns at a time therefore saves unnecessary operations that are needed to access single bits within a byte. This is true at least, when the matrices are stored in a row-major order. The size of each generated chunk is therefore $n - k$ bytes instead of $(n - k)/8$ bytes.

Our implementation has a memory overhead of $17/8(n-k)$ bytes, including the output buffer and intermediary results (but excluding control variables). Table 4 also illustrates the memory footprint for each parameter set.

Table 4. Timings for retrieving the public key with Algorithm 2. We include the biggest contributor to its runtime, the k matrix-vector-multiplications with the $(n-k) \times (n-k)$ matrix S. We also list the total memory footprint of our implementation.

Parameter set	Algorithm 2		k mat-vec-muls		Memory overhead bytes
	Cycles	s	Cycles	s	
mceliece348864	667,392,425	3.97	623,672,694	3.71	1632
mceliece460896	2,250,917,383	13.40	1,965,249,172	11.70	2652
mceliece6688128	5,820,127,974	34.64	5,152,221,701	30.67	3536
mceliece8192128	7,558,882,087	44.99	6,694,439,348	39.85	3536

5.4 Streaming Encapsulation

We implemented a variant of the encapsulation algorithm by adapting it to use the single-column encoding subroutine (Algorithm 3). For the same reason as before, we work on chunks of eight columns instead of single columns, again leading to chunks of $n-k$ bytes instead of $(n-k)/8$ bytes. Table 5 lists the runtime and the memory footprint of our implementation for the encoding subroutine. The memory footprint includes the error vector and the chunk of eight columns as the input buffers and the syndrome as the output buffer and amounts to $n/8 + 9/8(n-k)$ bytes. We note that processing the public key in row-major order can be implemented faster than processing it in column-major order. In comparison to the reference implementation that processes the public key in row-major order, our implementation is around twenty to fifty percent slower (depending on the parameter set).

Table 5. Measured speed of the streaming encapsulation operation. Columns 2 and 3 give the timings when operating on a local buffer in the RAM of the device. This is given as a reference point for the speed of the operation itself. Column 4 depicts the timing when streaming the public key to the board over a TCP/IP connection.

Parameter set Pubkey origin	Algorithm 3 local buffer	Algorithm 3 local buffer	Algorithm 3 network	Memory overhead –
	Cycles	ms	ms	bytes
mceliece348864	3,106,183	18.49	92.37	1300
mceliece460896	5,868,529	34.93	183.14	1980
mceliece6688128	11,464,900	68.24	358.67	2708
mceliece8192128	14,696,239	87.48	463.64	2896

6   TLS 1.2 Implementation

We implemented the algorithms in Sects. 3 and 4 into the mbedTLS library[5] by defining a new cipher suite for TLS 1.2. The current version of mbedTLS supports only TLS 1.2 and a prototype implementation of TLS 1.3 is work in progress. Our algorithms function both for TLS 1.2 and TLS 1.3 because the changes between these two versions do not affect them. In addition TLS 1.3 also does not have accepted standards for PQC yet. Later in this section we discuss the relevant changes for a TLS 1.3 implementation. We do not describe our implementation in full detail but outline our prototype that serves as a proof of concept. The cipher suite uses Classic McEliece as a key exchange algorithm and a server certificate with a SPHINCS+ key [14].

In our cipher suite, the server generates an ephemeral extended private key for Classic McEliece, using Algorithm 1. In the *server key exchange* message the public key is streamed to the client by utilizing Algorithm 2. A SPHINCS+ signature is appended to the key. The client performs the streaming encapsulation operation (Algorithm 3) and verifies the signature. The premaster secret is then generated analogously to RSA cipher suites by turning the Classic McEliece scheme into a PKE scheme through a KEM-DEM conversion [19, Section 5]. That is, the key from the encapsulation is used as an AES-256 key which is then used to encrypt a 48-byte premaster secret, which is defined and used analogously to the RSA-encrypted premaster secret. The client sends the encrypted premaster secret in the *client key exchange* message. If the server can successfully decrypt the premaster secret, both parties form the same master secret.

The parameter sets that we use in our cipher suite are *mceliece348864* and *SPHINCS+-256f*. For Classic McEliece, the size of the public key is 261,120B and the size of the required memory for the matrix inversion during the key generation is 73,728 B. A *SPHINCS+-256f* signature amounts to 49,216 B. The client verifies two of these signatures: One in the server certificate, since we chose to generate a root CA with a *SPHINCS+-256f* key in order to have a full post-quantum handshake, and one in the *server key exchange* message. While SPHINCS+ signatures can in principle be processed in a streaming fashion [13], our implementation stores the signature in a buffer on the device's memory.

We report the timings for the handshake in Table 6. The SPHINCS+ operations on the board take about 86.86% and 88.85% of the total handshake time. Since we focus on a memory-efficient implementation of Classic McEliece, we do not optimize the SPHINCS+ operations. We chose to set the number of key generation attempts fixed to three by choosing appropriate seeds. This approximates the mean of 3.4 key generation attempts but avoids the need to measure a vast amount of handshakes only to average the variance in key generation. The number of round-trips is the same as in common TLS 1.2 connections, i.e., two full round-trips before application data is sent.

With regard to using our approach in TLS 1.3, the following differences have to be considered: First, in TLS 1.3, to maintain the 1-RTT benefit over TLS

---

[5] https://tls.mbed.org/.

Table 6. Total handshake time (client hello to second finished message) including noteworthy sub-operations. Sign and Verify refer to the SPHINCS$^+$ sign and verify operation. The client verifies two signatures, the server certificate signature and the signed public key. The other listed operations are performed by the server. The last column depicts the measured time to send the server certificate (containing a SPHINCS$^+$ signature), as well as the signed Classic McEliece public key (the public key retrieval algorithm is used). Results are averaged and we chose seeds for the key generation that result in three key generation attempts.

Board as Server

	KeyGen	Decapsulation	Sign	2x Verify	send CERT+PK+SIG
Server	10.83 s	0.99 s	109.71 s	–	4.29 s
Client	–	–	–	0.01s	–

Total Handshake Time **126.30 s**

Board as Client

	KeyGen	Decapsulation	Sign	2x Verify	send CERT+PK+SIG
Server	0.14 s	0.00 s	0.11 s	–	0.34 s
Client	–	–	–	5.18s	–

Total Handshake Time **5.83 s**

1.2, the client would have to generate the key pair. This might be unwanted for embedded-client scenarios. Second, in TLS 1.3 sending a Classic McEliece public key is not straightforward. The natural place to convey the public key and the ciphertext is the *key_exchange*-field in the *KeyShareEntry* struct which is part of the *key_share*-extension. However, the field only holds keys of size up to $2^{16} - 1$ B. Classic McEliece keys exceed this limit. Therefore, an implementer would have to consider a strategy to circumvent this limit. Other than that, we see only minor changes for the sake of employing our proof of concept implementation in TLS 1.3.

A complete handshake has been performed with the outlined cipher suite on our development board. Both, the server side and the client side can be executed on the development board that features only 256 KiB RAM. Our proof of concept implementation demonstrates that our results can be applied in the real world and leave enough room to handle large signatures, as well as the memory overhead in the TLS and TCP stack.

Acknowledgements. This work was partially funded by the German Federal Ministry of Education and Research (BMBF) under the project "QuantumRISC" (ID 16KIS1037 and ID 16KIS1039). Moreover, JK was funded by the Deutsche Forschungsgemeinschaft (DFG, German Research Foundation) – SFB 1119 – 236615297. The authors thank Stathis Deligeorgopoulos for his preliminary work on TLS.

References

1. Augot, D., et al.: Initial recommendations of long-term secure post-quantum systems (2015)
2. Baldi, M., Bodrato, M., Chiaraluce, F.: A new analysis of the McEliece cryptosystem based on QC-LDPC codes. In: Ostrovsky, R., De Prisco, R., Visconti, I. (eds.) Security and Cryptography for Networks, pp. 246–262. Springer, Berlin Heidelberg (2008)
3. Baldi, M., Santini, P., Chiaraluce, F.: Soft McEliece: MDPC code-based McEliece cryptosystems with very compact keys through real-valued intentional errors. In: Proceedings of the IEEE International Symposium on Information Theory (ISIT 2016), pp. 795–799, July 2016. https://doi.org/10.1109/ISIT.2016.7541408
4. Bernstein, D., et al.: Classic McEliece Supporting Documentation (2019)
5. Bernstein, D.J., Lange, T.: McTiny: fast high-confidence post-quantum key erasure for tiny network servers. Cryptology ePrint Archive, Report 2019/1395 (2019). https://eprint.iacr.org/2019/1395
6. Cayrel, P.L., Hoffmann, G., Persichetti, E.: Efficient implementation of a CCA2-secure variant of McEliece using generalized srivastava codes. In: Fischlin, M., Buchmann, J., Manulis, M. (eds.) Public Key Cryptography - PKC 2012, pp. 138–155. Springer, Berlin Heidelberg (2012)
7. Eisenbarth, T., Güneysu, T., Heyse, S., Paar, C.: MicroEliece: McEliece for embedded devices. In: Clavier, C., Gaj, K. (eds.) Cryptographic Hardware and Embedded Systems - CHES 2009, pp. 49–64. Springer, Heidelberg (2009)
8. Faugère, J.C., Otmani, A., Perret, L., de Portzamparc, F., Tillich, J.P.: Structural cryptanalysis of McEliece schemes with compact keys. Designs Codes Crypt. **79**(1), 87–112 (2016). https://doi.org/10.1007/s10623-015-0036-z
9. Golub, G.H., van Loan, C.F.: Matrix Computations, 4 edn. JHU Press (2013). http://www.cs.cornell.edu/cv/GVL4/golubandvanloan.htm
10. Heyse, S.: Low-Reiter: Niederreiter encryption scheme for embedded microcontrollers. In: Sendrier, N. (ed.) PQCrypto 2010. LNCS, vol. 6061, pp. 165–181. Springer, Heidelberg (2010). https://doi.org/10.1007/978-3-642-12929-2_13
11. Heyse, S.: Implementation of McEliece based on quasi-dyadic Goppa codes for embedded devices. In: Yang, B.-Y. (ed.) PQCrypto 2011. LNCS, vol. 7071, pp. 143–162. Springer, Heidelberg (2011). https://doi.org/10.1007/978-3-642-25405-5_10
12. Heyse, S., von Maurich, I., Güneysu, T.: Smaller keys for code-based cryptography: QC-MDPC McEliece implementations on embedded devices. In: Bertoni, G., Coron, J.-S. (eds.) CHES 2013. LNCS, vol. 8086, pp. 273–292. Springer, Heidelberg (2013). https://doi.org/10.1007/978-3-642-40349-1_16
13. Hülsing, A., Rijneveld, J., Schwabe, P.: ARMed SPHINCS. In: Cheng, C.-M., Chung, K.-M., Persiano, G., Yang, B.-Y. (eds.) PKC 2016. LNCS, vol. 9614, pp. 446–470. Springer, Heidelberg (2016). https://doi.org/10.1007/978-3-662-49384-7_17
14. Hülsing, A., et al.: Sphincs+. https://sphincs.org/
15. van Lint, J.H.: Introduction to Coding Theory, 3rd edn. Springer, Heidelberg (1998). https://doi.org/10.1007/978-3-642-58575-3
16. McEliece, R.J.: A public-key cryptosystem based on algebraic coding theory. Deep Space Network Prog. Rep. **42**(44), 114–116 (1978)

17. Misoczki, R., Barreto, P.S.L.M.: Compact McEliece keys from Goppa codes. In: Jacobson, M.J., Rijmen, V., Safavi-Naini, R. (eds.) SAC 2009. LNCS, vol. 5867, pp. 376–392. Springer, Heidelberg (2009). https://doi.org/10.1007/978-3-642-05445-7_24
18. Niederreiter, H.: Knapsack-type cryptosystems and algebraic coding theory. Prob. Control Inf. Theory **15**, 159–166 (1986)
19. Shoup, V.: A proposal for an ISO standard for public key encryption (version 2.1), January 2002. https://www.shoup.net/papers/iso-2_1.pdf
20. Strenzke, F.: Solutions for the storage problem of McEliece public and private keys on memory-constrained platforms. In: Gollmann, D., Freiling, F.C. (eds.) ISC 2012. LNCS, vol. 7483, pp. 120–135. Springer, Heidelberg (2012). https://doi.org/10.1007/978-3-642-33383-5_8

Efficient Implementations

A Fast and Compact RISC-V Accelerator for Ascon and Friends

Stefan Steinegger$^{(\boxtimes)}$ and Robert Primas

Graz University of Technology, Graz, Austria
{stefan.steinegger,robert.primas}@iaik.tugraz.at

Abstract. Ascon-p is the core building block of Ascon, the winner in the lightweight category of the CAESAR competition. With Isap, another Ascon-p-based AEAD scheme is currently competing in the 2nd round of the NIST lightweight cryptography standardization project. In contrast to Ascon, Isap focuses on providing hardening/protection against a large class of implementation attacks, such as DPA, DFA, SFA, and SIFA, entirely on mode-level. Consequently, Ascon-p can be used to realize a wide range of cryptographic computations such as authenticated encryption, hashing, pseudorandom number generation, with or without the need for implementation security, which makes it the perfect choice for lightweight cryptography on embedded devices.

In this paper, we implement Ascon-p as an instruction extension for RISC-V that is tightly coupled to the processors register file and thus does not require any dedicated registers. This single instruction allows us to realize all cryptographic computations that typically occur on embedded devices with high performance. More concretely, with Isap and Ascon's family of modes for AEAD and hashing, we can perform cryptographic computations with a performance of about 2 cycles/byte, or about 4 cycles/byte if protection against fault attacks and power analysis is desired.

As we show, our instruction extension requires only 4.7 kGE, or about half the area of dedicated Ascon co-processor designs, and is easy to integrate into low-end embedded devices like 32-bit ARM Cortex-M or RISC-V microprocessors. Finally, we analyze the provided implementation security of Isap, when implemented using our instruction extension.

Keywords: Authenticated encryption · Ascon · Isap · Hardware acceleration · RISC-V · RI5CY · CV32E40P · Side-channels · Fault attacks · Leakage resilience

1 Introduction

Motivation. Implementation attacks such as fault attacks [3,4] or power analysis [5,22,25] are among the most relevant threats for implementations of cryptographic schemes. To counteract such attacks, cryptographic devices like smart cards typically implement dedicated countermeasures, both on hardware and algorithmic level.

© Springer Nature Switzerland AG 2021
P.-Y. Liardet and N. Mentens (Eds.): CARDIS 2020, LNCS 12609, pp. 53–67, 2021.
https://doi.org/10.1007/978-3-030-68487-7_4

The most prominent examples of algorithmic countermeasures are masking against power analysis [18, 26, 28], and the usage of some form of redundancy against fault attacks [1]. Redundant computations are usually used to detect and prevent the release of erroneous cryptographic computations, that could otherwise be exploited with techniques like Differential Fault Attacks (DFA) [4] or Statistical Fault Attacks (SFA) [15].

With these attacks in mind, the National Institute of Standards and Technology (NIST) recently started an effort to standardize lightweight authenticated encryption schemes for usage in embedded or IoT scenarios [6]. Amongst others, the submission requirements state that the possibility of adding implementation attack countermeasures at low cost is highly desired. To meet this criteria, many of the submitted schemes are based upon lightweight cryptographic primitives, while DryGASCON [27], and ISAP [9] can even give certain guarantees against implementation attacks purely on mode-level. While DryGASCON is based, amongst others, on a modified variant of ASCON-p, ISAP can be instantiated directly with ASCON-p, the core building block of ASCON. Consequently, acceleration of ASCON-p can speed up the computations of both, ASCON and ISAP, thereby achieving speed-ups for a wide variety of symmetric cryptographic tasks, including those that require protection from implementation attacks.

Our Contribution. In this work, we propose an instruction extension for ASCON-p that utilizes tight integration into a processors register file to significantly speed up various symmetric cryptographic computations at a comparably low cost. Most notably, our instruction extension can be used for applications with/without the need for protection against implementation attacks, simply by choosing the appropriate AEAD mode in software.

As a proof of concept, we integrate our instruction extension into the 32-bit RI5CY core. We provide various hardware metrics and, amongst others, show that our accelerator can be realized with about 4.7 kGE, or about half the area of dedicated co-processor designs.

Given this built-in acceleration for ASCON-p, we create assembly versions of the ASCON/ISAP modes that utilize our instruction extension and present benchmarks for authenticated encryption, hashing, and pseudorandom number generation. As we show, we achieve speed-up factors of about 50 to 80, when compared to corresponding pure software implementations.

Finally, we discuss the provided implementation security of ISAP, when implemented using our accelerator.

Open Source. Our hardware design is publicly available in the following Github repository: https://github.com/Steinegger/riscv_asconp_accelerator.

Outline. In Sect. 2, we cover the required background for this work: (1) the RISC-V instruction set architecture (ISA) (2) the RI5CY core for our a proof of concept (3) the two AEAD modes ASCON and ISAP. In Sect. 3, we describe the design of our accelerator, its software interface, our modifications to the RI5CY core and various hardware metrics. In Sect. 4 we then discuss how the hardware acceleration for Ascon-p can be used to build fast software implementations for hashing, pseudorandom number generation, and authenticated encryption, with or without protection from physical attacks and present various performance metrics. The provided implementation security of Isap, when implemented using our instruction extension, is analyzed in Sect. 5. Finally, we conclude the paper in Sect. 6.

2 Background

2.1 RI5CY Core

The RI5CY core[1] (as of late known as CV32E40P) is a free and publicly available RISC-V CPU design that implements the RV32IMFC instruction set and features a 4-stage in-order pipeline (Instruction Fetch, Instruction Decode, Execute, and Write-Back). It features an instruction prefetcher and is able to serve one instruction per cycle to the decode stage. The core performs similarly to the ARM Cortex M4 [30] and is part of the PULP platform[2], a silicon-proven ASIC design.

2.2 Ascon

Ascon is a sponge-based AEAD scheme that was selected as the primary choice for lightweight authenticated encryption in the final portfolio of the CAESAR competition [11]. Ascon operates on a 320-bit state that is organized into 5×64 bit lanes, and updated by the permutation Ascon-p. Ascon-p consists of 3 steps: a round constant addition, a substitution layer, and a linear layer, that are consecutively applied on the state in each round. Ascon's mode describes how state and permutation can be used to build an authenticated encryption scheme, hashing functionality Ascon-Hash and Ascon-Xof [12].

2.3 Isap

Isap is a mode for authenticated encryption with a focus on providing built-in hardening/protection against various kinds of implementation attacks. Isap was originally published at FSE 2017 [10], and currently competes in the 2nd round of the NIST Lightweight Cryptography project [9].

The authors propose 4 variations of Isap, however, we only focus on the Ascon-p based parametrizations Isap-A-128a and Isap-A-128. The claimed cryptographic security of all Isap instances is the same as for Ascon, i.e., 128 bit for confidentiality of plaintext, as well as integrity of plaintext, associated data, and nonce.

In contrast to Ascon, Isap is a two-pass scheme that performs authenticated encryption in an Encrypt-then-MAC manner. The main design goal of Isap is to provide inherent protection from DPA attacks. For a more detailed discussion of Isap's protection against physical attacks we refer to Sect. 5.

---

[1] https://github.com/pulp-platform/riscv.
[2] https://pulp-platform.org/.

3 Hardware Acceleration for Ascon-p

In this section we explain the design of our Ascon-p accelerator, as well as the integration into the RI5CY microprocessor. Sect. 3.1 describes the design of the Ascon-p accelerator itself and how it can be accessed from software. In Sect. 3.2 we discuss hardware modifications of the RI5CY core that are necessary to integrate our accelerator. Finally, in Sect. 3.3 we present various hardware metrics.

3.1 Design of the Ascon-p Accelerator

Typical co-processor designs, like the one in [19], represent a straight forward way to achieve computation speed-ups in microprocessors. While dedicated co-processors are arguably easy to integrate, they also come with certain downsides. From an area perspective, dedicated co-processors require their own registers for holding the cipher state which is comparably expensive on low-end microprocessors. From a performance perspective, moving data to and from the co-processor requires additional cycles. This effect can be alleviated to some extend with direct memory access, albeit at the expense of additional hardware for read/write ports and memory arbitration that is typically not reported. Besides that, dedicated co-processors usually only support one specific cipher operation which does not make them very flexible, and hence, leads to situations where, e.g., hardware support for both, AES and SHA-256 needs to be implemented.

These issues motivate our choice to implement our Ascon-p instruction extension by tightly coupling the accelerator into the register file. This way, one can reuse the register file for holding the cipher state, thus eliminating the need for additional registers and communication/synchronization overhead. In other words, we only need to add the combinatorial logic of the permutation[3] which is typically the only computationally expensive building block of permutation-based cryptographic design. The concrete AEAD mode can be implemented purely in software and is thus flexible.

3.2 Modifications to the RI5CY Core

To extend the existing RI5CY hardware and to make the instruction available to applications, we first design the instruction, add it to the existing opcode-space and later to RI5CY's decode stage. We then connect the Ascon-p accelerator to the register file.

Instruction Encoding. For our Ascon-p instruction, we propose an I-type instruction to be used. The 12-bit immediate allows us to encode the number of rounds with bits 10 to 8 and the 8-bit round constant with bits 7 to 0. The remaining bit can be used to specify the endianness of the data representation

---

[3] Our accelerator is based on Ascon's reference hardware implementation (https://github.com/IAIK/ascon_hardware.)

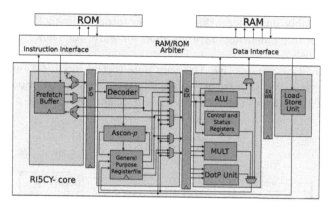

Fig. 1. Block diagram of the RI5CY core with hardware acceleration for ASCON-p. The blocks labelled **IF ID**, **ID EX** and **EX WB** refer to the registers between the pipeline stages instruction fetch (**IF**), instruction decode (**ID**), execute (**EX**) and write-back (**WB**)

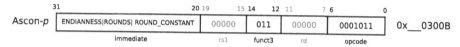

Fig. 2. Structure of our RISC-V ASCON-p instruction.

in the registers to allow for correct interpretation by the accelerator. We use fixed registers for the operation, hence, the **rd** and **rs** of the instruction remain unused.

To accommodate the instruction, we use the previously unused opcode 0x0B with 0x3 as the **funct3**. The resulting structure is illustrated in Fig. 2.

Register Adaptations. Our accelerator re-purposes parts of the existing CPU register file for holding the state of ASCON-p. This design choice is motivated by the fact that CPU registers, especially on small embedded devices, are one of the main contributing factors to the resulting hardware area. To store the full 320-bit state of ASCON-p, 10 out of the 32 available 32-bit registers are required. Conveniently, two such registers combined can store one lane of the ASCON state and can be directly passed to the accelerator as such. When looking at other ISAs like RV32E or ARMv7, they only offer 16 32-bit registers, which is however more than enough to hold the entire ASCON state and still allows to implement the mode itself without usage of excessive amounts of write/load operations.

For a low-area design, allowing arbitrary registers to store the ASCON state is inefficient since this would lead to a significant increase in the number of read and write ports on the register file. Therefore, we propose using a set of fixed registers, in our case **x12** to **x17** and **x28** to **x31**, to accommodate the ASCON state, as shown in Fig. 3. Note that our choice here is to some extend arbitrary. Our chosen registers are defined to be "caller saved" by the RISC-V calling convention which could improve the compatibility with C code. However, when using pure assembly implementations for the cryptographic modes, which is the standard way of implementing cryptographic software, the choice of registers is up to the designer.

From a hardware perspective, the only noteworthy modification here is the addition of toggle logic that can, depending on the current instruction, switch the input signal of 10 registers between the write port and the ASCON-p accelerator.

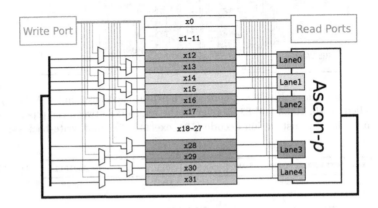

Fig. 3. The register file with the ASCON-p accelerator, as well as read/write ports.

Decode Stage Adaptations. To make our ASCON-p instruction accessible to applications we add the opcode to the decoder. When an instruction decodes as our ASCON-p instruction a signal enables the ASCON-p accelerator and switches the multiplexers of our fixed set of registers seen in Fig. 3 to update from the accelerator.

As seen in Fig. 1, the arithmetic logic unit (ALU) and load-store unit forward their result to the next instruction before updating the registers. This prevents pipeline stalls. However, an instruction altering any of the 10 ASCON state registers must not directly precede our permutation instruction. Load operations to these registers must not happen in the two preceding instructions. Alternatively, this could also be handled in and at the cost of additional hardware by adapting the forwarding to directly feed into the ASCON-p accelerator, or by stalling the pipeline for up to two cycles.

3.3 Hardware Metrics

Benchmarking Platform. We use the RI5CY core commit 528ddd4 as the basis for our modifications. The source files are compiled by the Cadence Encounter RTL Compiler v14.20-s064_1 and routed with NanoRoute 16.13-s045_1. The used process is umc065LL 1P10M. We deactivate the floating-point unit in the hardware design as it is not required for our evaluation. To build the benchmarking platform, we connect the RI5CY core to a 64 kbit FSE0K_A_SH single-port SRAM macro by Faraday Technology, and to a ROM (implemented as a logic vector) that holds the executable code.

The RI5CY core has a separated bus for data and instruction memory. However, as this is not meant to implement a Harvard architecture [29], we add an arbitration module to allow access from the data port to the instruction ROM. The RI5CY core incorporates an instruction prefetch buffer. Hence, for accesses to the ROM, requests by the data port are prioritized over requests by the prefetching, buffered instruction port.

We operate the RI5CY core at a clock frequency of 50 MHz to keep single cycle RAM and ROM accesses with our design-flow without increasing the overall complexity. To determine the area of the implementation, we set the ungroup-ok attribute to false in our design-flow for the RI5CY core and the ASCON-p accelerator. This might result in a reduced area optimization of the overall result, however, as the modules are not ungrouped into their parent modules, more consistent area estimates can be shown and especially prevent the RAM and ROM modules from affecting the area numbers of the core.

Area Estimations. To evaluate the area overhead of our design, we compare RI5CY in its base configuration against our modified design that can perform 1 round of ASCON-p within a single clock cycle. The result can be seen in Table 1. The numbers for the RI5CY core refer to the core part only, as illustrated in Fig. 1.

The unmodified RI5CY core serves as our baseline and requires 45.6 kGE. When using 1-round ASCON-p acceleration, the overall core size increases to 50.3 kGE, with the accelerator itself making up 4.2 kGE. The remaining difference of 0.5 kGE can be attributed to the addition of multiplexers to parts of the register file, additional instruction decoding as well as overall variations in optimizations by the toolchain.

To put these numbers into perspective, we can refer to implementation results from Gross et al. who provide area numbers for ASCON co-processor designs, with (9.4 kGE) and without (7.1 kGE) the CAESAR hardware API [19, 20]. When compared to these numbers, our 1-round ASCON-p accelerator requires only about half that area, due to the fact that we can directly operate on parts of the register file. The authors of ISAP also roughly estimate the area requirement of a dedicated ISAP co-processor to be around 12 kGE, which is also noticeable larger than our design. Do note that our numbers also include the integration cost of the accelerator while the other designs will likely require higher integration costs due to the additionally needed interconnected for the data exchange.

Critical Path. In order to determine if our proposed ASCON-p acceleration could increase the critical path delay of the RI5CY core, we performed experiments with modified hardware accelerator designs that can perform up to 6 rounds of ASCON-p within one clock cycle while keeping the clock frequency constant at 50 MHz. In these cases, the core area increases to up to 70.8 kGE with the ASCON-p accelerator taking up to 24.7 kGE, showing a linear growth in size

Table 1. Comparison between the RI5CY core with/without 1-round Ascon-*p* accelerator (HW-A) and dedicated co-processor designs of Ascon and Isap.

Design	kGE	
	Standalone	Integration
RI5CY base design	45.6	0
This work	4.2	0.5
Ascon co-processor [19]	7.1	?
Ascon co-processor [17,20]	9.4	?
Isap co-processor (estimated) [9]	≤12.8	?

for this range of configurations. Since our Ascon-*p* accelerator met the timing constraints in all configuration, we conclude that the 1-round variant should not pose any problems for clock frequencies up to about 300 MHz.

4   Performance Evaluation

4.1   AEAD and Hashing with Ascon

For the performance evaluation of Ascon and Ascon-Hash we focus on the primary, recommended parametrization Ascon-128 [11]. Our accelerator is configured to perform 1 permutation round per clock cycle and the software implementations are implemented in RISC-V assembly so we can make sure that the state is always kept in the registers x12 to x17 and x28 to x31. Examples of the actual message processing loop are shown in Code 1 and Code 2.

Code 1. Encrypt Block Loop

```
 1: <encrypt_block_start>:
 2:   lw t1,0(t0)
 3:   lw s1,4(t0)
 4:   xor a2,a2,t1
 5:   xor a3,a3,s1
 6:   sw a2,0(s8)
 7:   sw a3,4(s8)
 8:   ASCON-P(ROUND_CONSTANT)

     : 6-times

14:   addi t0,t0,8
15:   addi s8,s8,8
16:   bgeu t2,t0, <encrypt_block_start>
```

Code 2. Absorb Block Loop

```
 1: <absorb_block_start>:
 2:   lw t1,0(t0)
 3:   lw s1,4(t0)
 4:   xor a2,a2,t1
 5:   xor a3,a3,s1
 6:   addi t0,t0,8
 7:   ASCON-P(ROUND_CONSTANT)

     : 12-times

19:   bgeu t2,t0 <absorb_block_start>
```

In our benchmarks, we consider the case of encrypting/hashing messages of various lengths (0 bytes of associated data), as well as pseudorandom number generation using the XOF mode. We compare our results with the efficient C implementations from the Ascon team[4], compiled with −O3, mainly due to the

---

[4] https://github.com/ascon/ascon-c

lack of available RISC-V optimized implementations As shown in Table 2, the hardware-accelerated implementations achieve speed-ups by about a factor of 50 for ASCON and factor 80 for ASCON-HASH. At the same time, hardware acceleration reduces the binary sizes significantly, even when compared to the size-optimized C versions (-Os).

Table 2. Runtime and code size comparison of ASCON and ISAP, with/without 1-round ASCON-p hardware acceleration (HW-A)

Implementations	Cycles/Byte			Binary size (B)
	64 B	1536 B	Long	
Ascon-C (-O3)	164.3	110.6	108.3	11 716
Ascon-C (-Os)	269.7	187.1	183.5	2 104
Ascon-ASM + HW-A	4.2	2.2	2.1	888
AsconHash-C (-O3)	306.9	208.0	203.8	20 244
AsconHash-C (-Os)	423.3	268.0	261.3	1528
AsconHash-ASM + HW-A	4.6	2.6	2.5	484
AsconXOF-ASM + HW-A	4.0	2.3	2.3	484
ISAP-A-128a-C (-O3)	1 184.3	386.9	352.3	11 052
ISAP-A-128a-C (-Os)	2 024.1	616.0	554.8	3 744
ISAP-A-128a-ASM + HW-A	29.1	5.2	4.2	1 844
ISAP-A-128-ASM + HW-A	73.6	7.7	5.0	2 552

4.2   AEAD with ISAP

When deriving performance numbers for ISAP, we mainly refer to the parameterization of ISAP-A-128A [9], since it is recommended over the more conservative ISAP-A-128 instance by the designers. We do, however, state concrete performance numbers for both variants in Table 2. For the C implementation we use the `opt_32` implementation of ISAP[5]. The runtime of ISAP is comprised of the re-keying function ISAPRK, as well as the processing of message blocks in ISAPENC and ISAPMAC. Since ISAP is an Encrypt-then-MAC scheme that calls ISAPRK both during ISAPENC and ISAPMAC, the runtime of ISAPRK needs to be counted twice [9].

Comparison. Table 2 contains runtimes for encrypting messages of various lengths and 0 bytes of associated data. As expected, the runtime of shorter 64 byte messages is affected by the comparably slow initialization. However, this effect diminishes with increasing message length and approaches a performance of 4.2 and 5.0 cycles/byte for ISAP-A-128A and ISAP-A-128 respectively. Given

---

[5] https://github.com/isap-lwc/isap-code-package.

the provided protection from implementation attacks (cf. Sect. 5), the performance penalty of about factor 2 for somewhat longer messages, is comparably low compared to Ascon. Also note that, with hardware acceleration, the binary size of Isap can be lower than an unprotected, size-optimized, pure software implementation of Ascon.

5   Implementation Security of Isap

In this section we first briefly discuss the provided security of the Isap mode against implementation attacks such as DPA/DFA/SFA/SIFA. We then provide a more detailed discussion of Isap's SPA security when hardware acceleration for Ascon-p is used.

5.1   Differential Fault Analyis (DFA)

DFA attacks exploit the difference between results of repeated executions of cryptographic computations, with and without fault injection. During authenticated encryption, fresh nonces ensure that the session keys K_A^* and K_E^* are unique for each encryption, which prevents DFA attacks.

In the case of authenticated decryption, the attacker can perform multiple queries with the same ciphertext/nonce/tag, and thus force a repeated decryption of constant inputs with the same key. Since tag verification in Isap happens before decryption, a DFA on the encryption phase of IsapEnc is, in principle, possible. However, when following a similar attack strategy as shown by Luo et al. [23] for Keccak-based MAC constructions, targeting IsapEnc alone is not sufficient since the long term key is only used within IsapRk. IsapRk by itself can also not be directly attacked since the attacker never gets to see any direct output. A multi-fault strategy, as outlined in [14], is still possible but requires roughly the quadratic amount of faulted decryptions, when compared to the numbers reported in [23], and more importantly, precise combinations of multiple fault injections, both in terms of timing and location.

5.2   Differential Power Analysis (DPA)

One of the main design goals of Isap is inherent protection from side-channel attacks, such as DPA. This is achieved through the usage of the leakage-resilient re-keying function IsapRk [9] that derives unique session keys K^* for encryption/authentication from the long term key K and the nonce N. IsapRk can be viewed as a sponge variant of the classical GGM construction [16]. By limiting the rate r_B during the absorption of Y, one can reduce the number of possible inputs to a permutation call to 2, which renders classical DPA attacks impractical.

5.3   Statistical (Ineffective) Fault Attacks (SFA/SIFA)

SFA and SIFA are fault attack techniques that, in contrast to DFA, are applicable to many AEAD schemes, including online/single-pass variants, and without assumptions such as nonce repetition or release of unverified plaintext. These attacks are especially interesting since it was shown that they are also applicable to (higher-oreder) masked implementations, whereas SIFA can even work in cases where masking is combined with typical fault countermeasure techniques [8].

Both attacks have in common that they require the attacker to call a certain cryptographic building block (e.g. permutation) with varying inputs. In principle, SFA is applicable whenever AEAD schemes perform a final key addition before generating an output [7], which is not the case in ISAP. SIFA, on the other side, can be used in the initialization phase of almost all AEAD schemes, similarly to as shown for the KECCAK-based AEAD schemes KETJE and KEYAK [13]. However, in the case of ISAP, the 1-bit rate during ISAPRK limits the number of inputs per permutation call to 2 and thus severely limits the capabilities of SIFA which usually requires a couple hundred calls with varying inputs [13].

5.4   Simple Power Analysis (SPA)

Simple Power Analysis (SPA) describes a class of power analysis attacks that, in contrast to DPA, can work in scenarios where the attacker is limited to observing power traces of cryptographic computations with constant inputs [5]. Consequently, SPA attacks are, in principle, applicable to ISAP and thus require a more thorough discussion. For simplicity, we focus on the authenticated decryption procedure of ISAP, including the re-keying ISAPRK, but excluding the tag verification within ISAPMAC. In this scenario, the attacker is in control of the nonce N and can directly observe the outputs of the computation (the later is not the case in ISAPMAC).

When arguing about SPA protection of ISAP's long term key K, we can first take a look at mode-level properties of ISAP's decryption procedure, which is depicted in Fig. 4. Since K is only used during ISAPRK, which by itself is hard-to-invert, an attacker is forced to target ISAPRK directly. Within ISAPRK, we can observe that different parts of the computation leak different amounts of information, depending on the number of bits that are processed in parallel. In general, when looking at permutation-based cryptographic designs, the sizes of the rate r and the capacity c naturally reflect how much information about the state an attacker is allowed to learn, without gaining any noticeable advantage in performing state recoveries. Intuitively, side-channel information decreases the more data is processed concurrently. For example, as shown by Medwed et al., a simple AES-based GGM construction can be broken on an 8-bit microcontroller using template attacks [24]. While the 32-bit RI5CY core should already provide noticeably better SPA protection, there still exist a few works that show that SPA attacks on 16 or 32-bit implementations could be successful [2,21]. Nevertheless, we do expect leakage stemming from the processing of 320 bits in parallel, i.e. during the usage of the ASCON-p accelerator, to be very hard to exploit .

Given this, and the fact that ISAP uses $r \leq 64$ and $c \geq 256$, we can see in Fig. 4 that, after the initial state setup, there is no point in time where the attacker can observe easy to exploit leakage (indicated in green/yellow) of state chunks that are larger than r. In other words, the ASCON-p accelerator ensures that leakage of at least c bits of the state is hard to exploit (red), which should render simple SPA-based state recovery attacks impractical. This leaves the initial state setup phase as the only supposedly easy SPA attack target. In the following, we take a closer look at this state setup phase and estimate the amount of information about K that an attacker could learn there under reasonable assumptions.

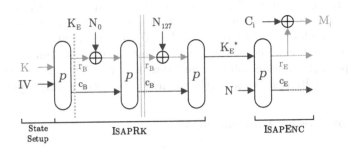

Fig. 4. Authenticated decryption of ISAP: SPA leakage when utilizing hardware acceleration for ASCON-p. Green values are public (or leak fully), orange values create some leakage in 32-bit chunks, red values result in hard to exploit leakage (Given, e.g., a decapped chip, high resolution EM probes, and averaged power measurements, it could be possible to still gain usable SPA leakage. If such powerful attackers are a concern, we recommend using hiding/shuffling in the ASCON-p accelerator and in software.). (Color figure online)

Entropy Loss of K during State Setup. The state setup consists of 10 load operations that move the initial state from RAM into the respective CPU registers. In other words, an attacker can observe the leakage of K, when split into the four 32-bit chunks $K_0 \ldots K_3$ while all other values are public. If we further assume an observable leakage that corresponds to the noise-free Hamming weight (HW) of each K_i, thereby essentially simulating the case of averaged power traces on a typical 32-bit microprocessor [21], we can estimate the entropy loss of K as follows:

First, we need to find the probability that a uniformly chosen K_i has a certain HW x. Since the number of 32-bit values with HW $= x$ is exactly $\binom{32}{x}$, we can calculate $p(\mathrm{HW}(K_i) = x)$ simply as $\binom{32}{x}/2^{32}$. The corresponding entropy loss of knowing $x = \mathrm{HW}(K_i)$ is then $32 - \log_2\binom{32}{x}$. To give two concrete examples, $p(\mathrm{HW}(K_i) = 0)$ is $1/2^{32}$ with entropy loss of 32 bits, while $p(\mathrm{HW}(K_i) = 16)$ is 0.14 with entropy loss of 2.83 bits.

If we now want to determine the maximum entropy loss of the entire 128-bit key K, while ignoring unrealistic events, we need to consider a *combined* event that consists of the individual and independent leakage events for $K_0 \ldots K_3$. Their combined probability is simply the product of the individual probabilities, while their combined entropy loss is summed up.

Finally, we can fix a certain probability and search for the maximum entropy loss among all combined events with at least that probability. More concretely, if we are interested in cases with, e.g., a combined probability above $1/10^6$ ($1/10^9$) we can derive that an attacker cannot learn more than 20 (30) bits of K. If we oppose these results with the fact that K has a total entropy of 128 bits, we can conclude that, under our assumptions, the probability of learning any meaningful amount of information about K is negligible.

Further Increasing SPA Protection. As discussed in the previous section, hardware acceleration for ASCON-p alone can already significantly increase the SPA protection of ISAP's software implementations. Nevertheless, further simple steps can still be taken to additionally harden the implementation against SPA attacks.

For once, software shuffling/hiding during ISAPRK's state setup helps to reduce the amount of averaging an attacker can perform, thereby essentially decreasing the signal-to-noise ratio of power measurements.

And secondly, instead of using K and IV during ISAPRK's state setup, one could also opt for storing the equivalent 320-bit key K_E instead (cf. Fig. 4). In this case, K_E is the initial state of ISAPRK, and would not contain any values that are known by the attacker.

6 Conclusion

In this paper, we presented an instruction extension for ASCON-p that allows us to significantly speed up a variety of cryptographic computations that are typically needed on embedded devices at low cost. More concretely, with ISAP and ASCON's family of cryptographic modes, we can perform authenticated encryption, hashing, and pseudorandom number generation with a performance of about 2 cycles/byte, or about 4 cycles/byte if implementation security is desired.

When using ISAP, protection/hardening against implementation attacks such as DPA/DFA/SIFA is already provided on mode-level. We additionally analyze the case of SPA protection which is significantly increased thanks to ASCON-p acceleration. As a proof of concept, we integrated our accelerator into the 32-bit RI5CY core and present various hardware/performance metrics.

Acknowledgments. This project has received funding from the European Research Council (ERC) under the European Union's Horizon 2020 research and innovation programme (grant agreement No 681402), the Austrian Research Promotion Agency (FFG) via the K-project DeSSnet, which is funded in the context of COMET – Competence Centers for Excellent Technologies by BMVIT, BMWFW, Styria and Carinthia, and the Austrian Research Promotion Agency (FFG) via the project ESPRESSO, which is funded by the province of Styria and the Business Promotion Agencies of Styria and Carinthia.

References

1. Bar-El, H., Choukri, H., Naccache, D., Tunstall, M., Whelan, C.: The Sorcerer's apprentice guide to fault attacks. Proc. IEEE **94**(2), 370–382 (2006)
2. Bellizia, D., et al.: Mode-level vs. implementation-level physical security in symmetric cryptography: a practical guide through the leakage-resistance jungle. IACR Cryptol. ePrint Arch. 2020, 211 (2020)
3. Biham, E., Shamir, A.: Differential fault analysis of secret key cryptosystems. In: Kaliski, B.S. (ed.) CRYPTO 1997. LNCS, vol. 1294, pp. 513–525. Springer, Heidelberg (1997). https://doi.org/10.1007/BFb0052259
4. Boneh, D., DeMillo, R.A., Lipton, R.J.: On the importance of checking cryptographic protocols for faults. In: Fumy, W. (ed.) EUROCRYPT 1997. LNCS, vol. 1233, pp. 37–51. Springer, Heidelberg (1997). https://doi.org/10.1007/3-540-69053-0_4
5. Chari, S., Rao, J.R., Rohatgi, P.: Template attacks. In: Kaliski, B.S., Koç, K., Paar, C. (eds.) CHES 2002. LNCS, vol. 2523, pp. 13–28. Springer, Heidelberg (2003). https://doi.org/10.1007/3-540-36400-5_3
6. Committee, N.L.: NIST lightweight cryptography project (2019). https://csrc.nist.gov/Projects/lightweight-cryptography/
7. Dobraunig, C., Eichlseder, M., Korak, T., Lomné, V., Mendel, F.: Statistical fault attacks on nonce-based authenticated encryption schemes. In: Cheon, J.H., Takagi, T. (eds.) ASIACRYPT 2016. LNCS, vol. 10031, pp. 369–395. Springer, Heidelberg (2016). https://doi.org/10.1007/978-3-662-53887-6_14
8. Dobraunig, C., Eichlseder, M., Korak, T., Mangard, S., Mendel, F., Primas, R.: SIFA: exploiting ineffective fault inductions on symmetric cryptography. IACR Trans. Cryptogr. Hardw. Embed. Syst. **2018**(3), 547–572 (2018)
9. Dobraunig, C., et al.: ISAP v2.0. Submission to the NIST Lightweight Crypto Competition (2019). https://csrc.nist.gov/CSRC/media/Projects/lightweight-cryptography/documents/round-2/spec-doc-rnd2/isap-spec-round2.pdf
10. Dobraunig, C., Eichlseder, M., Mangard, S., Mendel, F., Unterluggauer, T.: ISAP - towards side-channel secure authenticated encryption. IACR Trans. Symmetric Cryptol. **2017**(1), 80–105 (2017)
11. Dobraunig, C., Eichlseder, M., Mendel, F., Schläffer, M.: Ascon v1.2. Submission to the CAESAR Competition (2016). https://web.archive.org/web/20200715142917/ascon.iaik.tugraz.at/files/asconv12.pdf
12. Dobraunig, C., Eichlseder, M., Mendel, F., Schläffer, M.: Ascon v1.2. Submission to the NIST Lightweight Crypto Competition (2019). https://csrc.nist.gov/CSRC/media/Projects/lightweight-cryptography/documents/round-2/spec-doc-rnd2/ascon-spec-round2.pdf
13. Dobraunig, C., Mangard, S., Mendel, F., Primas, R.: Fault attacks on nonce-based authenticated encryption: application to Keyak and Ketje. In: Cid, C., Jacobson Jr., M. (eds.) SAC Lecture Notes in Computer Science, vol. 11349, pp. 257–277. Springer, Cham (2018)
14. Dobraunig, C., Mennink, B., Primas, R.: Exploring the golden mean between leakage and fault resilience and practice. Cryptology ePrint Archive, Report 2020/200 (2020). https://eprint.iacr.org/2020/200
15. Fuhr, T., Jaulmes, É., Lomné, V., Thillard, A.: Fault attacks on AES with faulty ciphertexts only. In: FDTC, pp. 108–118. IEEE (2013)
16. Goldreich, O., Goldwasser, S., Micali, S.: How to construct random functions. J. ACM **33**(4), 792–807 (1986)

17. Groß, H.: Caesar hardware API reference implementation. https://github. com/IAIK/ascon_hardware/tree/master/caesar_hardware_api_v_1_0_3/ASCON_ ASCON. Accessed Dec 2019
18. Gross, H., Mangard, S., Korak, T.: An efficient side-channel protected AES implementation with arbitrary protection order. In: Handschuh, H. (ed.) CT-RSA 2017. LNCS, vol. 10159, pp. 95–112. Springer, Cham (2017). https://doi.org/10.1007/ 978-3-319-52153-4_6
19. Groß, H., Wenger, E., Dobraunig, C., Ehrenhöfer, C.: Suit up! - made-to-measure hardware implementations of ASCON. In: DSD, pp. 645–652. IEEE (2015)
20. IAIK: Ascon 128 implementations. https://web.archive.org/web/20200107135835/ ascon.iaik.tugraz.at/implementations.html. Accessed Jan 2020
21. Kannwischer, M.J., Pessl, P., Primas, R.: Single-trace attacks on keccak. IACR Trans. Cryptograph. Hardware Embed. Syst. **2020**(3), 243–268 (2020). https:// doi.org/10.13154/tches.v2020.i3.243-268
22. Kocher, P., Jaffe, J., Jun, B.: Differential power analysis. In: Wiener, M. (ed.) CRYPTO 1999. LNCS, vol. 1666, pp. 388–397. Springer, Heidelberg (1999). https://doi.org/10.1007/3-540-48405-1_25
23. Luo, P., Fei, Y., Zhang, L., Ding, A.A.: Differential fault analysis of SHA-3 under relaxed fault models. J. Hardw. Syst. Secur. **1**(2), 156–172 (2017)
24. Medwed, M., Standaert, F.-X., Joux, A.: Towards super-exponential side-channel security with efficient leakage-resilient PRFs. In: Prouff, E., Schaumont, P. (eds.) CHES 2012. LNCS, vol. 7428, pp. 193–212. Springer, Heidelberg (2012). https:// doi.org/10.1007/978-3-642-33027-8_12
25. Quisquater, J.-J., Samyde, D.: ElectroMagnetic analysis (EMA): measures and counter-measures for smart cards. In: Attali, I., Jensen, T. (eds.) E-smart 2001. LNCS, vol. 2140, pp. 200–210. Springer, Heidelberg (2001). https://doi.org/10. 1007/3-540-45418-7_17
26. Reparaz, O., Bilgin, B., Nikova, S., Gierlichs, B., Verbauwhede, I.: Consolidating masking schemes. In: Gennaro, R., Robshaw, M. (eds.) CRYPTO 2015. LNCS, vol. 9215, pp. 764–783. Springer, Heidelberg (2015). https://doi.org/10.1007/978-3-662-47989-6_37
27. Riou, S.: Drygascon. Submission to the NIST Lightweight Crypto Competition (2019). https://csrc.nist.gov/CSRC/media/Projects/lightweight-cryptography/ documents/round-2/spec-doc-rnd2/drygascon-spec-round2.pdf
28. Rivain, M., Prouff, E.: Provably secure higher-order masking of AES. In: Mangard, S., Standaert, F.-X. (eds.) CHES 2010. LNCS, vol. 6225, pp. 413–427. Springer, Heidelberg (2010). https://doi.org/10.1007/978-3-642-15031-9_28
29. Schuiki, F., team, P.: The parallel ultra low power platform (2019). https://web. archive.org/web/20191219152925/pulp-platform.org/docs/HC31_T7_Pulp.pdf. Accessed Dec 2019
30. Traber, A., et al.: Pulpino: a small single-core RISC-V SoC (2016). https:// web.archive.org/web/20200103103911/riscv.org/wp-content/uploads/2016/01/ Wed1315-PULP-riscv3_noanim.pdf. Accessed Jan 2020

Optimized Software Implementations for the Lightweight Encryption Scheme ForkAE

Arne Deprez[1(✉)], Elena Andreeva[1], Jose Maria Bermudo Mera[2], Angshuman Karmakar[2], and Antoon Purnal[2]

[1] Alpen-Adria University, Klagenfurt, Austria
arne.deprez1@gmail.com, elena.andreeva@aau.at
[2] imec-COSIC, KU Leuven, Kasteelpark Arenberg 10, Bus 2452, 3001 Leuven-Heverlee, Belgium
{jose.mariabermudomera,angshuman.karmakar,antoon.purnal}@esat.kuleuven.be

Abstract. In this work we develop optimized software implementations for ForkAE, a second round candidate in the ongoing NIST lightweight cryptography standardization process. Moreover, we analyze the performance and efficiency of different ForkAE implementations on two embedded platforms: ARM Cortex-A9 and ARM Cortex-M0.

First, we study portable ForkAE implementations. We apply a decryption optimization technique which allows us to accelerate decryption by up to 35%. Second, we go on to explore platform-specific software optimizations. In platforms where cache-timing attacks are not a risk, we present a novel table-based approach to compute the SKINNY round function. Compared to the existing portable implementations, this technique speeds up encryption and decryption by 20% and 25%, respectively. Additionally, we propose a set of platform-specific optimizations for processors with parallel hardware extensions such as ARM NEON. Without relying on parallelism provided by long messages (cf. bit-sliced implementations), we focus on the primitive-level ForkSkinny parallelism provided by ForkAE to reduce encryption and decryption latency by up to 30%. We benchmark the performance of our implementations on the ARM Cortex-M0 and ARM Cortex-A9 processors and give a comparison with the other SKINNY-based schemes in the NIST lightweight competition – SKINNY-AEAD and Romulus.

Keywords: Authenticated encryption · Lightweight implementation · ForkAE · NIST LWC

1 Introduction

The immense growth of small embedded devices that are connected in the Internet of Things (IoT) mandates the adequate development of their respective security mechanisms. To secure the communication between such devices one most

© Springer Nature Switzerland AG 2021
P.-Y. Liardet and N. Mentens (Eds.): CARDIS 2020, LNCS 12609, pp. 68–83, 2021.
https://doi.org/10.1007/978-3-030-68487-7_5

commonly requires the use of lightweight symmetric authenticated encryption schemes. The competition for dedicated standards for lightweight symmetric authenticated encryption (AE) and/or hashing algorithms that is run at present by the U.S. National Institute of Standards and Technology (NIST) is a clear indication of the benefits and demand for such algorithms in practice. Besides security, achieving good performance in software implementations is an important criterion for all candidates in the second round of this standardization process. In their call for submissions, NIST states that the algorithms should preferably be "...optimized to be efficient for short messages (e.g., as short as 8 bytes)." and "Compact hardware implementations and embedded software implementations with low RAM and ROM usage should be possible." In this work we focus on ForkAE [1,2], a NIST lightweight cryptography (LWC) second round candidate which is particularly optimized for the processing of such short messages. ForkAE uses a novel building block called forkcipher [2,3] which enables one primitive call per data block for secure authenticated ecnryption with associated data AEAD. Forkcipher in ForkAE is instantiated with the ForkSkinny primitive which reuses the SKINNY [5] round and tweakey functions. The SKINNY-based nature of ForkSkinny gives us a natural reference point for comparison with the rest of the SKINNY-based candidates in the competition SKINNY-AEAD [6] and Romulus [9]. Moreover, software implementation results come with distinct advantages and optimization techniques when one deals with general versus specific platforms. In this work we aim to illustrate the advantages of ForkAE in all those aspects.

Contributions. Our contributions in this work are as follows.

1. We analyze portable ForkAE implementations across a range of platforms and show that decryption latency can be significantly reduced (up to 35%) by preprocessing the tweakey schedule. Our new decryption approach achieves code size reduction (up to 31%) in addition to speed-up, at the cost of higher memory usage.
2. We explore platform-specific optimizations. Our first implementation, suitable for systems where (cache-) timing attacks are not applicable, accelerates ForkAE encryption and decryption by 20% to 25%, respectively, by representing the forward and inverse round functions as a series of table lookups. We also explore the speed-memory trade-off for this implementation strategy.
3. We provide a second platform-specific implementation which targets platforms with SIMD (Single Instruction Multiple Data) parallel hardware extensions. Our implementation is developed to exploit the data-level parallelism present in ForkAE. Our results indicate that the efficiency and performance of ForkAE on such platforms can be significantly increased, reducing encryption and decryption latency by up to 30%.
4. We benchmark the performance of our implementations on the ARM Cortex-M0 and ARM Cortex-A9 processors, illustrating the improved software performance of ForkAE. Benchmark results are compared with the other

SKINNY-based schemes in the second round of the NIST LWC standardization process SKINNY-AEAD and Romulus. All implementations described in this paper are publicly available at [8].

2   Background on ForkAE

ForkAE uses a forkcipher primitive that was specifically designed for use in authenticated encryption of short messages. More concretely, it produces a $2n$-bit output from an n-bit input block via the secret key K and a public tweak T. The forward computation corresponds to calculating two independent permutations of the input block at a reduced computational cost (compared to two tweakable block cipher calls). A forkcipher can be obtained following the so-called *iterate-fork-iterate* [2] paradigm by using a round based (tweakable) block cipher to transform the input block M a fixed number of rounds into the intermediate state M' which is then "forked" (duplicated) and further iterated in two separate branches, producing the outputs C_0 and C_1. M can be computed backwards from C_0 or C_1 and in addition, either of the ciphertext blocks can be computed from the other via the so-called reconstruction functionality.

2.1   The Tweakable Forkcipher ForkSkinny

ForkAE uses the ForkSkinny forkcipher primitive which is based on the lightweight tweakable block cipher SKINNY [5]. The key and tweak are processed following the TWEAKEY approach [10]. ForkSkinny uses the SKINNY round function (RF) and tweakey schedule (TKS) to update its intermediate state and tweakey. The state of the second branch is also modified by an additional branch constant value (BC). The general processing of M under tweakey $K\|T$ to $C_0\|C_1$ in ForkSkinny is depicted in Fig. 1 and all details can be found in the ForkAE submission document [1].

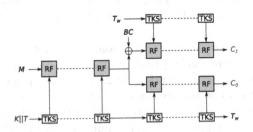

Fig. 1. Outline of ForkSkinny.

ForkSkinny comes in four instances [1], differing in the block (64- and 128-bit) and the tweakey (192-, 256- and 288-bit) sizes. Each instance is denoted as ForkSkinny-n-t where n and t are the block- and the tweakey size, respectively, in bits. The size of the key (128 bits) is the same for all instances. Each instance has a fixed number of r_{init} rounds before the forking step and a fixed number of $r_0 = r_1$ rounds in each branch after the forking point.

2.2   The ForkSkinny Round Function and Tweakey Schedule

The ForkSkinny round function (RF) consists of the same five operations as the SKINNY round function and they are described by their effect on the internal state. The internal state (IS) is represented by a 4×4 matrix where each cell contains 8 bits (if $n = 128$) or 4 bits ($n = 64$) of data. In the beginning of the cipher evaluation, the input block is loaded into the internal state in a row-wise manner. The operations of the round function are listed below:

SubCells: Each cell of the internal state is substituted according to the SKINNY S-boxes [5].

AddConstants: Constants are added to the first column of the IS. These constants are generated by a Linear-Feedback-Shift-Register (LFSR) [1].

AddRoundTweakey: Round-tweakey material is added to the internal state in the first two rows.

ShiftRows: The cells in the second row of the internal state are rotated one position to the right. The third row is rotated 2 cells and the fourth row 3 cells.

MixColumns: Each column of the internal state is modified by a multiplication with a binary matrix M [5].

At the beginning of the encryption procedure, a tweakey state is created as a set of 4×4 matrices with cells of the same size as those of the internal state. The tweakey matrices are then filled row-wise with the tweak and the key. This results in the matrices TK1, TK2 and possibly TK3. In each round, the first two rows of each of the matrices are jointly added to the first two rows of the internal state (*i.e.*, in AddRoundTweakey). After that, the tweakey state is updated to create the next round-tweakey. The update consists of a permutation of the cells and modification of the first two rows of TK2 and TK3 (if any) with an LFSR.

The ForkAE submission specifies two different modes of operation for domain extension of ForkSkinny: a parallel PAEF and a sequential SAEF [1]. The presented optimizations in this work are focused at the primitive level (*i.e.*, Fork-Skinny) due to its higher impact on short message processing.

3   Portable Implementations of ForkAE

When carefully designing software in a low-level language, it is possible to obtain efficient and secure implementations that can be compiled for a broad range of platforms. In the design of such software, careful attention should be spent to efficiently use the memory and avoid side-channel vulnerabilities.

In a concurrent work, Weatherley [15] explores efficient software for lightweight cryptographic primitives on general 32-bit platforms. This includes implementations of all instances of ForkAE. These implementations aim to perform well on 32-bit embedded microprocessors and are designed to execute in constant time with constant-cache behaviour [15]. In this section, we propose an optimization that increases the performance of ForkAE decryption in these implementations.

3.1 Decryption Optimization

For decryption, the evaluation of ForkSkinny requires the final round-tweakey to be computed. In the existing portable implementation from [15], this is achieved by fast-forwarding the tweakey state until the end of the tweakey schedule. The resulting round-tweakey is then inverted on-the-fly every round. By introducing many duplicate calculations, this approach causes ForkSkinny decryption to be significantly slower than encryption.

Duplicate calculations can be avoided when the tweakey schedule is iterated once and the portion of the round-tweakey that needs to be added to the internal state is saved in memory. This way, the correct round-tweakey can be directly accessed during the round function evaluation. This ensures that the tweakey schedule is only calculated once and significantly reduces the decryption time. This implementation strategy introduces a higher memory usage as the round-tweakeys needs to be stored in memory. However, instead of storing the full round-tweakeys, we show that it is sufficient to store only the relevant rows of the tweakey state. Moreover, these can readily be added together to reduce the memory footprint even more (cf. Sect. 2.2).

This new decryption approach achieves a significant speed-up and code size reduction, at the expense of higher memory usage. The ROM size is reduced because the round function code no longer needs to include tweakey calculations.

4 Lookup Table Implementations of ForkAE

Lookup tables can be used to speed up the calculations without introducing a security risk in platforms that are not vulnerable to cache-timing attacks. The original proposal of the Rijndael cipher for the Advanced Encryption Standard (AES) proposes very efficient implementations for 32-bit platforms, by combining multiple steps of the round function in table look ups [7]. In this section we show how, in a similar way, the SKINNY round function in ForkAE can be translated into a combination of table look ups. For the inverse round function, such a transformation is more complex. Here, the different steps of the inverse round must first be reordered, defining a modified inverse round function for which a table-base implementation can be derived.

4.1 Tabulating the Round Function

We represent the internal state at the beginning of the SKINNY round function by the matrix A (Eq. 1). For variants of ForkSkinny with a block size $n = 128$, the elements $a_{i,j}$ of this matrix are 8-bit values. In Eq. 5, we write the effect of the round function on a column a_j to obtain the column b_j of the state $B = (b_0\ b_1\ b_2\ b_3)$ at the end of the round. In this equation $S[a]$ denotes the output of the S-box of the SubCells step for input a. The binary matrix M (Eq. 2) defines the MixColumns operation and the matrix X contains the constants that are added in the AddConstants step (Eq. 3). The addition is always a bit-wise addition. This corresponds to an XOR operation and is denoted with the operator $\oplus$. Indices should be taken modulo 4, as the `ShiftRows` operation is a rotation. The values $TK_{i,j}$ contain the round-tweakey material that is added in the `AddRoundTweakey` step (Eq. 4).

$$A = \begin{pmatrix} a_{0,0} & a_{0,1} & a_{0,2} & a_{0,3} \\ a_{1,0} & a_{1,1} & a_{1,2} & a_{1,3} \\ a_{2,0} & a_{2,1} & a_{2,2} & a_{2,3} \\ a_{3,0} & a_{3,1} & a_{3,2} & a_{3,3} \end{pmatrix} \quad (1)$$

$$X = \begin{pmatrix} c_0 & 0 & 2 & 0 \\ c_1 & 0 & 0 & 0 \\ 2 & 0 & 0 & 0 \\ 0 & 0 & 0 & 0 \end{pmatrix} \quad (3)$$

$$M = \begin{pmatrix} 1 & 0 & 1 & 1 \\ 1 & 0 & 0 & 0 \\ 0 & 1 & 1 & 0 \\ 1 & 0 & 1 & 0 \end{pmatrix} \quad (2)$$

$$TK_{i,j} = TK1_{i,j} \oplus TK2_{i,j}(\oplus TK3_{i,j}) \quad (4)$$

Unfortunately, constants and tweakey material should be added before `ShiftRows` and `MixColumns`. We solve this problem by splitting the round function in three terms and distributing the matrix multiplication with M.

$$b_j = \begin{pmatrix} b_{0,j} \\ b_{1,j} \\ b_{2,j} \\ b_{3,j} \end{pmatrix} = M \cdot \left(\begin{pmatrix} S[a_{0,j}] \\ S[a_{1,j-1}] \\ S[a_{2,j-2}] \\ S[a_{3,j-3}] \end{pmatrix} \oplus \begin{pmatrix} x_{0,j} \\ x_{1,j-1} \\ x_{2,j-2} \\ x_{3,j-3} \end{pmatrix} \oplus \begin{pmatrix} TK_{0,j} \\ TK_{1,j-1} \\ 0 \\ 0 \end{pmatrix} \right) \quad (5)$$

With the lookup tables $T_0...T_3$ defined in Eq. 6, we can now calculate the first term as in Eq. 7. For ForkSkinny instances with $n = 128$, each of these tables has 256 entries of 32-bit (one for every possible input a) and thus takes up 1 kB of memory. To avoid having to store 4 kB of tables in memory, it is possible to store only one table $T = (S[a]\ S[a]\ S[a]\ S[a])^{\top}$ and mask it according to the needed vector. This approach needs an extra 4 logical AND operations per column, but has a smaller ROM size because only one table of 1 kB needs to be stored.

$$T_0[a] = \begin{pmatrix} S[a] \\ S[a] \\ 0 \\ S[a] \end{pmatrix}, \quad T_1[a] = \begin{pmatrix} 0 \\ 0 \\ S[a] \\ 0 \end{pmatrix}, \quad T_2[a] = \begin{pmatrix} S[a] \\ 0 \\ S[a] \\ S[a] \end{pmatrix}, \quad T_3[a] = \begin{pmatrix} S[a] \\ 0 \\ 0 \\ 0 \end{pmatrix} \quad (6)$$

$$M \cdot \begin{pmatrix} S[a_{0,j}] \\ S[a_{1,j-1}] \\ S[a_{2,j-2}] \\ S[a_{3,j-3}] \end{pmatrix} = T_0[a_{0,j}] \oplus T_1[a_{1,j-1}] \oplus T_2[a_{2,j-2}] \oplus T_3[a_{3,j-3}] \quad (7)$$

The second term corresponds to the values added in the `AddConstants` step and can be calculated by applying the `Shiftrows` and `MixColumns` step to the matrix X, resulting in the matrix from Eq. (8). For $j = 0, 1, 2$ the j-th column of this matrix AC_j needs to be added with the first term. The first two columns of this matrix are different for every round, but can also be stored in a lookup table.

The final term involves the application of ShiftRows and MixColumns to the round-tweakey. This corresponds to an addition of the column K_j (Eq. (9)).

$$AC = \begin{pmatrix} c_0 & 0 & 0 & 0 \\ c_0 & 0 & 2 & 0 \\ 0 & c_1 & 2 & 0 \\ c_0 & 0 & 0 & 0 \end{pmatrix} \quad (8) \qquad K_j = \begin{pmatrix} TK_{0,j} \\ TK_{0,j} \\ TK_{1,j-1} \\ TK_{0,j} \end{pmatrix} \quad (9)$$

Finally, every column b_j of the output of the round function can be calculated as in Eq. 10, requiring 5 table lookups and 5 XOR operations per column. For the third column, the constant lookup can be omitted as it is always the same. The final column does not feature any constants, saving another lookup and XOR. This results in a total cost for calculating the round function of 18 table lookups, 19 XOR operations and the cost of constructing the columns K_j.

$$b_j = T_0[a_{0,j}] \oplus T_1[a_{1,j-1}] \oplus T_2[a_{2,j-2}] \oplus T_3[a_{3,j-3}] \oplus AC_j \oplus K_j \quad (10)$$

4.2   The Inverse Round Function

In order to be able to implement the inverse round function in a similar way as the forward round, the SubCells step needs to be the first step of the inverse round and the ShiftRows step needs to come before the MixColumns step, which is not the case. In order to obtain an inverse round function where the SubCells_inv steps comes first, steps of consecutive rounds need to be combined in a new round and a different first and final round need to be defined. We illustrate this in Fig. 3. However, in this approach the ShiftRows_inv step still comes after the MixColumns_inv step and designing an efficient table-lookup implementation is still not possible. To solve this problem we noted that the sequence of operations from Fig. 2a, can be also be calculated with the sequence of operations from Fig. 2b, allowing to delay the ShiftRows_inv step. Here, we shift in advance the round-tweakey material and the constants, so that they are added to the correct part of the row that is not yet shifted.

When the ShiftRows_inv operation is calculated after the addition of shifted round-tweakey material and shifted constants, it comes before the SubCells_inv step. Now, the SubCells_inv and ShiftRows_inv can easily be swapped because the ShiftRows_inv step does not modify the value within a cell and SubCells_inv operates on individual cells [7]. With this reordering of operations, it becomes possible to define the new inverse rounds as in Fig. 4. In the calculation of these $n - 1$ new inverse rounds the first three steps can now be combined into table lookups. The table-based implementation is even more simple here, because the round-tweakey material and constants are added at the end of the round and their columns do not need to be mixed in advance. The tables are different than for the forward round, but also here the possibility exists to use only one table to reduce the memory size of the implementation.

First round

| MixColums_inv |
| ShiftRows_inv |
| AddRoundTweakey |
| AddConstants |

First round

| MixColums_inv |
| AddRoundTweakey_shifted |
| AddConstants_shifted |

(n-1) rounds

| SubCells_inv |
| ShiftRows_inv |
| MixColums_inv |
| AddRoundTweakey_shifted |
| AddConstants_shifted |

(n-1) rounds

| SubCells_inv |
| MixColums_inv |
| ShiftRows_inv |
| AddRoundTweakey |
| AddConstants |

| ShiftRows_inv |
| AddRoundTweakey |
| AddConstants |

(a)

| AddRoundTweakey_shifted |
| AddConstants_shifted |
| ShiftRows_inv |

(b)

Final round

| SubCells_inv |

Final round

| SubCells_inv |
| ShiftRows_inv |

Fig. 2. Delaying the ShiftRows_inv step in the inverse round function.

Fig. 3. Definition of a new inverse round that starts with the SubCells_inv step.

Fig. 4. Definition of new inverse round with delayed ShiftRows_inv step.

4.3 64-Bit Instance

The round function transformation can also be applied to the instance where $n = 64$ and the cells of the internal state contain 4-bit values. However, with a single byte containing two cells of the internal state, designing software that calculates this table-based round function becomes more difficult. A lot of overhead is needed to transform the state to a column representation, to select the correct 4-bit values, to construct the round-tweakey columns, etc. A possible solution to this is to split the cells of the internal state in separate bytes, i.e. using bytes that are half empty. Both ways of implementing the 64-bit lookup table round function were tested, but could not provide a speed-up.

5 Parallel Implementations of ForkAE

Cryptographic algorithms often feature data-level parallelism. As a result, they can be made more efficient or achieve higher performance when Single Instruction, Multiple Data (SIMD) hardware is available. Examples of such implementations are the bit-sliced implementation of AES from [11] using x86 Streaming SIMD Extensions (SEE) instructions, or the SKINNY implementation from [12] using x86 Advanced Vector Extensions (AVX). These bit-sliced implementations exploit the parallelism of processing multiple input blocks of long messages. As such, they are not well-suited for processing short messages.

To increase efficiency for the short messages typical for lightweight applications, the performance of a single primitive call needs to be improved. This section explores the data-level parallelism in ForkSkinny, and how it can be exploited in a SIMD-enabled processor. Specifically, we use the ARM NEON extension, available in the ARM Cortex-A9 processor of the Zynq ZYBO platform [4].

5.1   Parallelism in the Round Function

When looking at the round function, the S-box layer is the most promising subject for SIMD acceleration, because it works on the entire state in parallel and because it is the most computationally heavy part of the round function. In the portable C implementations, the S-box layer accounts for 60–80% of the execution time of round function and tweakey schedule combined.

For ForkSkinny instances with blocksize $n = 128$, the internal state fits perfectly in a NEON 128-bit quadword register. This effectively allows four times as much data to be processed in parallel. The S-box can be fully calculated for all cells of the internal state with a set of ± 60 NEON instructions. This reduces the execution time for the S-box from 169 to 83 clock cycles, a reduction of $\pm 50\%$.

The $n = 64$ ForkSkinny instance requires just one 64-bit NEON halfword register for its internal state. It also features a simpler S-box than the 128-bit instances, requiring roughly half the amount of instructions. We reduce its execution time from 117 clock cycles to 72 clock cycles, a reduction of $\pm 60\%$.

5.2   The Parallelism of the Fork

During encryption, forking after r_{init} rounds introduces data-level parallelism because the same round function is calculated in two independent branches. This parallelism has already been shown to increase performance in hardware implementations [13]. We now demonstrate that, if the processor features SIMD instructions, such primitive-level parallelism can also be exploited in software.

Although the state and round functions of both branches are independent, the tweakey schedule is serial. We overcome this apparent problem by calculating the round-tweakeys in advance and storing them (cf. decryption in Sect. 3.1). While this increases memory usage, round-tweakeys are now instantly available and the calculations for both branches are again completely independent.

The combined size of the internal state in both branches of ForkSkinny-64-192 is $2 \times 64 = 128$ bits. As this fits in a single NEON quadword register, the S-box can be calculated for both states in parallel, with only one set of NEON instructions. We already reduced S-box execution time from 117 to 72 clock cycles, and doing this for both branches would require 144 cycles. By leveraging the parallel branches with NEON, we manage to reduce this further to 85 cycles.

For instances with block size $n = 128$, the parallel hardware is already maximally exploited for the S-box calculation. As a consequence, executing two round functions in parallel will not speed up that part of the round function. For other parts of the round function a parallel execution does not improve performance because of the overhead introduced by using the NEON hardware. In processors with 256-bit (or higher) SIMD hardware (e.g., AVX on x86), both states can again be processed in parallel, similarly as for the 64-bit instance.

6   Performance Analysis

We analyze the performance of the ForkAE implementations on two different platforms. The first platform is the ZYBO development platform, containing the Xilinx Z-7010 system-on-chip (SoC). The Xilinx Z-7010 contains a 650 MHz dual-core ARM Cortex-A9, 240 kB RAM and 512 MB ROM. We use a single core for the evaluation. The second platform is the STM32F0 microcontroller, which incorporates a 32-bit 48 MHz ARM Cortex-M0, 8 kB RAM and 64 kB ROM.

    We always compile the C code with `gcc` and compiler option `-Os` (*i.e.*, optimizing for implementation size). We report the three most important performance metrics: speed, implementation size (ROM) and memory usage (RAM). Speed is evaluated by measuring the execution time for different input sizes, and expressed in the common metric of cycles/byte. The number that is reported is the average amount of cycles/byte needed for encryption or decryption of messages with sizes ranging from 1 block (64 or 128 bit depending to the instance) to 8 blocks. The size of the implementation, or ROM size, is expressed in bytes and corresponds to the memory necessary to store all compiled code needed for encryption or decryption. It also includes the storage of constant data such as the round constant. The memory usage, or RAM size, is also expressed in bytes and corresponds to the total amount of RAM memory that is used during encryption/decryption. This consists mainly of variables and data structures.

Constant-Time Execution: We followed the best practices for constant-time software implementation. Our implementation does not have any secret-dependent control flow. Furthermore, we used the `dudect` tool [14] to verify the constant-time execution of the optimized portable and parallel implementations.

6.1   Portable Implementations

The performance of the portable 32-bit C implementations is analysed on the Cortex-M0 and Cortex-A9 processors, and summarized in Table 1. It is clear that the duplicate tweakey calculations in the original approach (cf. Sect. 3) have a significant impact on the execution time. On the Cortex-A9, decryption with the fast-forwarding approach takes 30–55% more cycles per byte than encryption. On the Cortex-M0, the difference is even 45–70%. Another downside of this approach is the increased code size and higher memory usage compared to encryption.

    Our implementation with preprocessed tweakey schedule (cf. Sect. 3.1) reduces this decryption time. For 128-bit instances with two tweakey matrices, the cycles per byte on the A9 are reduced with 17% compared to

Table 1. Implementation figures for ForkAE encryption/decryption with portable 32-bit C implementations. Implementations from [15].

Encryption	Cortex-A9			Cortex-M0		
	c/B	ROM	RAM	c/B	ROM	RAM
PAEF-FS-64-192	1669	3067	107	4002	2067	107
PAEF-FS-128-192	1072	3187	161	2457	2251	161
PAEF-FS-128-256	1074	3219	169	2458	2247	169
PAEF-FS-128-288	1408	3483	189	3408	2541	189
SAEF-FS-128-19	1075	3015	161	2475	2187	161
SAEF-FS-128-256	1076	3043	169	2476	2173	169
Decryption						
PAEF-FS-64-192	2596	3999	140	6767	2819	140
PAEF-FS-128-192	1397	3735	210	3562	2715	210
PAEF-FS-128-256	1393	3767	218	3563	2707	218
PAEF-FS-128-288	2001	4399	254	5305	3243	254
SAEF-FS-128-192	1398	3599	210	3580	2771	210
SAEF-FS-128-256	1397	3603	218	3579	2757	218
Decryption (preprocessed tweakey schedule)						
PAEF-FS-64-192	1684	2927	392	4167	1955	392
PAEF-FS-128-192	1165	3131	810	2970	2303	810
PAEF-FS-128-256	1162	3163	818	2971	2295	818
PAEF-FS-128-288	1491	3363	950	4010	2571	950
SAEF-FS-128-192	1166	2995	810	2988	2359	810
SAEF-FS-128-256	1164	2999	818	2987	2345	818

the decryption implementation from [15]. For three tweakey matrices, the speed-up is even greater: 25% for PAEF-ForkSkinny-128-288 and 35% for PAEF-ForkSkinny-64-192. Similar observations hold for the M0. While decryption is still slower than encryption, the difference between the two is now much smaller. Our approach achieves a speed-up and code size reduction in exchange for a higher memory usage. The ROM size is reduced because the code to iterate through the entire tweakey schedule takes less space than when the tweakey schedule is calculated both in the ForkSkinny decryption and in the inverse round function. The consequence is that the round-tweakey material is stored in a buffer, which introduces a bigger RAM size. This buffer needs to be $(r_{init} + 2 \times r_0) \times \frac{n}{16}$ bytes big to store all round-tweakeys. The buffer is largest for PAEF-ForkSkinny-128-288, where 696 bytes of memory are needed to store the preprocessed tweakey.

In Fig. 5 and Fig. 5a, we compare the performance of ForkAE with other SKINNY-based AEAD schemes Romulus and SKINNY-AEAD. We compare the primary instances of the NIST LWC submission for small messages with different

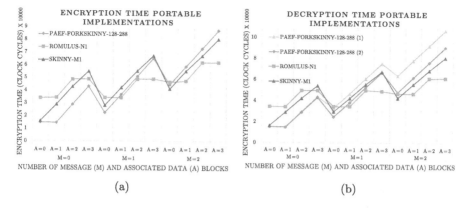

Fig. 5. Performance comparison of SKINNY based ciphers on Cortex-A9. Encryption with implementations from [15]. Decryption with SKINNY, Romulus and PAEF-ForkSkinny-128-288(1) implementations from [15] and PAEF-ForkSkinny-128-288(2) implementation with preprocessed tweakey schedule.

Table 2. Implementation figures for the table-based ForkAE encryption implementation on the ARM Cortex-M0.

Encryption	Tables in ROM			Tables in RAM		
4 lookup tables	c/B	ROM	RAM	c/B	ROM	RAM
PAEF-FS-128-192	2110	6752	192	2016	1960	4984
PAEF-FS-128-256	2111	6748	200	2017	1956	4992
PAEF-FS-128-288	2859	7034	220	2739	2242	5012
SAEF-FS-128-192	2128	6688	192	2035	1896	4984
SAEF-FS-128-256	2129	6674	200	2035	1882	4992
1 lookup table						
PAEF-FS-128-192	2138	3692	192	2030	1972	1912
PAEF-FS-128-256	2139	3688	200	2031	1968	1920
PAEF-FS-128-288	2919	3980	220	2805	2260	1940
SAEF-FS-128-192	2157	3628	192	2049	1908	1912
SAEF-FS-128-256	2157	3614	200	2049	1894	1920

number of message (M) and associated data (A) blocks. These figures highlight the advantage of a forkcipher over a blockcipher for encryption of small messages.

6.2   Table-Based Implementations

The lookup table round function described in Sect. 4 is implemented on the STM32F0 platform with the ARM Cortex-M0 processor as an example lightweight platform with no cache. We explore the different trade-offs between speed, code size and memory usage. Table 2 lists the results for an implementation with 4 different lookup tables. Compared to the portable implementations of Sect. 3, it needs up to 16% fewer clock cycles when the tables are stored in ROM. When the tables are stored in RAM, this gain is almost 20%.

We gain in speed in exchange for a higher memory cost. Particularly, when four lookup tables are used in combination with two tables containing the mixed and shifted round constants, a total of 4.7 kB of memory is needed. We show that the impact of the lookup table implementation on the memory usage can be greatly reduced when only one T-table is used instead four. The performance results for this method are listed in Table 2. This approach introduces some extra calculations in the round function, but as can be seen from the results, the impact on the computation time is only a few cycles per byte. The reduction in memory cost of 3 kB is significant and can be very important for the resource-constrained devices in embedded applications.

To study the gain of tabulating the inverse round function, the performance of one specific implementation for table-based decryption is analysed. The implementation uses one lookup-table that is stored in ROM and a preprocessed tweakey schedule that is stored in RAM. The performance metrics are listed in Table 3. When this is compared with the portable decryption implementation, it can be seen that using lookup tables can significantly speed-up decryption, as the amount of cycles that are needed is reduced with up to 25%. This speed-up is higher than for encryption because of the simpler inverse round function where the addition of the round tweakey and constants can be done at the end.

Table 3. Implementation figures for the table-based ForkAE decryption implementation on the ARM Cortex-M0.

Decryption	c/B	ROM	RAM
PAEF-FS-128-192	2241	3261	818
PAEF-FS-128-256	2241	3253	826
PAEF-FS-128-288	3156	3529	958
SAEF-FS-128-192	2259	3317	818
SAEF-FS-128-256	2257	3303	826

6.3   Parallel Implementations

In Table 4 we list the performance of ForkAE encryption and decryption on the ZYBO platform when the NEON SIMD implementations are used. For Fork-Skinny instances with a block-size $n = 128$, the S-box and its inverse are replaced with the 128-bit NEON implementation. For PAEF-ForkSkinny-64-192, the ForkSkinny implementation with parallel round function is used for encryption. Its decryption only features the parallel S-box layer, as it cannot benefit from parallelism in the round function.

For the 128-bit instances with the NEON S-box implementation, we observe a reduction in the amount of cycles for encryption and decryption of approximately 30% when compared to the portable implementations of Sect. 3. For the PAEF-ForkSkinny-128-288 instance with three tweakey matrices, this speed-up is a bit lower (27%). This can be explained by the larger relative importance of the tweakey calculations in this instance. The ROM size is reduced by approximately 500 bytes in all 128-bit instances. This follows from the smaller code size of the round function, which now uses the parallel NEON S-box implementation. The amount of RAM needed for encryption or decryption remains the same.

Table 4. Implementation figures for the NEON SIMD implementations of ForkAE on the ZYBO platform.

	Encryption			Decryption		
	c/B	ROM	RAM	c/B	ROM	RAM
PAEF-FS-64-192	1184	3235	331	1390	2653	392
PAEF-FS-128-192	736	2619	161	807	2551	810
PAEF-FS-128-256	737	2651	169	806	2583	818
PAEF-FS-128-288	1026	2863	189	1078	2783	950
SAEF-FS-128-192	743	2491	161	812	2415	810
SAEF-FS-128-256	743	2519	169	810	2419	818

The execution time of PAEF-ForkSkinny-64-192 encryption improves with almost 500 cycles per byte, $i.e.$, 29%, when compared to the portable implementation from [15]. For decryption, the speed-up is smaller as the degree of parallelism is lower. With the NEON inverse S-box implementation, we still accelerate decryption with 17%.

A single round of the 64-bit SKINNY round function with a NEON S-box implementation executes in 95 clock cycles on the ARM Cortex-A9. With 17 rounds before the forking point and 23 rounds after the forking point, a single branch of the ForkSkinny primitive, which is equal to the execution of the SKINNY primitive, needs 40 of these rounds. Producing twice as much output by calculating both branches requires $17 + 2 \times 23 = 63$ such rounds, or $\frac{63}{40} = 1.58$ times the amount of computations. When the S-box is calculated in parallel for the branches after the forking point, two rounds are calculated in 112 clock cycles instead of 2×95. This way producing the double output requires only 1.10 times the amount of execution time of a single branch.

Other SKINNY-based candidates need $M + 1$ calls to the SKINNY primitive for M message blocks, while ForkAE, which has no fixed cost, needs M calls to the ForkSkinny primitive (with 1.10 times the computational cost). As a result, for implementations where no mode parallelism is exploited (e.g., for serial modes, like Romulus), ForkAE encryption will be faster for messages of up to 10 blocks. This is illustrated in Fig. 6. We note that the SKINNY-AEAD and Romulus submissions to the NIST LWC competition do not include an instance with 64-bit blocks. However, when 256-bit SIMD hardware is available, this result could also be extended to the 128-bit instances.

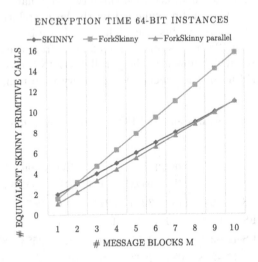

Fig. 6. Comparison of encryption time of 64-bit ForkAE implementations with SKINNY-AEAD, expressed in number of equivalent calls to SKINNY primitive.

7 Conclusion

This paper studied the design of software implementations for the lightweight authenticated encryption scheme ForkAE. First, portable 32-bit implementations were described and analyzed on different platforms. We presented a method to significantly speed-up the decryption of ForkAE in these implementations.

In order to increase performance, two specialized implementations for two different target platforms were designed. The first implementation is designed for platforms where cache-timing attacks are not possible. It was shown that on these platforms the SKINNY round function and inverse round function can be transformed into a combination of table-lookups. This allowed for a significant increase in performance. The impact on the amount of memory needed for this implementation can be minimised by reducing the number of tables.

A second platform-specific implementation targets platforms with a NEON SIMD hardware extension. This paper described how in these platforms, the data-level parallelism in the ForkSkinny primitive can be exploited in efficient implementations with reduced latency. We exploited the first level of parallelism found in the SKINNY round function, and a second level of parallelism introduced by the forking step in ForkSkinny.

References

1. Andreeva, E., Lallemand, V., Purnal, A., Reyhanitabar, R., Roy, A., Vizár, D.: Forkae, vol. 1 (2019). https://csrc.nist.gov/CSRC/media/Projects/lightweight-cryptography/documents/round-2/spec-doc-rnd2/forkae-spec-round2.pdf
2. Andreeva, E., Lallemand, V., Purnal, A., Reyhanitabar, R., Roy, A., Vizar, D.: Forkcipher: a new primitive for authenticated encryption of very short messages. Cryptology ePrint Archive, Report 2019/1004 (2019). https://eprint.iacr.org/2019/1004
3. Andreeva, E., Reyhanitabar, R., Varici, K., Vizár, D.: Forking a blockcipher for authenticated encryption of very short messages. Cryptology ePrint Archive, Report 2018/916 (2018). https://eprint.iacr.org/2018/916
4. ARM: Cortex^{TM}-A9 NEON^{TM} Media Processing Engine, Technical Reference Manual (2012)
5. Beierle, C., et al.: The SKINNY family of block ciphers and its low-latency variant MANTIS. In: Robshaw, M., Katz, J. (eds.) CRYPTO 2016. LNCS, vol. 9815, pp. 123–153. Springer, Heidelberg (2016). https://doi.org/10.1007/978-3-662-53008-5_5
6. Beierle, C., et al.: Skinny-aead and skinny-hash v1.1. Submission to Round 1 of the NIST Lightweight Cryptography Standardization process (2019)
7. Daemen, J., Rijmen, V.: AES proposal: Rijndael (1999)
8. Deprez, A.: ForkAE-SW. GitHub repository (2020). https://github.com/ArneDeprez1/ForkAE-SW
9. Iwata, T., Khairallah, M., Minematsu, K., Peyrin, T.: Romulus v1.2. submission to the NIST lightweight cryptography standardization process (2019)
10. Jean, J., Nikolić, I., Peyrin, T.: Tweaks and keys for block ciphers: the TWEAKEY framework. In: Sarkar, P., Iwata, T. (eds.) ASIACRYPT 2014. LNCS, vol. 8874, pp. 274–288. Springer, Heidelberg (2014). https://doi.org/10.1007/978-3-662-45608-8_15
11. Käsper, E., Schwabe, P.: Faster and timing-attack resistant AES-GCM. In: Clavier, C., Gaj, K. (eds.) CHES 2009. LNCS, vol. 5747, pp. 1–17. Springer, Heidelberg (2009). https://doi.org/10.1007/978-3-642-04138-9_1
12. Kölbl, S.: AVX implementation of the skinny block cipher. GitHub repository (2018). https://github.com/kste/skinny_avx
13. Purnal, A., Andreeva, E., Roy, A., Vizár, D.: What the fork: implementation aspects of a forkcipher. In: NIST Lightweight Cryptography Workshop (2019)
14. Reparaz, O., Balasch, J., Verbauwhede, I.: Dude, is my code constant time? In: Design, Automation & Test in Europe Conference & Exhibition (2017)
15. Weatherley, R.: NIST lightweight cryptography primitives. GitHub repository (2020). https://github.com/rweather/lightweight-crypto

Secure and Efficient Delegation
of Pairings with Online Inputs

Giovanni Di Crescenzo[1]([⊠]), Matluba Khodjaeva[2], Delaram Kahrobaei[3],
and Vladimir Shpilrain[4]

[1] Perspecta Labs Inc., Basking Ridge, NJ, USA
gdicrescenzo@perspectalabs.com
[2] CUNY John Jay College of Criminal Justice, New York, NY, USA
mkhodjaeva@jjay.cuny.edu
[3] University of York, Heslington, York, UK
delaram.kahrobaei@york.ac.uk
[4] City University of New York, New York, NY, USA
vshpilrain@ccny.cuny.edu

Abstract. Delegation of pairings from a computationally weaker client to a computationally stronger server has been advocated to expand the applicability of pairing-based cryptographic protocols to computation paradigms with resource-constrained devices. Important requirements for such delegation protocols include privacy of the client's inputs and security of the client's output, in the sense of detecting, with high probability, any malicious server's attempt to convince the client of an incorrect pairing result. In this paper we show that pairings with inputs only available in the online phase can be efficiently, privately and securely delegated to a single, possibly malicious, server. We present new protocols in 2 different scenarios: (1) the two pairing inputs are publicly known; (2) privacy of both pairing inputs needs to be maintained (left open in previous papers; e.g., [27]). In both cases, we improve the online-phase client's runtime with respect to previous work. In the latter case, we show the first protocol where the client's online-phase runtime is faster than non-delegated computation for all of the most practical known curves. In previous work, the client's runtime was worse, especially for one of the most practical elliptic curves underlying the pairing function (i.e., BN-12).

Keywords: Applied cryptography · Secure delegation · Pairings · Bilinear maps · Elliptic curves · Group theory

1 Introduction

Server-aided cryptography is an active research direction addressing the problem of computationally weaker clients delegating the most expensive cryptographic computations to more powerful servers. Recently, this area has seen an increased interest in reducing computation in client devices, including smart cards, smart phones, and even more resource-constrained devices, motivated by

© Springer Nature Switzerland AG 2021
P.-Y. Liardet and N. Mentens (Eds.): CARDIS 2020, LNCS 12609, pp. 84–99, 2021.
https://doi.org/10.1007/978-3-030-68487-7_6

shifts in modern computation paradigms, towards more smart-card computing, cloud/edge/fog computing, etc.

The first formal model for secure delegation protocols was presented in [18], where a secure delegation protocol is formally defined as a secure function evaluation (a concept first proposed in [28]) of the client's function delegated to the server. In follow-up models from [9,12,14], separate requirements of correctness, (input) privacy and (output) security are defined. In this paper we use a model of the latter type, since it allows a more granular parameterized description of solution properties (but note that our solutions can be proved in both model types). In this model, we have a client C, with inputs A, B, who delegates to a single server the computation of a pairing function e on the client's input, and the main desired requirements are:

1. δ-*correctness*: if both parties follow the protocol, C's output y at the end of the protocol, is equal to the value obtained by evaluating pairing e on its input (A, B), with probability at least δ (for some high δ value);
2. *input ϵ_p-privacy*: for any malicious algorithm Adv returning possible input pairs (A_0, B_0) or (A_1, B_1), playing as S in the protocol with C, and trying to guess which of these two pairs is being used by C as input, Adv's guess is only correct with probability $1/2 \pm \epsilon_p$ (for some small ϵ_p value);
3. *output ϵ_s-security*: for any malicious algorithm Adv returning input pair (A, B), playing as S in the protocol with C on input (A, B), and trying to convince C to return an incorrect output y', the probability that $y' \neq e(A, B)$ is at most ϵ_s (for some small ϵ_s value);
4. *efficiency with parameters* $(t_F, t_C, t_S, t_P, cc, mc)$: the protocol performance is upper-bounded by these functions: t_F, the runtime to compute pairing e without delegation; t_C, C's runtime in the online phase; t_S, S's runtime; t_P, C's runtime in the offline phase; cc, the communication exchanged between C and S; and mc, the number of messages exchanged between C and S.

As in previous work in the area, somewhat expensive computation can be performed in an *offline phase* (i.e., before the pairing result is used in a cryptographic protocol) and stored on the client's device (say, at device deployment time), and the reduction in the client's computation is mainly required in the *online phase* (i.e., when the pairing result is used in a cryptographic protocol). In this paper we focus on input scenarios where inputs A, B to pairing e are only available in the online phase, which is the case of interest in some important cryptographic protocols (most notably, Joux's 3-party key agreement protocol [19]). This paper can be seen as a follow-up to [13], where we mainly studied the technically simpler input scenarios where at least one of inputs A, B is also available in the offline phase, and briefly discussed that direct compositions of those protocols can be used to design protocols in technically more complex scenarios of online inputs. Here, we use different techniques, such as new probabilistic tests, and design 2 new protocols in the scenarios of online inputs, which improve over both previous work and direct compositions of protocols for other input scenarios.

Our Contributions. In this paper we show that when both inputs are only available in the online phase, bilinear-map pairings can be efficiently, privately and securely delegated to a single, possibly malicious, server. Our results include 2 new protocols, each for a different input scenario, improving the main performance metric (client's online runtime), with respect to all 4 of the practical elliptic curves proposed and benchmarked in [7]. In both our protocols, the client's online program only performs 1 exponentiation to a short (e.g., 128-bit) exponent in the most computationally intensive curve's target group. This improves over all previous protocols, where the client required either a larger number of exponentiations to short exponents or exponentiations to longer exponents, or pairing operation (which are even more expensive).

Our first protocol, presented in Sect. 3, considers the case where both inputs A, B are publicly available. Here, in the online phase, the client only performs 1 short-exponent exponentiation in the target pairing group, 1 scalar multiplication in A's group and 1 short-scalar multiplication in B's group (and other lower-order operations). Previously, a protocol with at least 1 long-exponent exponentiation was proved in [8,10], and a protocol with 2 short-exponent exponentiations was briefly discussed in [13], as a direct composition of protocols in scenarios where at least one input is known in the offline phase.

Our second protocol, presented in Sect. 4, considers the case where privacy of A, B needs to be guaranteed. Here, in the online phase, the client only performs 1 short-exponent exponentiation in the target pairing group, 3 scalar multiplications in A's group and 2 scalar multiplications, of which 1 short, in B's group (and other lower-order operations). This protocol is the first where the client's online runtime is faster than non-delegated computation with respect to all 4 of the elliptic curves benchmarked in [7]. Previously, this was provably achieved for 1 curve in [8] and an approach was briefly discussed in [13] achieving the same for 3 curves, using a direct composition of protocols in scenarios where at least one input is known in the offline phase.

In our protocols client and server only have a single communication exchange and only send a constant (specifically, 6 and 11) number of group elements. Indeed, reducing the exchanged communication is also of much interest to reduce energy consumed by resource-constrained devices (see, e.g., [24]).

Related Work. Pairing delegation to a single server was first studied by Girault et al. [15]. However, they only considered input secrecy but no output security against a malicious server. Guillevic et al. [16] proposed a more efficient scheme but their method increases communication complexity between client and server and their scheme does not provide security against a malicious server. Single-server protocols with this latter property for delegating $e(A, B)$ have first been provided by Chevallier-Mames et al. [10] and later by Kang et al. [21]. Canard et al. [8] improved these constructions and proposed more efficient and secure pairing delegation protocols. In particular, in [8] the authors showed that in their protocols the client's runtime is strictly lower than non-delegated computation of a pairing on the so-called KSS-18 curve [20]. Later, Guillevic et al. [16] showed that in protocols in [8] the client is actually less efficient than in a non-delegated computation of the pairing for the optimal ate pairing on the Barreto-Naehrig curve (BN-12).

2   Pairing Definitions

In this section we recall the definition and a number of useful facts about pairings, including current most practical realizations, as well as definitions and benchmark values to evaluate the efficiency of our protocols.

Bilinear Maps. Let $\mathcal{G}_1$, $\mathcal{G}_2$ be additive cyclic groups of order l and $\mathcal{G}_T$ be a multiplicative cyclic group of the same order l, for some large prime l. A *bilinear map* (also called *pairing* and so called from now on) is an efficiently computable map $e : \mathcal{G}_1 \times \mathcal{G}_2 \to \mathcal{G}_T$ with the following properties:

1. *Bilinearity:* for all $A \in \mathcal{G}_1$, $B \in \mathcal{G}_2$ and any $r, s \in \mathbb{Z}_l$, it holds that $e(rA, sB) = e(A, B)^{rs}$
2. *Non-triviality:* if U is a generator for $\mathcal{G}_1$ and V is a generator for $\mathcal{G}_2$ then $e(U, V)$ is a generator for $\mathcal{G}_T$

The last property is there to rule out the trivial case where e maps all of its inputs to 1. We denote a conventional description of the bilinear map e as $desc(e)$.

The currently most practical *pairing realizations* use an ordinary elliptic curve E defined over a field $\mathbb{F}_p$, for some large prime p, as follows. Group $\mathcal{G}_1$ is the l-order additive subgroup of $E(\mathbb{F}_p)$; group $\mathcal{G}_2$ is a specific l-order additive subgroup of $E(\mathbb{F}_{p^k})$ contained in $E(\mathbb{F}_{p^k}) \setminus E(\mathbb{F}_p)$; and group $\mathcal{G}_T$ is the l-order multiplicative subgroup of $\mathbb{F}_{p^k}$. Here, k is the embedding degree; i.e., the smallest positive integer such that $l | (p^k - 1)$. After the Weil pairing was considered in [4], more efficient constructions have been proposed as variants of the Tate pairing, including the more recent ate pairing variants (see, e.g., [26] for more details on the currently most practical pairing realizations).

For *asymptotic efficiency* evaluation of our protocols, we will use the following definitions:

- a_1 (resp. a_2) denotes the runtime for addition in $\mathcal{G}_1$ (resp. $\mathcal{G}_2$);
- $m_1(\ell)$ (resp. $m_2(\ell)$) denotes the runtime for scalar multiplication of a group value in $\mathcal{G}_1$ (resp. $\mathcal{G}_2$) with an ℓ-bit scalar value;
- m_T denotes the runtime for multiplication of group values in $\mathcal{G}_T$;
- $e_T(\ell)$ denotes the runtime for an exponentiation in $\mathcal{G}_T$ to an ℓ-bit exponent;
- p_T denotes the runtime for the bilinear pairing e;
- i_l denotes the runtime for multiplicative inversion in $\mathbb{Z}_l$;
- t_M denotes the runtime for testing membership of a value to $\mathcal{G}_T$;
- σ denotes the computational security parameter (i.e., the parameter derived from hardness studies of the underlying computational problem);
- λ denote the statistical security parameter (i.e., a parameter such that events with probability $2^{-\lambda}$ are extremely rare).

We recall some well-known facts about these quantities, of interest when evaluating the efficiency of our protocols. First, for large enough ℓ, $a_1 \ll m_1(\ell)$, $a_2 \ll m_2(\ell)$, $m_T(\ell) \ll e_T(\ell)$, and $e_T(\ell) < p_T$. Also, using a double-and-add (resp., square-and-multiply) algorithm, one can realize scalar multiplication (resp., exponentiation) in additive (resp., multiplicative) groups using, for random scalars (resp., random exponents), about 1.5ℓ additions (resp., multiplications). Finally, membership of a value w in $\mathcal{G}_T$ can be tested using one exponentiation in $\mathcal{G}_T$ to the l-th power (i.e., checking that $w^l = 1$), or, for some specific elliptic curves, including some of the most recommended in practice, using about 1 multiplication in $\mathcal{G}_T$ and lower-order Frobenius-based simplifications (see, e.g., [3,25]).

For *concrete efficiency* estimate of our protocols, we will set $\lambda = 128$ and use benchmark results from [7] for the runtime of an optimal ate pairing and of the other most expensive operations (i.e., scalar multiplication in groups $\mathcal{G}_1, \mathcal{G}_2$ and exponentiation in $\mathcal{G}_T$) for the some of the most practical curve families, also recalled in Table 1 below, as well as for the values of σ for each curve family, recalled in Tables 2 and 3. We will also neglect lower-order operations such as equality testing, assignments, Frobenius-based simplifications, etc.

Table 1. Benchmark results (obtained by [7] on an Intel Core i7-3520M CPU averaged over thousands of random instances) for scalar multiplications in $\mathcal{G}_1, \mathcal{G}_2$ and exponentiations in $\mathcal{G}_T$ relative to an optimal ate pairing based on some of the most practical curve families, measured in millions (M) of clock cycles.

Family-k	Pairing e	Scalar mult. in $\mathcal{G}_1$	Scalar mult. in $\mathcal{G}_2$	Expon. in $\mathcal{G}_T$
BN-12	7.0	0.9	1.8	3.1
BLS-12	47.2	4.4	10.9	17.5
KSS-18	63.3	3.5	9.8	15.7
BLS-24	115.0	5.2	27.6	47.1

3   Delegating Pairings with Online Public Inputs

In this section we investigate client-server protocols for pairing delegation, in the scenario where the two pairing inputs are known to both parties, and not before the online phase. Our main result is a new protocol with desirable security and efficiency properties. In what follows, we give a formal statement of our result, an asymptotic and concrete efficiency comparison with the previous most efficient protocols in the same input scenario, an informal description of the ideas behind the protocol, a formal description of the protocol and a proof of the protocol's correctness and security properties.

Our first protocol satisfies the following

Theorem 1. Let e be a pairing, as defined in Sect. 2, let σ be its computational security parameter, and let λ be a statistical security parameter. There exists (constructively) a client-server protocol (C, S) for delegating the computation of e, when inputs A and B are both publicly known in the online phase which satisfies 1-correctness, $2^{-\lambda}$-security, 0-privacy, and efficiency with parameters $(t_F, t_S, t_P, t_C, cc, mc)$, where

- $t_F = p_T$, $t_S = 3\, p_T$ and $t_P = p_T + m_2(\sigma) + i_l$;
- $t_C \leq a_1 + a_2 + m_1(\sigma) + m_2(\lambda) + 2\, m_T + e_T(\lambda) + 2\, t_M$;
- $cc = 1$ value in $\mathcal{G}_1 + 2$ values in $\mathcal{G}_2 + 3$ values in $\mathcal{G}_T$ and $mc = 2$.

The main takeaway from this theorem is that C can securely and efficiently delegate to S the computation of a bilinear pairing where both inputs A and B are publicly known but only available in the online phase. In particular, in the online phase C only performs 1 exponentiation to a λ-bit (thus, shorter) exponent in $\mathcal{G}_T$, 1 scalar multiplication in $\mathcal{G}_1$, 1 multiplication in $\mathcal{G}_2$ by a short, λ-bit scalar, and other lower-order operations. See Table 2 for a comparison with closest previous work, also showing estimated ratios of C's online runtime to a non-delegated pairing calculation ranging between 0.158 and 0.326 depending on the curve used. Additionally, C only computes 1 pairing in the offline phase, S only computes 3 pairings, and C and S only exchange 2 messages containing 6 group values.

Table 2. Protocols comparison in the input scenario with public A and B. (The expression of t_C only includes higher-order functions e_T, m_1, m_2. The estimated ratio t_C/t_F also counts terms based on functions a_1, a_2, m_T, t_M and uses $\lambda = 128$.)

Protocols	t_C	Ratio: t_C/t_F			
		BN-12 $\sigma = 461$	BLS-12 $\sigma = 635$	KSS-18 $\sigma = 508$	BLS-24 $\sigma = 629$
[10] §5.2	$3e_T(\sigma) + m_1(\sigma) + m_2(\sigma)$	1.719	1.439	0.956	1.517
[8] §4.1	$e_T(\sigma) + m_1(\sigma)$	0.832	0.697	0.460	0.697
[13] §4.1	$2\, e_T(\lambda) + m_2(\lambda) + m_1(\sigma) + m_1(\lambda)$	0.485	0.310	0.235	0.272
This paper Sect. 3	$e_T(\lambda) + m_1(\sigma) + m_2(\lambda)$	0.326	0.216	0.158	0.179

Protocol Description. Note that in the input scenario where both A and B are public, a protocol satisfying correctness is trivial: C sends A, B, and S replies with $e(A, B)$. Also, there is no privacy property to satisfy, and so the challenge remains to modify this protocol so to efficiently satisfy output security. Our approach for that is based on a new probabilistic test which involves computation of 2 additional pairings from S, the first with inputs A and a masked version of

B, and the second with inputs a masked version of A and a differently masked version of B. Masks are chosen carefully so to achieve some cancellation effect and to allow efficient verification from C, while especially minimizing the use of exponentiations in $\mathcal{G}_T$ to only 1 exponentiation to a short, λ-bit, exponent.

A formal description follows.
Offline Input to C and S: $1^\sigma, 1^\lambda$, $desc(e)$
Offline phase instructions:

1. C randomly chooses $U \in \mathcal{G}_1$, $P \in \mathcal{G}_2$, $c \in \{1, \ldots, 2^\lambda\}$ and $r \in \mathbb{Z}_l^*$
2. C sets $\hat{r} = r^{-1} \mod l$, $Q_0 := \hat{r} \cdot P$, $v := e(U, P)$ and $ov = (c, r, U, P, Q_0, v)$

Online Inputs: $A \in \mathcal{G}_1$ and $B \in \mathcal{G}_2$ to both C and S, and ov to C
Online phase instructions:

1. C sets $Z := r(A - U)$, $Q_1 := c \cdot B + P$ and sends Z, Q_0, Q_1 to S
2. S computes $w_0 := e(A, B)$, $w_1 := e(A, Q_1)$, $w_2 := e(Z, Q_0)$
   S sends w_0, w_1, w_2 to C
3. (Membership Test:)C checks that $w_0, w_2 \in \mathcal{G}_T$
   (Probabilistic Test:)C checks that $w_1 = (w_0)^c \cdot w_2 \cdot v$
   (with this test, C implicitly checks that $w_1 \in \mathcal{G}_T$)
   If any of these tests fails, C **returns** $\perp$ and the protocol halts
   C **returns** $y = w_0$

Properties of the Protocol (C, S)**:** *The efficiency properties* are verified by protocol inspection. In particular, as for C's online runtime, note that the probabilistic test requires 1 exponentiation to a short, λ-bit, exponent in $\mathcal{G}_T$; the computation of Z requires 1 scalar multiplication in $\mathcal{G}_1$; the computation of Q_1 requires 1 multiplication in $\mathcal{G}_2$ by a short, λ-bit scalar. Additional lower-order operations include 2 addition/subtractions in $\mathcal{G}_1$ or $\mathcal{G}_2$, 2 multiplications and a small number of Frobenius-based simplifications in $\mathcal{G}_T$.

The *correctness* property follows by showing that if C and S follow the protocol, C always outputs $y = e(A, B)$. We show that the 2 tests performed by C are always passed. The membership test is always passed by the pairing definition. The probabilistic test is always passed since

$$
\begin{aligned}
w_0^c \cdot w_2 \cdot v &= e(A, B)^c \cdot e(Z, Q_0) \cdot e(U, P) \\
&= e(A, B)^c \cdot e(r(A - U), r^{-1} \cdot P) \cdot e(U, P) \\
&= e(A, B)^c \cdot e(A - U, P) \cdot e(U, P) \\
&= e(A, c \cdot B) \cdot e(A, P) \cdot e(U, P)^{-1} \cdot e(U, P) \\
&= e(A, c \cdot B + P) = e(A, Q_1) = w_1
\end{aligned}
$$

This implies that C never returns $\perp$, and thus returns $y = w_0 = e(A, B)$.

To prove the *security* property against any malicious S we need to compute an upper bound ϵ_s on the security probability that S convinces C to output a y such that $y \neq e(A, B)$. We obtain that $\epsilon_s \leq 2^{-\lambda}$ as a consequence of the following 3 facts, which we later prove:

1. the tuple (Z, Q_0, Q_1) leaks no information about c to S;
2. for any S's message (w_0, w_1, w_2) different than what would be returned according to the protocol instructions, there is only one c for which the tuple (w_0, w_1, w_2) satisfies both membership and probabilistic tests in step 3;
3. for any S's message (w_0, w_1, w_2) different than what would be returned according to the protocol instructions, the probability that (w_0, w_1, w_2) satisfies the probabilistic test is $\leq 2^{-\lambda}$.

Towards proving Fact 1, recall that $\mathcal{G}_1, \mathcal{G}_2$ are cyclic groups, and let G_1 be a generator of $\mathcal{G}_1$, and G_2 be a generator of $\mathcal{G}_2$. Also, let a, b be values such that $A = aG_1, B = bG_2$, and let u, z, p, q_0, q_1 be values such that

$$U = uG_1, Z = zG_1, P = pG_2, Q_0 = q_0G_2, Q_1 = q_1G_2.$$

Note that $(Z, Q_0, Q_1) = (zG_1, q_0G_2, q_1G_2)$, and, since $\mathcal{G}_1, \mathcal{G}_2$ are cyclic groups of prime order l, to prove Fact 1, it suffices to show that the distribution of the triple (z, q_0, q_1) is independent on c, for all $a, b \in \mathbb{Z}_l$ and any $c \in \{0, \ldots, 2^\lambda\}$. The latter is proved as follows: first observe that q_1 is uniformly distributed in $\mathbb{Z}_l$ since so is p and $q_1 = cb + p \mod l$; next, observe that q_0 is either $= 0$ when $p = 0$ or is uniformly distributed in $\mathbb{Z}_l^*$, even conditioned on q_1, since so is r and $q_0 = r^{-1}p \mod l$; and finally, observe that z is uniformly distributed in $\mathbb{Z}_l$, even conditioned on q_0, q_1, since so is u and $z = r(a - u) \mod l$.

Towards proving Fact 2, let (w_0, w_1, w_2) be the values that would be returned by S according to the protocol, and assume a malicious algorithm Adv, corrupting S returns a different triple (w_0', w_1', w_2'). Because $\mathcal{G}_T$ is cyclic, we can consider a generator g for $\mathcal{G}_T$ and write $w_i = g^{a_i}$, for $i = 0, 1, 2$. Note that if the membership and probabilistic test are passed by (w_0', w_1', w_2'), all values w_0', w_1', w_2' are verified to be in $\mathcal{G}_T$. Then we can write

$$\forall i = 0, 1, 2, \ \exists u_i \in \mathbb{Z}_l \quad w_i' = g^{u_i} \cdot w_i \text{ such that for some } u_i \neq 0.$$

Now, note that in Fact 2 we study the case $u_0 \neq 0 \mod l$ (or else $y = w_0' = w_0 = e(A, B)$), and consider the following equivalent rewritings of the probabilistic test, obtained by variable substitutions and simplifications:

$$w_1' = (w_0')^c \cdot w_2' \cdot v$$
$$g^{u_1} \cdot w_1 = (g^{u_0} \cdot w_0)^c \cdot g^{u_2} \cdot w_2 \cdot v$$
$$g^{u_1} \cdot w_1 = g^{cu_0 + u_2} \cdot w_0^c \cdot w_2 \cdot v$$
$$g^{u_1} = g^{cu_0 + u_2}$$
$$u_1 = cu_0 + u_2 \mod l,$$

where the 4th equality follows since $w_1 = w_0^c \cdot w_2 \cdot v$. Now, if there exist two distinct c_1 and c_2 such that

$$u_1 = c_1u_0 + u_2 \mod l, \text{ and } u_1 = c_2u_0 + u_2 \mod l$$

then $u_0(c_1 - c_2) = 0 \mod l$, and finally $c_1 - c_2 = 0 \mod l$ (i.e $c_1 = c_2$), since $u_0 \neq 0 \mod l$. This shows that c is unique when $u_0 \neq 0 \mod l$, proving Fact 2.

Towards proving Fact 3, note that, by Fact 1, C's message Z, Q_0, Q_1 does not leak any information about c. This implies that all values in $\{1, \ldots, 2^\lambda\}$ are still equally likely for c even when conditioning over messages Z, Q_0, Q_1. Then, by using Fact 2, the probability that S's message (w_0, w_1, w_2) satisfies the probabilistic test, is 1 divided by the number 2^λ of values of c that are still equally likely when conditioning over message Z, Q_0, Q_1. This proves Fact 3.

4   Delegating Pairings with Online Private Inputs

In this section we investigate client-server protocols for secure pairing delegation, in the scenario where both of the pairing inputs are only known to the client in the online phase, and need to remain private from the server. Our main result is a new protocol with desirable privacy, security and efficiency properties. In what follows, we give a formal statement of our result, an asymptotic and a concrete efficiency comparison with previous protocols in the same input scenario, an informal description of the ideas behind the protocol, a formal description of the protocol and a proof of the protocol's correctness, privacy and security properties. Formally, our second protocol satisfies the following

Theorem 2. Let e be a pairing, as defined in Sect. 2, let σ be its computational security parameter, and let λ be a statistical security parameter. There exists (constructively) a client-server protocol (C, S) for delegating the computation of e, when inputs A and B are both privately known to C in the online phase which satisfies 1-correctness, $2^{-\lambda}$-security, 0-privacy, and efficiency with parameters $(t_F, t_S, t_P, t_C, cc, mc)$, where

- $t_F = p_T$, $t_S = 4\,p_T$ and $t_P = 2\,p_T + 4\,m_2(\sigma) + 3\,i_l$;
- $t_C \leq 2\,a_1 + 2\,a_2 + 3\,m_1(\sigma) + m_2(\sigma) + m_2(\lambda) + 4\,m_T + e_T(\lambda) + 3\,t_M$;
- $cc = 3$ values in $\mathcal{G}_1 + 4$ values in $\mathcal{G}_2 + 4$ values in $\mathcal{G}_T$ and $mc = 2$.

The main takeaway from this theorem is that C can privately, securely and efficiently delegate to S the computation of a bilinear pairing in the input scenario where both A and B are only available to C, not before the online phase. In particular, in the online phase C only performs 1 exponentiation to a λ-bit (thus, shorter) exponent in $\mathcal{G}_T$, 3 scalar multiplications in $\mathcal{G}_1$, 2 scalar multiplications in $\mathcal{G}_2$, of which 1 with a λ-bit scalar, and other lower-order operations. See Table 3 for a concrete comparison with closest previous work, also showing estimated ratios of C's online runtime to a non-delegated pairing calculation ranging between 0.425 and 0.843 depending on the curve used. Additionally, C only computes 2 pairings in the offline phase, S only computes 4 pairings, and C and S only exchange 2 messages containing 11 group values.

Protocol(s) Description. In our investigation, we actually evaluated 5 protocols: a protocol based on new ideas, as well as protocols in past work, including ours, possibly combined with our result in Sect. 3. In what follows, we briefly and informally describe the first 4 protocols, and then formally describe the new protocol, which happens to be the only one where C's online runtime is smaller than a non-delegated computation, and which proves Theorem 2. In Table 3 we give a detailed comparison of all protocols, with respect to C's online runtime.

Protocol Π_0. This protocol combines a randomization technique appeared, for instance, in [8], with our pairing delegation protocol from Sect. 3. C randomly chooses $r, s \in \mathbb{Z}_l$, computes rA, sB and sends them to S. Then C and S run a protocol such as the one from Sect. 3 in the (A' public online, B' public online) input scenario, where $A' = rA$ and $B' = sB$. Finally, A computes the desired result $e(A, B)$ as $e(A', B')^{1/rs}$.

Protocol Π_1. This protocol has been mentioned in our previous paper [13] and combines a simple randomization technique with pairing delegation protocols for different input scenarios in that same paper. In the offline phase, C randomly chooses $r \in \mathbb{Z}_l$ and $U \in \mathcal{G}_1$ and set $s = r^{-1} \mod l$. Then C and S run a protocol in the (A' public online, B' public online) input scenario, where $A' = rA$ and $B' = r^{-1}(B - U)$, and a protocol in the (A'' private online, B'' private offline) input scenario, where $A'' = A$ and $B'' = U$. Finally, A computes the desired result $e(A, B)$ as $e(A', B')/(e(A'', B''))$.

Protocol Π_2. This protocol combines known input randomization techniques used, for instance, in [10, 21], with pairing delegation protocols for different input scenarios in [13]. In the offline phase, C randomly chooses points R_a, R_b and computes $e(R_a, R_b)$. In the online phase, C sets $A_r = A + R_a, B_r = B + R_b$ and sends A_r, B_r to S, which computes and sends $e(A_r, B_r)$ to C. Then, C uses the state-of-the-art protocol in [13] for the input scenario (A' private offline, B' private online), where $A' = R_a, B' = B$, to delegate the computation of $e(R_a, B)$, and the state-of-the-art protocol in [13] for the input scenario (A'' private online, B'' private offline), where $A'' = A, B'' = R_b$, to delegate the computation of $e(A, R_b)$. Finally, C computes the desired result $e(A, B)$ as $e(A_r, B_r)/(e(R_a, B) \cdot e(A, R_b) \cdot e(R_a, R_b))$.

Protocol Π_3. This protocol is a variant of Π_1 where we use our improved protocol in Sect. 3 as a subprotocol for the (A' public online, B' public online) scenario.

Our Final and Most Efficient Protocol. Note that all of the previously discussed 4 protocols combine some input randomization technique with one or more subprotocols for different input scenarios. We observe that there is some inherent inefficiency in such approaches, as the subprotocols typically compute further input randomizations. In our final protocol, we bypass inefficiencies due to such compositions, and design a new probabilistic test, tailored to this specific input scenario, which involves computation of 4 pairings from S, all with efficiently masked variants of inputs A, B. Masks are chosen carefully so to achieve various cancellation effects and to allow efficient verification from C, while especially reducing the use of exponentiations in $\mathcal{G}_T$ to only 1 exponentiation to a short, λ-bit, exponent, as well as scalar multiplications in $\mathcal{G}_2$, to only 1.

A formal description follows.

Offline Input to C and S: $1^\sigma, 1^\lambda, desc(e)$
Offline phase instructions:

1. C randomly chooses $U_0, U_1 \in \mathcal{G}_1$, $P_0, P_1 \in \mathcal{G}_2$, $c \in \{1, \dots, 2^\lambda\}$, $r_0, r_1, r_2 \in \mathbb{Z}_l^*$
2. C sets $v_i := e(U_i, P_i)$, $Q_i := \hat{r}_i \cdot P_i$ where $\hat{r}_i = r_i^{-1} \mod l$, for $i = 0, 1$
3. C sets $\hat{r}_2 := r_2^{-1}$, $Q_{2,1} = -r_2 \cdot P_0$ and $Q_{3,1} = r_2 \cdot P_1$
4. C sets $ov = (c, r_0, r_1, r_2, \hat{r}_2, U_0, U_1, P_0, P_1, Q_0, Q_1, Q_{2,1}, Q_{3,1}, v_0, v_1)$

Online Input to C: $A \in \mathcal{G}_1$, $B \in \mathcal{G}_2$, and ov
Online phase instructions:

1. C sets $Z_0 := r_0(A - U_0)$, $Z_1 := r_1(A - U_1)$, $Z_2 := \hat{r}_2 \cdot A$
2. C sets $Q_{2,0} = Q_{3,0} := r_2 \cdot B$, $Q_2 := Q_{2,0} + Q_{2,1}$, $Q_3 := c \cdot Q_{3,0} + Q_{3,1}$
3. C sends $Z_0, Z_1, Z_2, Q_0, Q_1, Q_2, Q_3$ to S
4. S computes and sends to C
$$w_0 := e(Z_0, Q_0), \ w_1 := e(Z_1, Q_1), \ w_2 := e(Z_2, Q_2), \ w_3 := e(Z_2, Q_3)$$
5. (Membership Test:)C checks that $w_0, w_1, w_2 \in \mathcal{G}_T$
   C computes $y = w_0 \cdot w_2 \cdot v_0$
   (Probabilistic Test:)C checks that $w_3 = (y)^c \cdot w_1 \cdot v_1$
      (with this test, C implicitly checks that $w_3 \in \mathcal{G}_T$)
   If any of these tests fails, C **returns** $\perp$ and the protocol halts
   C **returns** y

Properties of the Protocol (C, S): *The efficiency properties* are verified by protocol inspection. In particular, as for C's online runtime, note that the probabilistic test requires 1 exponentiation in $\mathcal{G}_T$ to a short, λ-bit, exponent; the computation of Z_0, Z_1, Z_2 requires 3 scalar multiplications in $\mathcal{G}_1$; the computation of Q_0, Q_1, Q_2, Q_3 requires 2 multiplications in $\mathcal{G}_2$, of which 1 is by a short, λ-bit, scalar. Other parts of these computations involve lower-order operations, such as 4 additions/subtractions in $\mathcal{G}_1$ or $\mathcal{G}_2$, 4 multiplications and a small number of Frobenius-based simplifications in $\mathcal{G}_T$. In Table 3 we compare our main protocol with protocols $\Pi_0, \dots, \Pi_3$ as well as previous work. There, the estimated ratios of C's online runtime to a non-delegated pairing calculation is shown to range between 0.425 and 0.843 depending on the curve used.

Table 3. Protocols comparison in the input scenario with private A and B. (The expression of t_C only includes higher-order functions e_T, m_1, m_2. The estimated ratio t_C/t_F also counts terms based on functions a_1, a_2, m_T, t_M and uses $\lambda = 128$.)

Protocols	t_C	Ratio: t_C/t_F			
		BN-12 $\sigma = 461$	BLS-12 $\sigma = 635$	KSS-18 $\sigma = 508$	BLS-24 $\sigma = 629$
[10] §4.1	$5\,e_T(\sigma) + m_2(\sigma)$	2.606	2.182	1.453	2.337
[21] §3	$3\,e_T(\sigma) + m_2(\sigma) + m_1(\sigma)$	1.719	1.439	0.956	1.517
[8] §5.1	$2\,e_T(\sigma) + 2\,m_2(\sigma) + 2\,m_1(\sigma)$	1.658	1.391	0.917	1.390
[13] Π_1	$3\,e_T(\lambda) + m_2(\sigma) + m_2(\lambda)$ $+3\,m_1(\sigma) + 2\,m_1(\lambda)$	1.161	0.823	0.578	0.697
This paper: Π_0	$e_T(\sigma) + e_T(\lambda) + m_2(\sigma)$ $+m_2(\lambda) + 2\,m_1(\sigma)$	1.155	0.911	0.617	0.874
This paper: Π_2	$3\,e_T(\lambda) + m_2(\sigma) + 2\,m_2(\lambda)$ $+2\,m_1(\sigma) + m_1(\lambda)$	1.072	0.760	0.550	0.694
This paper: Π_3	$2\,e_T(\lambda) + m_2(\sigma) + 2\,m_2(\lambda)$ $+1\,m_1(\sigma) + m_1(\lambda)$	1.002	0.729	0.502	0.604
This paper Sect. 4	$e_T(\lambda) + m_2(\sigma)$ $+m_2(\lambda) + 3\,m_1(\sigma)$	0.843	0.635	0.425	0.511

The *correctness* property follows by showing that if C and S follow the protocol, C always outputs $y = e(A, B)$. We first show that if C returns y, then this returned value y is the correct output $e(A, B)$. This is proved as follows:

$$
\begin{aligned}
y = w_0 \cdot w_2 \cdot v_0 &= e(Z_0, Q_0) \cdot e(Z_2, Q_2) \cdot e(U_0, P_0) \\
&= e(r_0(A - U_0), r_0^{-1} P_0) \cdot e(r_2^{-1} A, r_2(B - P_0)) \cdot e(U_0, P_0) \\
&= e(A - U_0, P_0) \cdot e(A, B - P_0) \cdot e(U_0, P_0) \\
&= e(A, P_0) \cdot e(U_0, P_0)^{-1} \cdot e(A, B) \cdot e(A, P_0)^{-1} \cdot e(U_0, P_0) = e(A, B).
\end{aligned}
$$

We now show that the 2 tests performed by C are always passed. The membership test is always passed by the pairing definition. To see that the probabilistic test is always passed, first note that $Q_2 = Q_{2,0} + Q_{2,1} = r_2(B - P_0)$, and $Q_3 = Q_{3,0} + Q_{3,1} = r_2(c \cdot B + P_1)$. Then we have that

$$
\begin{aligned}
y^c \cdot w_1 \cdot v_1 &= e(A, B)^c \cdot e(Z_1, Q_1) \cdot e(U_1, P_1) \\
&= e(A, B)^c \cdot e(r_1(A - U_1), r_1^{-1} \cdot P_1) \cdot e(U_1, P_1) \\
&= e(A, B)^c \cdot e(A - U_1, P_1) \cdot e(U_1, P_1) \\
&= e(A, c \cdot B) \cdot e(A, P_1) \cdot e(U_1, P_1)^{-1} \cdot e(U_1, P_1) \\
&= e(r_2^{-1} \cdot A, r_2(c \cdot B + P_1)) = e(Z_2, Q_3) = w_3
\end{aligned}
$$

This implies that C never returns $\bot$, and thus always returns $y = e(A, B)$.

The *privacy* property of the protocol against any malicious S follows by observing that C's only message $(Z_0, Z_1, Z_2, Q_0, Q_1, Q_2, Q_3)$ to S does not leak any information about C's inputs A, B. To prove this, we show the stronger property (also used later to show the security property of (C, S)) that for any A, B, c, the message sent by C in the protocol is a uniformly distributed 7-tuple in $\mathcal{G}_1^3 \times \mathcal{G}_2^4$. Towards proving this latter property, recall that $\mathcal{G}_1, \mathcal{G}_2$ are cyclic groups, and denoting as G_1 a generator for $\mathcal{G}_1$, and as G_2 a generator for $\mathcal{G}_2$, we can denote as $a, b, u, z_0, z_1, z_2, p_0, p_1, q_0, q_1, q_2, q_3$ the values in $\mathbb{Z}_l$ such that

- $A = aG_1, B = bG_2$
- $P_0 = p_0 G_2, P_1 = p_1 G_2$
- $Z_0 = z_0 G_1, Z_1 = z_1 G_1, Z_2 = z_2 G_1$
- $Q_0 = q_0 G_2, Q_1 = q_1 G_2, Q_2 = q_2 G_3, Q_3 = q_3 G_3$.

Note that to prove the above stronger property, rewriting C's message as

$$(Z_0, Z_1, Z_2, Q_0, Q_1, Q_2, Q_3) = (z_0 G_1, z_1 G_1, z_2 G_2, q_0 G_2, q_1 G_2, q_2 G_3, q_3 G_3),$$

and since $\mathcal{G}_1, \mathcal{G}_2$ are cyclic groups of prime order l, it suffices to show that the 7-tuple $(z_0, z_1, z_2, q_0, q_1, q_2, q_3)$ is uniformly distributed in $(\mathbb{Z}_l^*)^3 \times \mathbb{Z}_l^4$, for all $a, b \in \mathbb{Z}_l$ and any $c \in \{0, \ldots, 2^\lambda\}$. The latter is proved as follows:

- z_0 is uniformly distributed in $\mathbb{Z}_l$ since so is u_0 and $z_0 = r_0(a - u_0) \mod l$;
- z_1 is uniformly distributed in $\mathbb{Z}_l$, even conditioned on z_0, since so is u_1 and $z_1 = r_1(a - u_1) \mod l$;
- z_2 is $= 0$ if $a = 0$ or else is uniformly distributed in $\mathbb{Z}_l^*$, even conditioned on z_0, z_1, since so is r_2 and $z_2 = r_2^{-1}a \mod l$;
- q_0 is $= 0$ if $p_0 = 0$ or else is uniformly distributed in $\mathbb{Z}_l^*$, even conditioned on z_0, z_1, z_2, since so is r_0 and $q_0 = r_0^{-1}p_0 \mod l$
- q_1 is $= 0$ if $p_1 = 0$ or else is uniformly distributed in $\mathbb{Z}_l^*$, even conditioned on q_0, z_0, z_1, z_2, since so is r_1 and $q_1 = r_1^{-1}p_1 \mod l$;
- q_2 is uniformly distributed in $\mathbb{Z}_l$, even conditioned on q_0, q_1, z_2, z_0, z_1, since so is p_0 and $q_2 = r_2(b - p_0) \mod l$;
- q_3 is uniformly distributed in $\mathbb{Z}_l$, even conditioned on $q_0, q_1, q_2, z_2, z_0, z_1$, since so is p_1 and $q_3 = r_2(cb + p_1) \mod l$.

To prove the *security* property against any malicious S we need to compute an upper bound ϵ_s on the security probability that S convinces C to output a y such that $y \neq e(A, B)$. We obtain that $\epsilon_s \leq 2^{-\lambda}$ as a consequence of the following 3 facts, which we later prove:

1. the tuple $(Z_0, Z_1, Z_2, Q_0, Q_1, Q_2, Q_3)$ leaks no information about c to S;
2. for any S's message (w_0, w_1, w_2, w_3) different than what would be returned according to the protocol instructions, there is only one value of c for which (w_0, w_1, w_2, w_3) satisfies both the membership and the probabilistic test in step 3 of the protocol;
3. for any S's message (w_0, w_1, w_2, w_3) different than what would be returned according to the protocol instructions, the probability that (w_0, w_1, w_2, w_3) satisfies the probabilistic test in step 3 of the protocol is $\leq 2^{-\lambda}$.

The proof of Fact 1 follows from the stronger property established when proving the protocol's privacy property. Towards proving Fact 2, let (w_0, w_1, w_2, w_3) be the values that would be returned by S according to the protocol, and assume a malicious algorithm Adv, corrupting S returns a different pair (w'_0, w'_1, w'_2, w'_3). Because $\mathcal{G}_T$ is cyclic, we can consider a generator g for $\mathcal{G}_T$ and write $w_i = g^{a_i}$, for $i = 0, 1, 2, 3$. Note that if the membership and probabilistic tests are satisfied, all values in (w'_0, w'_1, w'_2, w'_3) are verified to be in $\mathcal{G}_T$. Then we can write

$$\forall i = 0, 1, 2, 3, \ \exists u_i \in Z_l \quad w'_i = g^{u_i} \cdot w_i \text{ such that for some } u_i \neq 0.$$

Now, assume wlog that $u_i \neq 0 \mod l$ and consider the following equivalent rewritings of the probabilistic test, via variable substitutions and simplifications:

$$w'_3 = y^c \cdot w'_1 \cdot v_1$$
$$w'_3 = (w'_0 \cdot w'_2 \cdot v_0)^c \cdot w'_1 \cdot v_1$$
$$g^{u_3} \cdot w_3 = (g^{u_0} \cdot w_0 \cdot g^{u_2} \cdot w_2 \cdot v_0)^c \cdot g^{u_1} \cdot w_1 \cdot v_1$$
$$g^{u_3} \cdot w_3 = g^{c(u_0+u_2)+u_1} \cdot (w_0 \cdot w_2 \cdot v_0)^c \cdot w_1 \cdot v_1$$
$$g^{u_3} \cdot w_3 = g^{c(u_0+u_2)+u_1} \cdot y^c \cdot w_1 \cdot v_1$$
$$g^{u_3} = g^{c(u_0+u_2)+u_1}$$
$$u_3 = c(u_0 + u_2) + u_1 \mod l,$$

where the 4th equality follows since $w_3 = y^c \cdot w_1 \cdot v_1$. Now, if there exist two distinct c_1 and c_2 such that

$$u_3 = c_1(u_0 + u_2) + u_1 \mod l \text{ and } u_3 = c_2(u_0 + u_2) + u_1 \mod l$$

then $(u_0 + u_2)(c_1 - c_2) = 0 \mod l$ which implies either $c_1 - c_2 = 0 \mod l$ (i.e. $c_1 = c_2$ and c is unique) or $u_0 + u_2 = 0 \mod l$ (i.e. $u_0 = -u_2 \mod l$). If $u_0 = -u_2 \mod l$ then $y = w'_0 \cdot w'_2 \cdot v_0 = g^{u_0} \cdot w_0 \cdot g^{u_1} \cdot w_2 \cdot v_0 = w_0 \cdot w_2 \cdot v_0 = e(A, B)$, and thus S is honest. If S is not honest then $c_1 = c_2$ and this proves Fact 2.

Towards proving Fact 3, note that, by Fact 1, no information about c is leaked by C's message $(Z_0, Z_1, Z_2, Q_0, Q_1, Q_2, Q_3)$. This implies that all values in $\{1, \ldots, 2^\lambda\}$ are still equally likely for c even when conditioning over C's message. Then, by using Fact 2, the probability that S's message (w_0, w_1, w_2, w_3) satisfies the probabilistic test, is 1 divided by the number 2^λ of values of c that are still equally likely even after conditioning over C's message. This proves Fact 3.

5 Conclusions

Pairings are important primitive operations in many public-key cryptosystems and, more generally, cryptographic protocols (see, e.g., [1, 4–6, 17, 19, 23]). In this paper we studied pairing delegation to a single, possibly malicious, server, in the input scenario where both inputs are not available until the online phase. We proposed new protocols improving online client's runtime over previous solutions in the scenario where (a) both inputs are publicly available; and (b) both inputs are known to the client but should remain private from the server. Both our protocols only require client and server to communicate a constant number (specifically, 6 and 11) of group elements. We showed the first protocol in case (b) which improves the client's online runtime with respect to non-delegated computation for all 4 practical curves for which benchmark runtimes are reported in [7]. In future versions of the paper, we plan to analyze our protocols with respect to practical curve implementations that satisfy desired security levels in light of the recent improved number field sieve attacks (see, e.g., [2,22]).

References

1. Al-Riyami, S.S., Paterson, K.G.: Certificateless public key cryptography. In: Laih, C.S. (eds.) Advances in Cryptology - ASIACRYPT (2003)
2. Barbulescu, R., Duquesne, S.: Updating key size estimations for pairings. J. Cryptol. **32**(4), 1298–1336 (2018). https://doi.org/10.1007/s00145-018-9280-5
3. Barreto, P.S.L.M., Costello, C., Misoczki, R., Naehrig, M., Pereira, G.C.C.F., Zanon, G.: Subgroup security in pairing-based cryptography. In: Lauter, K., Rodríguez-Henríquez, F. (eds.) Progress in Cryptology - LATINCRYPT (2015)
4. Boneh, D., Franklin, M.: Identity-based encryption from the Weil pairing. In: Kilian, J. (ed.) CRYPTO 2001. LNCS, vol. 2139, pp. 213–229. Springer, Heidelberg (2001). https://doi.org/10.1007/3-540-44647-8_13
5. Boneh, D., Di Crescenzo, G., Ostrovsky, R., Persiano, G.: Public key encryption with keyword search. In: Cachin, C., Camenisch, J.L. (eds.) EUROCRYPT 2004. LNCS, vol. 3027, pp. 506–522. Springer, Heidelberg (2004). https://doi.org/10.1007/978-3-540-24676-3_30
6. Boneh, D., Lynn, B., Shacham, H.: Short signatures from the Weil pairing. In: Boyd, C. (ed.) ASIACRYPT 2001. LNCS, vol. 2248, pp. 514–532. Springer, Heidelberg (2001). https://doi.org/10.1007/3-540-45682-1_30
7. Bos, J.W., Costello, C., Naehrig, M.: Exponentiating in pairing groups. In: Lange, T., Lauter, K., Lisoněk, P. (eds.) SAC 2013. LNCS, vol. 8282, pp. 438–455. Springer, Heidelberg (2014). https://doi.org/10.1007/978-3-662-43414-7_22
8. Canard, S., Devigne, J., Sanders, O.: Delegating a pairing can be both secure and efficient. In: Boureanu, I., Owesarski, P., Vaudenay, S. (eds.) ACNS 2014. LNCS, vol. 8479, pp. 549–565. Springer, Cham (2014). https://doi.org/10.1007/978-3-319-07536-5_32
9. Cavallo, B., Di Crescenzo, G., Kahrobaei, D., Shpilrain, V.: Efficient and secure delegation of group exponentiation to a single server. In: Mangard, S., Schaumont, P. (eds.) RFIDSec 2015. LNCS, vol. 9440, pp. 156–173. Springer, Cham (2015). https://doi.org/10.1007/978-3-319-24837-0_10
10. Chevallier-Mames, B., Coron, J.-S., McCullagh, N., Naccache, D., Scott, M.: Secure delegation of elliptic-curve pairing. In: Gollmann, D., Lanet, J.-L., Iguchi-Cartigny, J. (eds.) CARDIS 2010. LNCS, vol. 6035, pp. 24–35. Springer, Heidelberg (2010). https://doi.org/10.1007/978-3-642-12510-2_3
11. Chevalier, C., Laguillaumie, F., Vergnaud, D.: Privately outsourcing exponentiation to a single server: cryptanalysis and optimal constructions. In: Askoxylakis, I., Ioannidis, S., Katsikas, S., Meadows, C. (eds.) ESORICS 2016. LNCS, vol. 9878, pp. 261–278. Springer, Cham (2016). https://doi.org/10.1007/978-3-319-45744-4_13

12. Di Crescenzo, G., Khodjaeva, M., Kahrobaei, D., Shpilrain, V.: Practical and secure outsourcing of discrete log group exponentiation to a single malicious server. In: Proceedings of 9th ACM CCSW, pp. 17–28 (2017)
13. Di Crescenzo, G., Khodjaeva, M., Kahrobaei, D., Shpilrain, V.: Secure and Efficient Delegation of Elliptic-Curve Pairing. In: Conti, M., Zhou, J., Casalicchio, E., Spognardi, A. (eds.) ACNS 2020. LNCS, vol. 12146, pp. 45–66. Springer, Cham (2020). https://doi.org/10.1007/978-3-030-57808-4_3
14. Gennaro, R., Gentry, C., Parno, B.: Non-interactive verifiable computing: outsourcing computation to untrusted workers. In: Rabin, T. (ed.) CRYPTO 2010. LNCS, vol. 6223, pp. 465–482. Springer, Heidelberg (2010). https://doi.org/10.1007/978-3-642-14623-7_25
15. Girault, M., Lefranc, D.: Server-aided verification: theory and practice. In: Roy, B. (ed.) ASIACRYPT 2005. LNCS, vol. 3788, pp. 605–623. Springer, Heidelberg (2005). https://doi.org/10.1007/11593447_33
16. Guillevic, A., Vergnaud, D.: Algorithms for outsourcing pairing computation. In: Joye, M., Moradi, A. (eds.) CARDIS 2014. LNCS, vol. 8968, pp. 193–211. Springer, Cham (2015). https://doi.org/10.1007/978-3-319-16763-3_12
17. Hess, F.: Efficient identity based signature schemes based on pairings. In: Nyberg, K., Heys, H. (eds.) SAC 2002. LNCS, vol. 2595, pp. 310–324. Springer, Heidelberg (2003). https://doi.org/10.1007/3-540-36492-7_20
18. Hohenberger, S., Lysyanskaya, A.: How to securely outsource cryptographic computations. In: Kilian, J. (ed.) TCC 2005. LNCS, vol. 3378, pp. 264–282. Springer, Heidelberg (2005). https://doi.org/10.1007/978-3-540-30576-7_15
19. Joux, A.: A one round protocol for tripartite Diffie–Hellman. In: Bosma, W. (ed.) ANTS 2000. LNCS, vol. 1838, pp. 385–393. Springer, Heidelberg (2000). https://doi.org/10.1007/10722028_23
20. Kachisa, E.J., Schaefer, E.F., Scott, M.: Constructing Brezing-Weng pairing-friendly elliptic curves using elements in the cyclotomic field. In: Galbraith, S.D., Paterson, K.G. (eds.) Pairing 2008. LNCS, vol. 5209, pp. 126–135. Springer, Heidelberg (2008). https://doi.org/10.1007/978-3-540-85538-5_9
21. Kang, B.G., Lee, M.S., Park, J.H.: Efficient delegation of pairing computation. In: IACR Cryptology ePrint Archive, vol. 259 (2005)
22. Kim, T., Barbulescu, R.: Extended tower number field sieve: a new complexity for the medium prime case. In: Robshaw, M., Katz, J. (eds.) CRYPTO 2016. LNCS, vol. 9814, pp. 543–571. Springer, Heidelberg (2016). https://doi.org/10.1007/978-3-662-53018-4_20
23. Liu, J.K., Au, M.H., Susilo, W.: Self-generated-certificate public key cryptography and certificateless signature/encryption scheme in the standard model. In: Proceedings ACM Symposium on Information, Computer and Communications Security. ACM Press (2007)
24. Markantonakis, C.: Is the performance of smart card cryptographic functions the real bottleneck? In: Proceedings of IFIP/SEC, pp. 77–92 (2001)
25. Scott, M.: Unbalancing pairing-based key exchange protocols. In: IACR Cryptology ePrint Archive, vol. 688 (2013)
26. Vercauteren, F.: Optimal pairings. IEEE Trans. Inf. Theory **56**(1), 455–461 (2010)
27. Vergnaud, D.: Secure outsourcing in discrete-logarithm-based and pairing-based cryptography. In: Proceedings of WISTP, pp. 7–11 (2018)
28. Yao, A.: Protocols for secure computations. In: Proceedings of 23rd IEEE FOCS, pp. 160–168 (1982)

Physical Attacks

On the Security of Off-the-Shelf Microcontrollers: Hardware Is Not Enough

Balazs Udvarhelyi[⊠], Antoine van Wassenhove, Olivier Bronchain, and François-Xavier Standaert

Crypto Group, ICTEAM Institute, UCLouvain, Louvain-la-Neuve, Belgium
{balazs.udvarhelyi,antoine.wassenhove,olivier.bronchain,
francois-xavier.standaert}@uclouvain.be

Abstract. We complete the state-of-the-art on the side-channel security of real-world devices by analysing two 32-bit microcontrollers equipped with an unprotected co-processor. Our results show that (i) the lack of understanding of their hardware architecture can be circumvented with standard detection tools – for this purpose, we combine a simple variation of the Test Vector Leakage Assessment methodology with Signal-to-Noise Ratio estimations, which enables the efficient identification of attack vectors; (ii) standard distinguishers then lead to powerful key recoveries with less than 5,000 traces; and (iii) preprocessing like the continuous wavelet transform can be useful in such a black box evaluation context.

1 Introduction

Side-channel analysis is known to be a threat to the security of embedded systems. It has been the topic of intensive academic research over the last two decades and many powerful attacks have been put forward. Yet, most academic results are performed in well understood and controlled environments, and public security analyses of real-world deployed products is more sporadic. Among the examples of such more realistic attacks we are aware of, we note the ones against Keeloq [13], the Xilinx bitstream encryption [18,19], SIM cards [15,29], Hue Smart lamps [21] and Thread communication stacks [11]. Their common denominator is the presence of a long-term key shared among many devices, so that its recovery can be used to decrypt secret communications, forge software updates or clone devices. Technically, performing such attacks typically requires a (possibly long and tedious) reverse engineering effort, because of either badly documented components or limited public implementation details, which is followed by a side-channel attack. In all the aforementioned cases, the products turned out to be unprotected, leading to quite straightforward weaknesses.

We complete this state-of-the-art and extend the investigation of side-channel attacks against real-world devices to 32-bit microcontrollers (MCU), that are becoming increasingly popular for lightweight embedded systems. In particular,

© Springer Nature Switzerland AG 2021
P.-Y. Liardet and N. Mentens (Eds.): CARDIS 2020, LNCS 12609, pp. 103–118, 2021.
https://doi.org/10.1007/978-3-030-68487-7_7

we study the side-channel resistance of two off-the-shelf Cortex-M4 devices that include a hardware co-processor. We focus on MCUs from two different manufacturers, namely NXP Semiconductors (NXP) and STMicroelectronics (STM). We insist that none of them claimed to provide a high physical security level (although the NXP device includes some light countermeasure [23]). So our main goal is to evaluate the technical difficulty to identify attack vectors despite lacking a precise description of the target hardware architectures.

Our investigations show that this limited information does not prevent the identification of simple yet powerful attacks (while a better understanding of the targets could lead to further optimizations [6]). For this purpose, we first propose a variant of the Test Vector Leakage Assessment (TVLA) methodology, which we denote as "one-hot" and is well suited to the analysis of hardware implementations: it allows us to locate some target operations and to infer the co-processor architecture (e.g., the degree of parallelism) with low data complexity. We next show that standard distinguishers are sufficient to recover the full encryption key in less than 5,000 (power or EM) measurements. As an additional contribution, we put forward the interest of the continuous wavelet transform for such a black box security evaluation (as previously proposed in [10]).

2   Background

This section contains the necessary background used in the rest of the paper. We first introduce the notations. Second, two widely spread detections tools are recalled. Third, two profiled side-channel attacks are described. Finally, we detail our methodology for the pre-processing of the traces.

2.1   Notations

For the rest of the paper, random variables are denoted by a capital letter X and their realisations with x. The statistical expectation is denoted as $\mathsf{E}[\cdot]$ and estimators are denoted with a hat. A leakage trace will be written as l.

2.2   Detection Tools

The first step in side channel analysis is the detection of Points-Of-Interest (POIs). It consists in learning the location of the sensible information within the leakage traces. To do so, we make use of two methods.

The first one is a slightly tweaked version of the TVLA in [9,14] which is based on Welch's t-test [28]. The t-test is a statistical test used to highlight a difference between the means of two populations respectively denoted as μ_1 and μ_2. The test is performed by computing

$$t = \frac{\hat{\mu}_1 - \hat{\mu}_2}{\sqrt{\frac{\hat{\sigma}_1^2}{N_1} + \frac{\hat{\sigma}_2^2}{N_2}}}, \tag{1}$$

where σ_i and N_i are the standard deviation and the sample size of the population i. If the maximum $|t|$ is larger than 4.5, a difference between the means is very likely to be present (with a p-value smaller than 10^{-5}). In a side-channel context, it is generally used to highlight dependencies between the mean of the traces and the manipulated variables. To do so, the two tested populations are leakage traces l_i for two different sets of inputs. The t-test is then applied to all the time samples of the leakage traces independently.

The second detection tool we use is the Signal-to-Noise Ratio (SNR) [16]. It aims at quantifying the available signal about one (secret) intermediate variable within the side-channel measurements. Concretely, the SNR of a target intermediate variable X is estimated as

$$\hat{\mathrm{SNR}} = \frac{\hat{\mathrm{Var}}[\hat{\mu}_x]}{\hat{\mathrm{E}}[\hat{\sigma}_x^2]} , \tag{2}$$

where the estimated mean and variance of each possible value of X are denoted as $\hat{\mu}_x$, $\hat{\sigma}_x^2$. Similarly to the TVLA, the SNR is computed for every time sample. This metric is significant only at the locations where X (or values injectively depending of it) is (are) manipulated, which are its associated POIs.

2.3   Side-Channel Distinguishers

In this paper, key recovery attacks are performed against two targets. To do so, we make use of two distinguishers, namely Gaussian Template Attacks (TA) [7] and Correlation Power Analysis (CPA) [5]. Both are *Divide & Conquer*: they target the 16 bytes of the master key independently.

First, the TA is performed in two steps. It starts with a profiling phase. During this step, leakage traces and the corresponding plaintexts and keys are given to the adversary. Based on these, it estimates a Probability Density Function (PDF) of the leakage l given an intermediate state x at the POI. The leakage distribution is assumed to be Gaussian, so that this conditional distribution is

$$\hat{f}[l|x] = \frac{1}{\sqrt{(2\pi)^d|\Sigma_x|}} \exp\left(-\frac{1}{2}(l - \mu_x)'\Sigma_x(l - \mu_x)\right) , \tag{3}$$

where μ_x and Σ_x are the estimated mean vector and covariance matrix for the leakages of x. Next, during the attack phase, leakage traces and only the corresponding plaintext are given. Based on these and the estimated PDF, the adversary uses Bayes' theorem to estimate $\Pr[x|l]$ for each trace independently. From n measurements, he infers the key byte with maximum likelihood as

$$\hat{k} = \underset{k^*}{\mathrm{argmax}} \prod_{i=1}^{n} \Pr[p_i, k^*|l_i] , \tag{4}$$

where p_i is the plaintext corresponding to the l_i trace.

Second, the CPA is exploiting Pearson's Correlation $\hat{\rho}(\cdot, \cdot)$ between the observed traces l and a key-dependent leakage model $M_{k^*, p}$ [5]. The inferred key byte is the one leading to the highest correlation such that

$$\hat{k} = \underset{k^*}{\operatorname{argmax}} \quad \hat{\rho}(M_{k^*, p}, l). \tag{5}$$

Informally, it is expected that the most accurate model will be the one of the correct key. The model can be selected based on engineering intuition (e.g., assuming the leakages to be proportional to the Hamming weight of x), which we denote as the non-profiled CPA. In this paper, the model is rather profiled and corresponds to the estimated mean of the output of the first Sbox (i.e., the vectors μ_x of the TA). Compared to the profiled CPA, TA have the ability to exploit multivariate leakages. In a univariate setting with a sufficiently noisy environment, these two are equivalent [17].

2.4   Pre-processing Tools

Before launching the previously mentioned attacks on actual leakage traces, some pre-processing stages can be implemented. These can be used both for *noise reduction* and/or for *dimensionality reduction*.

Continuous Wavelet Transform. In order to reduce the impact of noise on the measurements, a Continuous Wavelet Transform (CWT) can be used [10]. Similarly to Fourier Transforms, the CWT is a representation of a given signal in another domain. The CWT domain can be interpreted as the frequency content (f) across time (t'). Formally, the CWT of a time signal $x(t)$ is written as

$$X_\omega(f, t') = \frac{1}{|f|} \int_{-\infty}^{\infty} x(t) \cdot \psi\left(\frac{t - t'}{f}\right) dt, \tag{6}$$

where $\psi(\cdot)$ is a given wavelet. It is therefore the convolution of the signal with a scaled wavelet. Several wavelets have been tested. The best results were obtained with the Ricker wavelet which we use for the rest of the paper. For computational reasons, we limited the wavelet width to the smallest one that was maintaining the signal. In the side-channel context, a CWT can be applied to the traces before any other processing.[1] Since the signal manipulated is then in the CWT domain, an SNR computed on it will highlight where the key-dependent signal lies across both time and frequency. This allows removing frequencies and time samples that are not signal-dependent, making it useful for noise reduction.

Principal Component Analysis. In order to reduce the number of samples over which an attack is executed, a Principal Component Analysis (PCA) can be used [1]. It is a profiled dimensionality reduction tool that takes high dimensional

---

[1] Concretely, we only evaluate Eq. 6 at a finite number of coordinates since exploring the entire continuous domain is unpractical.

signals and reduces them to a smaller, chosen number of dimensions. In the side-channel context, it is typically applied to the mean vectors, which maximizes the inter-class variance. Practically, before applying PCA, the SNR can be used (and was used in our experiments) to find and apply the PCA only on the POIs. This allows to speed up the convergence of the PCA.

3   Targets and Setup

First, this section gives a rationale behind the choice of two MCUs as well as their specificities. Second, it describes the conditions under which these were monitored during their security evaluation.

3.1   Targets

In this study, we are interested in the security of AES co-processors in low-cost off-the-shelf components. We found out that ARM Cortex-M4 devices are among the cheapest components with widely spread AES hardware acceleration. For diversity, we chose one component fulfilling these criteria from two well-known manufacturers in the MCU industry, namely NXP and STM.

NXP Kinetis. The selected MCU from NXP is the Kinetis K82 MK82FN256-VLL15 [23]. It comes with two cryptographic co-processors. The one under investigation is the LP Trusted Cryptography module. It reports a countermeasure that inserts noise into the power consumption with a random mask [24]. A DPAMaskSeed register is present to reseed the core, which is advised after 50,000 encryptions. This target has been mounted on a custom Printed Circuit Board (PCB) in order to limit potential noise due to additional components.

STM32. The selected MCU from STM is the STM32L422CB [25]. The AES co-processor of this processor does not have countermeasures against side-channel attacks mentioned. The target has been mounted on a custom PCB too.

3.2   Evaluation Setup

In order to cover a good range of threat models, we evaluated the two afore-mentioned targets under different conditions, also reflecting the fact that such low-cost MCUs can be used for a wide range of applications, going from low-energy to more computationally intensive tasks.

The first parameter of our evaluations is the clock frequency. Targets were evaluated with a low clock frequency of 8 [MHz] as well as close to their maximum frequency (i.e., 100 [MHz] for the NXP target and 80 [MHz] for the STM target). In both cases, the clock is derived from a 8 [MHz] on-board crystal.

Second, both the electromagnetic (EM) emanations and the power consumption were recorded for the evaluations. These two signals are simultaneously measured by a `Picoscope 5244d` at 500 [MSample/s] with an 8-bit resolution. The EM leakage was obtained using an H near-field probe from the HZ-15, probe set from Rohde&Schwartz. The EM probe used was impedance matched and preamplified using the Rohde&Schwartz HZ-16 preamplifier. Several positions were tested by hand for the probes and the position with the highest signal was kept. Therefore, the measurement was done above the target for the NXP MCU. For the STM, no exploitable emanations were observed above the chip. Hence, the measurements were made thanks to the emanations of a power line.

The power consumption was measured through a shunt resistor and without amplification. The resistor is of 5 [Ohm] for the NXP target and 10 [Ohm] for the STM target. These values were chosen as high as possible, leading to a greater signal, but without triggering a brown out reset. The MCUs are accessing the AES cores using the hardware abstraction layer (HAL) published by the manufacturers. The scope is triggered just before the HAL call.

4   Architecture Inference

In absence of detailed specifications of the target hardware architectures, a first step in the following side-channel attacks is to infer a sufficient understanding enabling us to identify good target intermediate variables. We next describe our methodology for this purpose, followed by its results on the two targets.

At a high-level, we use a (fast) variant of the TVLA to locate the encryption and the execution of the first-round Sboxes. Then, we use the (slower) SNR to precisely identify the time samples corresponding to each key byte.

4.1   Methodology

In order to detect POIs as well as inferring the level of parallelism used within the targets, we combined the two detection tools from Subsect. 2.2.

1. The first one is a variant of the non-specific TVLA which we next denote as one-hot TVLA. We perform 16 well-chosen fixed-vs-fixed t-tests [12], such that the two sets of inputs induce a difference of a single byte in the first round of the AES encryption (hence the one-hot terminology). An independent t-test is then executed for each byte of the AES state. Overall, this requires only 17 sets of measurements as one of the sets is common across all the t-tests. An illustration of this method is given in Fig. 1.

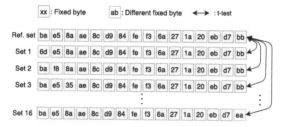

Fig. 1. Illustration of the one-hot TVLA.

2. Second, and as a complement, the SNR is evaluated for the first AES round (detected thanks to the first step), in order to obtain the POIs for each of the Sbox outputs, that are then considered for profiling.

Note that the one-hot TVLA lies between specific and non-specific t-tests. A non-specific t-test leaks everywhere on the leakage trace and is not suitable for POI detection. Non-specific t-tests can be fixed-vs-random as in [9,14] or fixed-vs-fixed as in [12]. They typically allow faster leakage detection thanks to their reduced number of classes. By contrast, specific t-tests (like SNR computations) allow POI detection at the cost of a higher number of classes to estimate. Due to the structure of the one-hot TVLA, leakage is detected only for the single byte which is different during the first operations of a block cipher. Then, for the later rounds, leakage is spotted everywhere due to the diffusion property. As a result, the one-hot TVLA is more specific for the first AES round and non-specific for the later rounds. By comparing the position of significant TVLA peaks for each byte, we can deduce the position of the first round of the AES.

Note also that such an intermediate between non-specific and specific tests was already proposed. For example, the semi-fixed vs. random test in [9] combines a random set and one set with "well-chosen" values for similar reasons. Yet, the one-hot approach has two advantages compared to this previous proposal. First, the semi-fixed vs. random test will become specific as the size of the semi-fixed test increases (while the one-hot TVLA works with two classes per target byte, which can reduce its data complexity). Second, the semi-fixed vs. random test works as long as the model assumptions used to select the "well-chosen" values are correct (while such good model assumptions may not be available at this stage of an evaluation and are anyway not desirable for detection).

The combination of the two proposed steps can be an interesting tradeoff for evaluators. While a good part of the most informative points' positions can be identified with the one-hot TVLA, it remains that the corresponding peaks do not have the quantitative meaning that the SNR carries, as for example discussed in [12]. Besides, while the first step could directly be based on the SNR, the TVLA has the advantage of requiring a small data and time complexity to be evaluated [22]. Since the SNR is not computed on the whole trace but only on the first round, it reduces the time/memory complexity required for the detection. For example, when performed on traces of the same size, the one-hot TVLA requires about 100 times less memory than the SNR computed for 256 classes.

4.2 NXP Kinetis

The results of the methodology presented above are shown in Fig. 2 with the
mean trace on Fig. 2a. We observe that a greater signal is present from samples

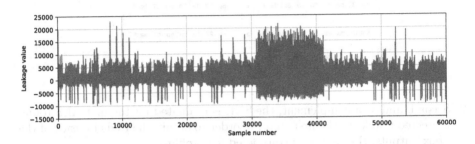

(a) Mean power leakage trace.

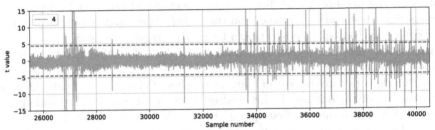

(b) Exemplary *t*-test on EM traces for byte 4.

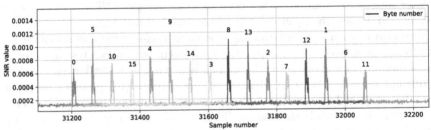

(c) SNR on EM traces. Each peak is annotated with its corresponding byte number.

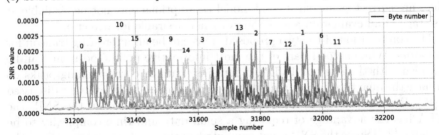

Fig. 2. Architecture inference methodology on the NXP target (low clock freq.).

30,000 to 40,000. This is equivalent to 160 MCU cycles, leading to the suggestion of an implementation serialized on 1 Sbox. This will be verified with measurements as NXP does not provide the cycle count for this AES core.

We observe that no leakage is spotted with the one-hot TVLA up to sample 25,000. This first part of the trace corresponds to the key scheduling of the AES (which we confirmed by using a set of inputs with different keys). More interestingly, three distinctly leaking parts can then be highlighted, confirming the interest of the one-hot TVLA: first, the loading of the plaintext around sample 27,000; second, the key addition and the Sbox execution (here given for an exemplary byte) which correspond to the two peaks between samples 28,000 and 32,000; finally, all the peaks after sample 33,000 which is where the test starts to be non-specific due to the diffusion happening after the first AES round.

We next estimated the SNR of the 16 AES Sboxes for all the samples corresponding to the first AES round identified with the one-hot TVLA. The results of Fig. 2c and Fig. 2d show that each Sbox leads to well identified peaks and these peaks are spaced by a single cycle. Information about all the bytes is therefore available. By computing the SNR on the second round Sbox, we finally observe on Fig. 3a that no cycles are lost between rounds. The MixColumns and key addition operations are therefore interleaved with the Sboxes.

As a result, the architecture is inferred to be serialized on 8 bits for the Sboxes and 32 bits for MixColumns (possibly performed in parallel to the Sboxes).

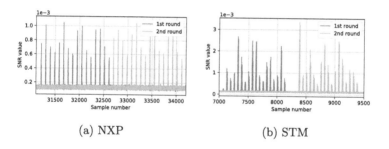

(a) NXP   (b) STM

Fig. 3. SNR on first and second rounds for both devices

4.3   STM32

The same methodology was applied to the STM target and is reported in Fig. 4. The mean power trace is given in Fig. 4a. A repeating pattern is present and its length corresponds to the 214 MCU cycles presented in the reference manual [26].[2] This again suggests an implementation serialized on 1 Sbox. The application of the one-hot TVLA in Fig. 4b leads to similar intuitions as for the NXP target and we can identify the plaintext loading (around sample 3500), the key addition and S-boxes (around samples 6000 and 7000) and the non-specific leakages after the first AES round (starting after sample 8,200).

---

[2] This number corresponds to the AES core and excludes data loadings.

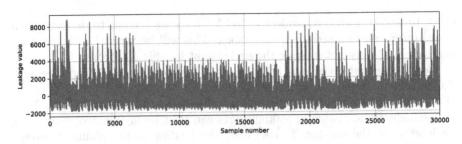

(a) Mean power leakage trace.

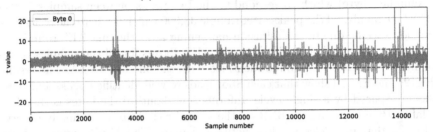

(b) Exemplary *t*-test on EM traces for byte 0.

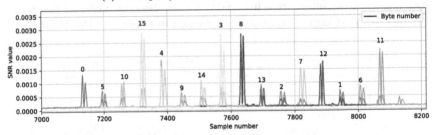

(c) SNR on EM traces. Each peak is annotated with its corresponding byte number.

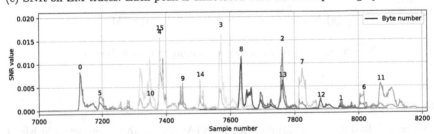

(d) SNR on power traces. Each peak is annotated with its corresponding byte number.

Fig. 4. Architecture inference methodology on the STM target (low clock freq.).

These preliminary results are then confirmed with the SNR estimations of Fig. 4c for EM measurements and Fig. 4d for power ones. Compared to the NXP target, we notice a more significant disparity between the peak SNR levels of the different bytes (this difference is observed for both power and EM leakages). The largest SNRs on each byte are spaced by exactly one cycle. The SNR on a byte is also significant (but smaller) one cycle after the first peak (except for bytes 10 and 15 with power leakage). Eventually, by computing the SNR on the second round, we deduce that the first round and the second one are spaced by 5 cycles, as represented on Fig. 3b.

Putting things together, the architecture can be inferred to be serialized on 8 bits for the Sbox layer. The MixColumns operation and key addition are serialized on 32 bits and are not interleaved with Sboxes. Such an architecture might also leak information through the distance between two consecutive Sboxes. We tried to exploit such leakages but did not obtained better SNRs.

Overall, by comparing the STM and the NXP targets, we can conclude that the two manufacturers propose quite similar architectures.

5 Attacks

In order to evaluate the side-channel security provided by the two targets, we performed key recovery with CPA with various leakage models and TA. Next, we first describe our attack strategy and then discuss attack results.

5.1 Attack Strategy

The different steps of the presented attacks we performed are illustrated in Fig. 5. All these steps (including the pre-processing) are performed independently on the key bytes. More precisely, these steps are described as follows.

– First, we use the results of the architecture inference from Fig. 4 to identify the most significant SNR peaks. For each attack, we reduce the trace length by two cycles before and four cycles after this peak.
– Second, the CWT (see Eq. 6) is optionally applied to the shorter traces. When applied, the next steps are performed in the wavelet domain.
– If applicable, and in order to identify the POIs in the wavelet domain, we compute again the SNR on the previously obtained signal.
– In all cases, we only keep the points that have significant SNR values. This is done by filtering all the points with SNR smaller than at $2 \cdot 10^{-4}$.
– Eventually, the two attacks from Subsect. 2.3 are performed on the pre-processed traces. The CPA is directly applied. For the TA, a PCA in additionally performed in order to reduce the signal to five dimensions. Five dimensions were chosen as a compromise between the computational efficiency of the resulting attack and the amount of information extracted.

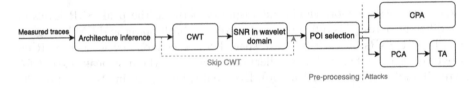

Fig. 5. General attack strategy.

The above attacks all use a profiled leakage model. For the CPA, it corresponds to the mean leakage of each output value of the Sboxes. CPAs with non profiled leakage models were also performed and are discussed below.

5.2   Attacks Results and Discussions

We now compare different attacks against our two targets for both low and high clock frequencies and for both EM and power traces. In all cases, we used $2 \cdot 10^6$ profiling traces. The results of these attacks are summarized in Table 1. It contains the number of traces we need to reduce the rank of the 128-bit master key below 2^{32}, using the rank estimation algorithm of [20].[3] As a complement, we also provide the graphs reporting the evolution of the guessing entropy for the best attack against each target in the full version of this paper.

We next discuss the influence of some parameters by looking at the minimum number of traces to reach a key rank lower than 2^{32}. We start with the targets' parameters and measurement setup, and follow with the attack strategy.

The **clock frequency** has a limited influence: for the NXP target, the best attack requires 3.5 more traces at high frequency than at low frequency; for the STM one, the best attacks are nearly equivalent at low and high frequencies. This is most likely due to the fact that these frequencies remain moderate and do not lead to particular challenges in terms of sampling frequencies.

The **power and EM** measurements do not differ strongly either (in terms of best attack complexity): both channels can lead to powerful key recoveries. Yet, the attack exploiting power leakage is roughly twice faster than the one based on EM traces in most of the cases. EM is only the best for the NXP target at high frequency, where it requires about 2.5 less traces than its power counterpart.

By contrast, **TA and the CPA** do not always lead to similar results. In most cases, the best attack is a CPA. This can be explained by the limited number of traces we used for profiling. That is, the CPA is a univariate attack and only requires estimating mean values. The TA is a multivariate attack (remember we kept 5 dimensions after PCA) and in most cases, exploiting these additional dimensions is not useful given our profiling effort. Interestingly, the only case where TA outperform the CPA is with the power traces of the NXP target. This

---

[3] For CPA attacks, as they do not output probabilities but correlation scores, the rank estimation algorithm is not optimal and may not represent the worst-case [8]. We then use it as a heuristic bound on the security level of our targets.

Table 1. Number of traces needed for every attack. The maximum number of traces was set to 40k traces. The best attack for each target is highlighted in a different color. N.A. signifies the need for more than 40k traces to succeed.

Device		2^{32} key rank		Full key recovery	
		CPA	TA	CPA	TA
NXP 8MHz	EM	27800	5200	N.A.	27400
	EM with CWT	3800	2400	7400	8800
	Power	6400	2000	15600	6200
	Power with CWT	12600	1200	27600	5400
NXP 100MHz	EM	26000	N.A.	N.A.	N.A.
	EM with CWT	4200	4400	11000	26600
	Power	N.A.	N.A.	N.A.	N.A.
	Power with CWT	10000	N.A.	N.A.	N.A.
STM32 8MHz	EM	16800	N.A.	N.A.	N.A.
	EM with CWT	3800	N.A.	11000	N.A.
	Power	4200	N.A.	17400	N.A.
	Power with CWT	1800	38000	5400	N.A.
STM32 80MHz	EM	30000	N.A.	N.A.	N.A.
	EM with CWT	2200	N.A.	7200	N.A.
	Power	1600	N.A.	7400	N.A.
	Power with CWT	1600	N.A.	6200	N.A.

quite nicely matches the intuition of Fig. 2d where we see that the signal is less sparse in this case. So for this target, the additional information of the additional dimensions is sufficient to compensate a more expensive profiling.

Note that with more profiling efforts, TA should at least reach the level of performance of CPA [17]). In view of the low complexity of the simple attacks we put forward in Table 1, we did not look for such further optimizations.

The **CWT** pre-processing is almost always improving attack complexity. The disparities observed between the different leakages are indeed reduced thanks to the CWT. We also note that the gain of the CWT in the EM case is of a factor between 4 and 10, while it never exceeds 2 in the power case. We assume this difference is due to the richer frequency content of the EM signals.

Although partially successful, our attacks without profiled leakage models were much worse. A combination of Hamming weight and Hamming distance models was necessary to recover the key on the STM target. Yet, the corresponding attack required 40,000 traces. As for the NXP target, a profiled model was necessary with our measurements and we were not able to recover any byte of the key with 75,000 traces. This suggest that both accelerators have leakages that are only weakly correlated to a Hamming Weight predictions.

Finally, we note that the **NXP core countermeasure** was activated. Namely, all the experiments against the NXP target reported in this section were performed while reseeding the `DPA Mask Seed` register after 50,000 encryptions, as stated in the reference manual. This setting was compared with two other ones where we either did not reseed the register or we reseeded it with the same value before each encryption in order to cancel the randomization. While slightly modifying the shape of the measurements, these variations did not appear to imply noticeable variations of the corresponding security levels.[4]

6   Conclusions

Our results first exhibit the limited security against side-channel attacks that unprotected hardware co-processors in mid-range 32-bit MCUs provide. Those co-processors should therefore be viewed as performance improvers, not as a direct solution for securing an embedded implementation. They also highlight that a lack of precise understanding of the target architectures does not prevent the simple identification of target intermediate variables in an implementation (though more optimized attacks could certainly be designed with a better understanding of the targets). The "one-hot" variation of the TVLA we propose is quite handy for this purpose. A similar statement holds for the CWT which seems to be an interesting addition in the side-channel analysis toolbox, as is quite systematically improved the attack results in our investigations. As an interesting direction for further research we mention the combination of hardware co-processors such as analyzed in this work with leakage-resistant modes of operation such as [3,4,27], as recently surveyed in [2].

Acknowledgments. We thank Colin O'Flynn for useful feedback about the paper. François-Xavier Standaert is a Senior Research Associate of the Belgian Fund for Scientific Research (FNRS-F.R.S.). Work funded in parts by the European Union through the ERC project SWORD (724725) and the European Union & Walloon Region FEDER USERMedia project 501907379156.

References

1. Archambeau, C., Peeters, E., Standaert, F., Quisquater, J.: Template attacks in principal subspaces. In: Goubin L., Matsui M. (eds.) Cryptographic Hardware and Embedded Systems - CHES 2006. CHES 2006. Lecture Notes in Computer Science, vol. 4249, pp. 1–14. Springer, Heidelberg (2006). https://doi.org/10.1007/11894063_1
2. Bellizia, D., et al.: Mode-level vs. implementation-level physical security in symmetric cryptography. In: Micciancio, D., Ristenpart, T. (eds.) CRYPTO 2020. LNCS, vol. 12170, pp. 369–400. Springer, Cham (2020). https://doi.org/10.1007/978-3-030-56784-2_13

---

[4] We are aware of two independent teams who observed similar results.

3. Berti, F., Guo, C., Pereira, O., Peters, T., Standaert, F.: TEDT, a leakage-resist AEAD mode for high physical security applications. IACR Trans. Cryptogr. Hardw. Embed. Syst. **2020**(1), 256–320 (2020)
4. Berti, F., Pereira, O., Peters, T., Standaert, F.: On leakage-resilient authenticated encryption with decryption leakages. IACR Trans. Symmetric Cryptol. **2017**(3), 271–293 (2017)
5. Brier, E., Clavier, C., Olivier, F.: Correlation power analysis with a leakage model. In: Joye, M., Quisquater, J.-J. (eds.) CHES 2004. LNCS, vol. 3156, pp. 16–29. Springer, Heidelberg (2004). https://doi.org/10.1007/978-3-540-28632-5_2
6. Bronchain, O., Standaert, F.: Side-channel countermeasures' dissection and the limits of closed source security evaluations. IACR Trans. Cryptogr. Hardw. Embed. Syst. **2020**, 1–25 (2020)
7. Chari, S., Rao, J.R., Rohatgi, P.: Template attacks. In: Kaliski, B.S., Koç, K., Paar, C. (eds.) CHES 2002. LNCS, vol. 2523, pp. 13–28. Springer, Heidelberg (2003). https://doi.org/10.1007/3-540-36400-5_3
8. Choudary, M.O., Poussier, R., Standaert, F.-X.: Score-based vs. probability-based enumeration – a cautionary note. In: Dunkelman, O., Sanadhya, S.K. (eds.) INDOCRYPT 2016. LNCS, vol. 10095, pp. 137–152. Springer, Cham (2016). https://doi.org/10.1007/978-3-319-49890-4_8
9. Cooper, J., Mulder, E.D., Goodwill, G., Jaffe, J., Kenworthy, G., Rohatgi, P.: Test vector leakage assessment (TVLA) methodology in practice. In: ICMC (2013)
10. Debande, N., Souissi, Y., Elaabid, M.A., Guilley, S., Danger, J.: Wavelet transform based pre-processing for side channel analysis. In: MICRO Workshops, pp. 32–38. IEEE Computer Society (2012)
11. Dinu, D., Kizhvatov, I.: EM analysis in the IoT context: lessons learned from an attack on thread. IACR Trans. Cryptogr. Hardw. Embed. Syst. **2018**, 73–97 (2018)
12. Durvaux, F., Standaert, F.-X.: From improved leakage detection to the detection of points of interests in leakage traces. In: Fischlin, M., Coron, J.-S. (eds.) EUROCRYPT 2016. LNCS, vol. 9665, pp. 240–262. Springer, Heidelberg (2016). https://doi.org/10.1007/978-3-662-49890-3_10
13. Eisenbarth, T., Kasper, T., Moradi, A., Paar, C., Salmasizadeh, M., Shalmani, M.T.M.: On the power of power analysis in the real world: a complete break of the KEELOQ code hopping scheme. In: Wagner, D. (ed.) CRYPTO 2008. LNCS, vol. 5157, pp. 203–220. Springer, Heidelberg (2008). https://doi.org/10.1007/978-3-540-85174-5_12
14. Goodwill, G., Jun, B., Jaffe, J., Rohatgi, P.: A testing methodology for side channel resistance validation. In: NIST Non-Invasive Attack Testing Workshop (2011)
15. Liu, J., et al.: Small tweaks do not help: differential power analysis of MILENAGE implementations in 3G/4G USIM cards. In: Pernul, G., Ryan, P.Y.A., Weippl, E. (eds.) ESORICS 2015. LNCS, vol. 9326, pp. 468–480. Springer, Cham (2015). https://doi.org/10.1007/978-3-319-24174-6_24
16. Mangard, S.: Hardware countermeasures against DPA – a statistical analysis of their effectiveness. In: Okamoto, T. (ed.) CT-RSA 2004. LNCS, vol. 2964, pp. 222–235. Springer, Heidelberg (2004). https://doi.org/10.1007/978-3-540-24660-2_18
17. Mangard, S., Oswald, E., Standaert, F.: One for all - all for one: unifying standard differential power analysis attacks. IET Inf. Secur. **5**, 100–110 (2011)
18. Moradi, A., Kasper, M., Paar, C.: Black-box side-channel attacks highlight the importance of countermeasures. In: Dunkelman, O. (ed.) CT-RSA 2012. LNCS, vol. 7178, pp. 1–18. Springer, Heidelberg (2012). https://doi.org/10.1007/978-3-642-27954-6_1

19. Moradi, A., Schneider, T.: Improved side-channel analysis attacks on Xilinx bit-stream encryption of 5, 6, and 7 series. In: Standaert, F.-X., Oswald, E. (eds.) COSADE 2016. LNCS, vol. 9689, pp. 71–87. Springer, Cham (2016). https://doi.org/10.1007/978-3-319-43283-0_5

20. Poussier, R., Standaert, F.-X., Grosso, V.: Simple key enumeration (and rank estimation) using histograms: an integrated approach. In: Gierlichs, B., Poschmann, A.Y. (eds.) CHES 2016. LNCS, vol. 9813, pp. 61–81. Springer, Heidelberg (2016). https://doi.org/10.1007/978-3-662-53140-2_4

21. Ronen, E., Shamir, A., Weingarten, A., O'Flynn, C.: IoT goes nuclear: Creating a Zigbee chain reaction. In: IEEE Symposium on Security and Privacy, pp. 195–212. IEEE Computer Society (2017)

22. Schneider, T., Moradi, A.: Leakage assessment methodology - extended version. J. Cryptogr. Eng. 6(2), 85–99 (2016)

23. Semiconductors, N.: Kinetis k82 datasheet (2015). https://www.nxp.com/docs/en/data-sheet/K82P121M150SF5.pdf

24. Semiconductors, N.: Kinetis k82 reference manual (2015). https://www.nxp.com/docs/en/reference-manual/K82P121M150SF5RM.pdf

25. ST: Stm32l422cb datasheet (2018). https://www.st.com/resource/en/datasheet/stm32l422cb.pdf

26. ST: Stm32l422cb reference manual (2018). https://www.st.com/resource/en/reference_manual/dm00151940-stm32l41xxx42xxx43xxx44xxx45xxx46xxx-advanced-armbased-32bit-mcus-stmicroelectronics.pdf

27. Unterstein, F., Schink, M., Schamberger, T., Tebelmann, L., Ilg, M., Heyszl, J.: Retrofitting leakage resilient authenticated encryption to microcontrollers. IACR Trans. Cryptogr. Hardw. Embed. Syst. 2020(4), 365–388 (2020)

28. Welch, B.L.: The generalization of 'student's' problem when several different population variances are involved. Biometrika 34, 28–35 (1947)

29. Zhou, Y., Yu, Yu., Standaert, F.-X., Quisquater, J.-J.: On the need of physical security for small embedded devices: a case study with COMP128-1 implementations in SIM cards. In: Sadeghi, A.-R. (ed.) FC 2013. LNCS, vol. 7859, pp. 230–238. Springer, Heidelberg (2013). https://doi.org/10.1007/978-3-642-39884-1_20

A Power Side-Channel Attack on the CCA2-Secure HQC KEM

Thomas Schamberger[(✉)], Julian Renner, Georg Sigl, and Antonia Wachter-Zeh

Technical University of Munich, Munich, Germany
{t.schamberger,julian.renner,sigl,antonia.wachter-zeh}@tum.de

Abstract. The Hamming Quasi-Cyclic (HQC) proposal is a promising candidate in the second round of the NIST Post-Quantum Cryptography Standardization project. It features small public key sizes, precise estimation of its decryption failure rates and contrary to most of the code-based systems, its security does not rely on hiding the structure of an error-correcting code. In this paper, we propose the first power side-channel attack on the Key Encapsulation Mechanism (KEM) version of HQC. Our attack utilizes a power side-channel to build an oracle that outputs whether the BCH decoder in HQC's decryption algorithm corrects an error for a chosen ciphertext. Based on the decoding algorithm applied in HQC, it is shown how to design queries such that the output of the oracle allows to retrieve a large part of the secret key. The remaining part of the key can then be determined by an algorithm based on linear algebra. It is shown in experiments that less than 10000 measurements are sufficient to successfully mount the attack on the HQC reference implementation running on an ARM Cortex-M4 microcontroller.

Keywords: Error correction · HQC · Post-Quantum Cryptography · Power analysis · Side-channel analysis

1 Introduction

In modern communication systems, asymmetric cryptography is widely applied to enable secure communication between multiple parties. Since it is well known that classic public-key algorithms such as ElGamal or RSA are vulnerable against Shor's quantum computer algorithm, the National Institute of Standards and Technology (NIST) has started a standardization process for post-quantum secure public-key cryptosystems [8]. The code-based system Hamming Quasi Cyclic (HQC) [7] is a promising candidate in the second round of this NIST competition, as it offers several advantages. Established code-based cryptosystems like McEliece or its derivatives rely on hiding the structure of the used error correcting code. In contrast, the structure of the error-correcting code as well as the efficient decoding algorithm used in HQC are publicly known and therefore its security does not rely on hiding this knowledge. Instead, the security of HQC can be reduced to instances of the Quasi-Cyclic Syndrome Decoding problem, which is a well-understood problem in coding theory. Furthermore, HQC

© Springer Nature Switzerland AG 2021
P.-Y. Liardet and N. Mentens (Eds.): CARDIS 2020, LNCS 12609, pp. 119–134, 2021.
https://doi.org/10.1007/978-3-030-68487-7_8

features attractive key sizes and allows precise estimations of its decryption failure rate. It has been shown that the IND-CPA secure version of HQC can be attacked requiring only a few thousand queries to the algorithm [5]. Nevertheless, the IND-CCA2 secure version is not vulnerable to these sorts of attacks as the decryption signals a failure if the ciphertext is not valid. Recent attacks on the IND-CCA2 variant of HQC [9,12] use a timing side-channel in the implementation of the used BCH decoder to gather information about the decryption despite its IND-CCA2 security. Utilizing this information both attacks are able to successfully retrieve the used secret key. Fortunately, this attack vector has been removed as the authors of [12] provide a constant-time implementation of a BCH decoder, which has been merged into the HQC reference implementation.

In this paper we build upon the work of Ravi et al. [11], which describes a power side-channel attack methodology against the error correction used in the two lattice-based cryptosystems LAC [6] and Round5 [1]. We identify a similar vulnerability in HQC and are the first to show a power side-channel attack against the cryptosystem. Our attack is able to retrieve the whole secret key despite the constant-time implementation of the BCH decoder. The attack works by observing that the BCH decoder of the reference implementation shows a characteristic and distinguishable power consumption dependent on whether an error has to be corrected.

Contributions. We show that the attack methodology from [11] can be used to construct an oracle through the power side-channel that is able to identify whether an error has to be corrected by the BCH decoder used in the HQC reference implementation. The oracle is based on a template matching approach using a sum of squared differences metric. The initialization of the oracle can be performed without the knowledge of the secret key, which allows a direct initialization on the device under attack. An evaluation of the oracle on our measurement platform consisting of an STM32F415RE ARM Cortex-M4 microcontroller indicated that a total of four traces is sufficient for the initialization. The efficiency of the oracle is shown by the correct evaluation of 20000 test traces.

Building on this oracle we are the first to show a successful power side-channel attack against the Key Encapsulation Mechanism (KEM) version of HQC. We show general formulas for all parameter sets of HQC describing how to construct ciphertext inputs to the algorithm that lead to exploitable behavior based on the value of the secret key. Through an evaluation of the oracle results for these ciphertexts, we are able to sequentially retrieve the secret key. Due to the fact that the secret key has a marginally larger size than the ciphertext, there are keys that can only be partially attacked with this technique. Using simulations, we observe that the probabilities for such a key cannot be neglected, e.g., the probability for HQC-128 is 29.23%, and provide a linear algebra solution that is able to find the remaining part of the secret key. In general, the success of our attack is highly dependent on the distribution of ones in the secret key. The described ciphertext inputs are sufficient to attack 93.20% of the possible keys in HQC-128, which we consider to be high enough to pose a significant threat to the system. Nevertheless, our attack methodology can be adapted to support a larger range of keys with the trade-off of a significant increase in required measurement traces. Although this trade-off exists, there are rare cases where we are not able to retrieve the entire key. For these cases, we propose a modification of information set decoding (ISD) that utilizes the obtained side-channel information and thus still results in an attack complexity far below the claimed security level.

Finally, we use our described attack and successfully retrieve the whole secret key of the HQC-128 reference implementation using our measurement setup. In addition to the required four initialization traces, the attack requires less than 10000 measurements of the decoding step during the HQC decryption.

2 Preliminaries

2.1 Notation

Let $\mathbb{F}_2$ be the finite field of size 2. Throughout this paper we use $\mathbb{F}_2^{m \times n}$ to denote the set of all $m \times n$ matrices over $\mathbb{F}_2$, $\mathbb{F}_2^n = \mathbb{F}_2^{1 \times n}$ for the set of all row vectors of length n over $\mathbb{F}_2$, and define the set of integers $[a, b] := \{i : a \le i \le b\}$. We index rows and columns of $m \times n$ matrices by $0, \ldots, m-1$ and $0, \ldots, n-1$, where the entry in the i-th row and j-th column of the matrix $\boldsymbol{A}$ is denoted by $A_{i,j}$.

The Hamming weight of a vector $\boldsymbol{a}$ is indicated by $\mathrm{HW}(\boldsymbol{a})$ and the Hamming support of $\boldsymbol{a}$ is denoted by $\mathrm{supp}(\boldsymbol{a}) := \{i \in \mathbb{Z} : a_i \neq 0\}$. A set $\mathcal{A}$ is called super support (ssupp) of $\boldsymbol{a}$ if $\mathcal{A} \supset \mathrm{supp}(\boldsymbol{a})$.

Let $\mathcal{V}$ be a vector space of dimension n over $\mathbb{F}_2$. We define the product of $\boldsymbol{u}, \boldsymbol{v} \in \mathcal{V}$ as $\boldsymbol{u}\boldsymbol{v} = \boldsymbol{u}\,\mathrm{rot}(\boldsymbol{v})^\top = \boldsymbol{v}\,\mathrm{rot}(\boldsymbol{u})^\top = \boldsymbol{v}\boldsymbol{u}$, where

$$
\mathrm{rot}(\boldsymbol{v}) := \begin{bmatrix} v_0 & v_{n-1} & \cdots & v_1 \\ v_1 & v_0 & \cdots & v_2 \\ \vdots & \vdots & \ddots & \vdots \\ v_{n-1} & v_{n-2} & \cdots & v_0 \end{bmatrix} \in \mathbb{F}_2^{n \times n}.
$$

As a consequence of this definition, elements of $\mathcal{V}$ can be interpreted as polynomials in the ring $\mathcal{R} := \mathbb{F}_2[X]/(X^n - 1)$.

2.2 HQC

The HQC scheme is based on two different codes. It consists of a public code $\mathcal{C} \subseteq \mathbb{F}_2^n$ of length n and dimension k, where it is assumed that both an efficient encoding algorithm **Encode** and an efficient decoding algorithm **Decode** are known publicly. Further, the decoding algorithm can correct δ errors with high probability but fails for errors of large weight. HQC is also based on a second code of length $2n$ and dimension n which has a parity-check matrix $(\boldsymbol{I}, \mathrm{rot}(\boldsymbol{h})) \in \mathbb{F}_2^{n \times 2n}$, where $\boldsymbol{I}$ denotes the $n \times n$ identity matrix. Contrary to $\mathcal{C}$, it is assumed that no party posses an efficient decoding algorithm for the second code. Note that decoding in the second code is neither required in the encryption nor in the decryption algorithm.

In the following we describe the IND-CPA secure HQC public key encryption scheme as it is submitted to the second round of the NIST PQC competition [7]. It consists of the three algorithms Key Generation, Encryption and Decryption, which are shown in Algorithms 1 to 3. The algorithms use the functions **Encode** and **Decode** which encode into and decode in $\mathcal{C}$. These functions are formally defined in Sect. 2.3. All parameter sets for different security levels are shown in Table 1. In [4], Hofheinz *et al.* show a generic method to transform an IND-CPA secure encryption scheme into an IND-CCA2 secure KEM. This transformation is applied in the HQC proposal and results in the encapsulation and decapsulation algorithms of the HQC KEM described in [7]. Note that our attack especially targets the KEM version of HQC as the IND-CPA secure PKE version has been shown to be vulnerable without using a side-channel [5]. Due to space restrictions we only show the PKE version, as the target of our attack, namely the decryption (c.f. Algorithm 3), is the first step during the decapsulation function of the KEM.

Table 1. Parameter sets proposed for HQC [7]

Instance	n_1	n_2	n	k	w	$w_r = w_e$	δ
HQC-128	766	31	23869	256	67	77	57
HQC-192	766	59	45197	256	101	117	57
HQC-256	796	87	69259	256	133	153	60

Algorithm 1: Key Generation

Input: param $= (n, k, \delta, w, w_r, w_e)$
Output: pk $= (h, s)$ and sk $= (x, y)$
1 choose $\mathcal{C}$
2 $h \xleftarrow{\$} \mathcal{R}$
3 $(x, y) \xleftarrow{\$} \mathcal{R}^2$ such that $\mathrm{HW}(x) = \mathrm{HW}(y) = w$
4 $s \leftarrow x + hy$
5 **return** pk $= (h, s)$, sk $= (x, y)$

Algorithm 2: Encryption

Input: pk $= (h, s)$, pt $= (m)$ and randomness θ
Output: ct $= (u, v)$
1 $e' \xleftarrow{\$} \mathcal{R}$ such that $\mathrm{HW}(e') = w_e$ using θ
2 $(r_1, r_2) \xleftarrow{\$} \mathcal{R}^2$ such that $\mathrm{HW}(r_1) = \mathrm{HW}(r_2) = w_r$ using θ
3 $u \leftarrow r_1 + hr_2$
4 $v \leftarrow \mathbf{Encode}(m) + sr_2 + e'$
5 **return** ct $= (u, v)$

Algorithm 3: Decryption

Input: sk $= (\boldsymbol{x}, \boldsymbol{y})$, ct $= (\boldsymbol{u}, \boldsymbol{v})$
Output: $\boldsymbol{m}$

1 $\boldsymbol{v}' \leftarrow \boldsymbol{v} - \boldsymbol{u}\boldsymbol{y}$
2 $\boldsymbol{m} \leftarrow \mathbf{Decode}(\boldsymbol{v}')$
3 return $\boldsymbol{m}$

2.3   Choice of the Error-Correcting Code $\mathcal{C}$

In the original proposal, $\mathcal{C}$ is constructed using a product code of a $[n_1, k]$ short-ened BCH code $\mathcal{C}_1$ with a generator matrix $\boldsymbol{G}_1 \in \mathbb{F}_2^{k \times n_1}$ and a $[n_2, 1]$ repetition code $\mathcal{C}_2$. Note that the HQC proposal was recently extended and contains now an additional variant called HQC-RMRS that uses a code concatenation of a Reed-Muller code and a Reed-Solomon code for the error-correcting code $\mathcal{C}$. The extension is not motivated by security concerns regarding the original HQC scheme but instead the new choice of $\mathcal{C}$ provides a better error correction capability and thus allows to reduce the parameter sizes. The new variant is out of the scope of this paper and for simplicity we denote the original proposal as HQC for the remainder of this paper.

Encoding Algorithm. The encoding is defined as

$$\mathbf{Encode} : \mathbb{F}_2^k \to \mathbb{F}_2^n,$$

$$\boldsymbol{m} \mapsto (\underbrace{m_0', \ldots, m_0'}_{n_2 \text{ times}}, \underbrace{m_1', \ldots, m_1'}_{n_2 \text{ times}}, m_2', \ldots, m_{n_1-1}', \underbrace{0, 0, \ldots, 0}_{n - n_1 n_2 \text{ times}}),$$

where $\boldsymbol{m}' = (m_0', \ldots, m_{n_1-1}') = \boldsymbol{m}\boldsymbol{G}_1$ and $\boldsymbol{G}_1 \in \mathbb{F}_2^{k \times n_1}$ is a generator matrix of the $[n_1, k]$ shortened BCH code $\mathcal{C}_1$.

Decoding Algorithm. Given an input vector $\boldsymbol{v}' = (v_0', \ldots, v_{n_1-1}', v_{n_1}') \in \mathbb{F}_2^n$, where $v_0', \ldots, v_{n_1-1}' \in \mathbb{F}_2^{n_2}$ and $v_{n_1}' \in \mathbb{F}_2^{n-n_1 n_2}$, the decoding algorithm $\mathbf{Decode} : \mathbb{F}_2^n \to \mathbb{F}_2^k$ consists of two steps. First the algorithm decodes the vectors $v_0', \ldots, v_{n_1-1}'$ separately in the repetition code $\mathcal{C}_2$ using majority decoding to a vector $\tilde{\boldsymbol{v}} = (\tilde{v}_0, \ldots, \tilde{v}_{n_1-1}) \in \mathbb{F}_2^{n_1}$, where $\tilde{v}_i$ is 1 if $\sum_{j=1}^{n_2} v_{ij}' \geq \lceil \frac{n_2}{2} \rceil$ and 0 other-wise. In the second step, the algorithm decodes $\tilde{\boldsymbol{v}}$ in the BCH code $\mathcal{C}_1$ to the vector $\boldsymbol{m} \in \mathbb{F}_2^k$. In the proposal, a key equation based approach is used for decoding in $\mathcal{C}_1$ which works as follows. First, the syndromes are computed using the transpose of the additive Fast Fourier Transformation as in [2]. Then the error locator poly-nomial is determined using a modification of Berlekamp's algorithm and the error values are computed with an additive Fast Fourier Transformation.

2.4   Security of HQC

For our proposed attack, it is important to recognize that retrieving the secret key sk $= (\boldsymbol{x}, \boldsymbol{y})$ from the public key pk $= (\boldsymbol{h}, \boldsymbol{s})$ is equal to solving an instance of the Computational 2-Quasi Cyclic Syndrome Decoding (QCSD) Problem. This can be seen by $s = x + hy = (x, y)(1, \mathrm{rot}(h))^\top = eH^\top$, where $e := (x, y) \in \mathbb{F}_2^{2n}$ with $\mathrm{HW}(x) = \mathrm{HW}(y) = w$ and $H := (1, \mathrm{rot}(h)) \in \mathbb{F}_2^{n \times 2n}$. The vector s can be interpreted as the syndrome of the error e and the parity-check matrix H.

Using our proposed side-channel attack, we gain information about the support of y that we can incorporate in an information set decoding (ISD) algorithm, like Prange's algorithm [10], to reduce its complexity. We will later state the exact information that we obtain by the side-channels. For now however, it is sufficient to consider a generalized version of the 2-QCSD problem. Let n', w', k' be integers with $1 \leq n' \leq n$, $1 \leq w' \leq w$ and $n' \leq k' \leq n$. Further, let $y' \in \mathbb{F}_2^{n'}$ with $\mathrm{HW}(y') = w'$, $H' \in \mathbb{F}_2^{(n+n'-k') \times (n+n')}$ be a parity-check matrix of an $[n + n', k']$ code and $s' := (x, y')H'^\top$. This can be solved by a modification of Prange's algorithm. As in the original algorithm, we are interested in finding an error-free information set, but we modify the method to guess the indices. Instead of choosing k' indices at random from $\{0, \ldots, n + n' - 1\}$, we randomly choose k_1' indices from $\{0, \ldots, n - 1\}$ and k_2' indices from $\{0, \ldots, n' - 1\}$, where $k_1' + k_2' = k'$. The probability of guessing an error-free information set is then approximately given by $\binom{n-k_1'}{w}/\binom{n}{w} \cdot \binom{n'-k_2'}{w'}/\binom{n'}{w'}$. It follows that the complexity of this modified algorithm evaluates to

$$\mathcal{W}_{\mathrm{MPr}} = n^3 \min_{\substack{k_1', k_2' \\ s.t. k_1' + k_2' = k'}} \frac{\binom{n}{w}\binom{n'}{w'}}{\binom{n-k_1'}{w}\binom{n'-k_2'}{w'}} = n^3 \min_{k_1'} \frac{\binom{n}{w}\binom{n'}{w'}}{\binom{n-k_1'}{w}\binom{n'-k'+k_1'}{w'}}.$$

where it is assumed that solving a linear system of equations is in $O(n^3)$.

3   Side-Channel Attack on HQC

In this section, we propose an attack to retrieve the secret key $y = (y^{(0)}, y^{(1)}) \in \mathbb{F}_2^n$, where $y^{(0)} \in \mathbb{F}_2^{n_1 n_2}$ and $y^{(1)} \in \mathbb{F}_2^{n-n_1 n_2}$. Please note that although the secret key additionally consists of x, it is sufficient to only retrieve y, as it is the only secret needed for a successful decryption (c.f. Sect. 2.2). We will first analyze the distribution of the non-zero positions in y and based on this analysis, we show an algorithm that is able to obtain $y^{(0)}$ with high probability, given a decoding oracle. A method to construct such an oracle through a power side-channel is described in Sect. 4. Afterwards, we present a method to determine $y^{(1)}$ assuming that $y^{(0)}$ was successfully recovered. Finally, we show the complexity of a modified information set decoding algorithm in the unlikely case that the support of y was only partly retrieved.

3.1   Support Distribution of y

The distribution of the non-zero position in the secret y is essential for our attack. To simplify the notation, we decompose the vector y as follows $y = (y_0^{(0)}, \ldots, y_{n_1-1}^{(0)}, y^{(1)}) \in \mathbb{F}_2^n$, where $y_0^{(0)}, \ldots, y_{n_1-1}^{(0)} \in \mathbb{F}_2^{n_2}$.

From the parameters in Table 1 it follows that y is a sparse vector and thus the vectors $y_0^{(0)}, \ldots, y_{n_1-1}^{(0)}, y^{(1)}$ have Hamming weight close to zero with high probability. We performed simulations, by generating one million secret keys, in order to estimate the weight distribution of $y_0^{(0)}, \ldots, y_{n_1-1}^{(0)}$. The results are shown in Table 2, where we observed that most of the secret keys have a $y_0^{(0)}, \ldots, y_{n_1-1}^{(0)}$ of Hamming weight at most 3. Simulations showed further that the probability that $\mathrm{HW}(y^{(1)}) > 0$ is approximately 29.23%, 0.69%, 1.52% for HQC-128, HQC-192 and HQC-256, respectively.

Table 2. Probabilities that y is generated such that the weight of $y_i^{(0)}$ for $i = 0, \ldots, n_1 - 1$ is at most 1, 2 or 3 for the different parameter sets.

$\max\{\mathrm{HW}(y_0^{(0)}), \ldots, \mathrm{HW}(y_{n_1-1}^{(0)})\}$	HQC-128	HQC-192	HQC-256
1	5.59%	0.11%	$\approx$0%
2	93.20%	77.98%	58.99%
3	99.86%	99.25%	97.99%

3.2 Retrieving $y^{(0)}$ Using a Decoding Oracle

In this section, we propose a chosen ciphertext attack that retrieves $y_i^{(0)}$ for $i = 0, \ldots, n_1 - 1$. Please note that our attack approach is similar to [12], but we are using a power instead of a timing side-channel. Our attack methodology works as follows.

First, we fix u to $(1, 0, \ldots, 0) \in \mathbb{F}_2^n$ such that the vector that is feed into the decoder of $\mathcal{C}$ is given by $v' = v - y$, as it can be seen in Algorithm 3. Then, we choose specific vectors v and use a decoding oracle $\mathcal{O}_{01}^{Dec}$ that is able to determine whether an error is corrected in the BCH code. After the oracle has been initialized it can be queried for different inputs v and returns 1 if an error had to be corrected and 0 otherwise. We give detailed information on how to construct such an oracle through a power side-channel in Sect. 4. Based on the oracle results for different inputs v, we can obtain $y^{(0)}$.

To derive the chosen vectors v, recall that the code $\mathcal{C}$ is a product code consisting of a BCH code $\mathcal{C}_1$ of length n_1 and a repetition code $\mathcal{C}_2$ of length n_2 and only the first $n_1 n_2$ positions of v' are decoded in $\mathcal{C}$. The decoder for $\mathcal{C}$ divides the first $n_1 n_2$ positions of v' into chunks $v'_0, \ldots, v'_{n_1-1}$ of size n_2 that are separately decoded in the repetition code. Decoding in $\mathcal{C}_2$ is performed by a majority voting, meaning vectors of Hamming weight at least $\lceil \frac{n_2}{2} \rceil$ are mapped to 1 and the remaining vectors are mapped to 0. The outputs of the repetition decoder are then decoded in the BCH code. Since the zero vector is in $\mathcal{C}_1$ and vectors of Hamming weight one[1] are not in $\mathcal{C}_1$, we observe the following. Setting

---

[1] This follows from the fact that the BCH code has a minimum distance larger than 1.

$\lceil\frac{n_2}{2}\rceil$ entries of v_i to 1 and v_j to the zero vector, where $j \in [0, n_1 - 1] \setminus \{i\}$, results in two cases that we can distinguish using $\mathcal{O}_{01}^{Dec}$:

1. $|\operatorname{supp}(y_i^{(0)}) \cap \operatorname{supp}(v_i)| > \frac{\mathrm{HW}(y_i^{(0)})}{2}$: This leads to $\mathrm{HW}(v_i') < \lceil\frac{n_2}{2}\rceil$ and the repetition decoder outputs 0. Then, no error is corrected in the BCH code.
2. $|\operatorname{supp}(y_i^{(0)}) \cap \operatorname{supp}(v_i)| \leq \frac{\mathrm{HW}(y_i^{(0)})}{2}$: This leads to $\mathrm{HW}(v_i') \geq \lceil\frac{n_2}{2}\rceil$ and the repetition decoder outputs 1, which is corrected in the BCH code.

This observation allows to determine the support of $y_i^{(0)}$ in a two-step approach, where we first determine a super support of $y_i^{(0)}$ and then refine these approximate locations to obtain the exact non-zero positions of $y_i^{(0)}$. Note that all $y_0^{(0)}, \ldots, y_{n_1-1}^{(0)}$ are examined separately in sequential manner.

Finding a Super Support of $y_i^{(0)}$. In the following, we derive how to choose v_i to determine a super support of $y_i^{(0)}$ under the assumption that $\mathrm{HW}(y_i^{(0)}) \leq 2$. As shown in Table 2, this already covers a large part of the possible keys. Nevertheless, a generalization of the proposed method to cases where $\mathrm{HW}(y_i^{(0)}) > 2$ works accordingly. Assuming $\mathrm{HW}(y_i^{(0)}) \leq 1$, a super support of $y_i^{(0)}$ can be found by using only two patterns of v_i. For pattern 0, we choose $\operatorname{supp}(v_i) = [0, \lceil\frac{n_2}{2}\rceil-1]$ and for pattern 1, we choose $\operatorname{supp}(v_i) = [\lceil\frac{n_2}{2}\rceil - 1, n_2 - 1]$. The patterns for $n_2 = 31$ (HQC-128) are illustrated in Fig. 1.

Fig. 1. Pattern of v_i to find a super support of $y_i^{(0)}$ for $n_2 = 31$ and $\mathrm{HW}(y_i^{(0)}) \leq 1$. The black part indicates positions with value 1 and the white part positions with value 0.

If the BCH decoder has to correct an error for both patterns, it follows that $\mathrm{HW}(y_i^{(0)}) = 0$ and in case no error was corrected by the BCH code in both cases, we conclude that $\operatorname{supp}(y_i^{(0)}) = \operatorname{ssupp}(y_i^{(0)}) = \{\lceil\frac{n_2}{2}\rceil - 1\}$. Furthermore, if the BCH decoder has to correct an error for the first pattern but not for the second pattern we know that $\operatorname{supp}(y_i^{(0)}) \cap \operatorname{ssupp}(y_i^{(0)}) = [\lceil\frac{n_2}{2}\rceil, n_2 - 1]$. Given the BCH decoder does not correct an error in the first case but in the second we know that $\operatorname{supp}(y_i^{(0)}) \cap \operatorname{ssupp}(y_i^{(0)}) = [0, \lceil\frac{n_2}{2}\rceil - 2]$.

For the case $\mathrm{HW}(y_i^{(0)}) \leq 2$ and $4 \mid (n_2 + 1)$, we can generalize the described method as follows[2]. Instead of only two patterns, we construct six different

---

[2] This condition is fulfilled for HQC-128, HQC-192 and HQC-256. In case of an HQC instance with $4 \nmid (n_2 + 1)$, the algorithm works similarly but the patterns need to be slightly modified.

patterns of $\boldsymbol{v}_i$. An illustration of the six patterns for $n_2 = 31$ together with the general formulas for the sets dependent on n_2 is given in Fig. 2.

Similar to before, we can determine a super support of $\boldsymbol{y}_i^{(0)}$ based on the output of the oracle for the different patterns of $\boldsymbol{v}_i$, where the logic is given in Table 3. In the table, either one or two sets per row are shown. The union of these sets give a super support of $\boldsymbol{y}_i^{(0)}$ and each set has a non-empty intersection with the support of $\boldsymbol{y}_i^{(0)}$. The latter property is important since it reduces the complexity of the next step.

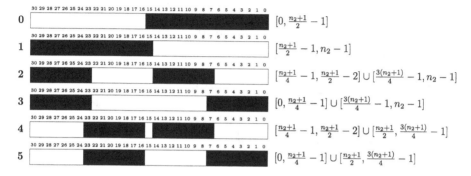

Fig. 2. Patterns of $\boldsymbol{v}_i$ to find a super support of $\boldsymbol{y}_i^{(0)}$ for $n_2=31$ and $\mathrm{HW}(\boldsymbol{y}_i^{(0)}) \leq 2$. The black part indicates positions with value 1 and the white part entries with value 0. In addition, the support of $\boldsymbol{v}_i$ dependent on n_2 is given.

Table 3. Super support of $\boldsymbol{y}_i^{(0)}$ depending on the oracle output for different patterns of $\boldsymbol{v}_i$ (see Fig. 2) and $\mathrm{HW}(\boldsymbol{y}_i^{(0)}) \leq 2$.

$\mathcal{O}_{01}^{Dec}$ (Pattern ⋆)						$\mathrm{ssupp}(\boldsymbol{y}_i^{(0)})$
0	1	2	3	4	5	
1	1	1	1	1	1	$\{\,\}$
0	1	–	–	–	–	$[0, \frac{n_2+1}{2} - 1]$
1	0	–	–	–	–	$[\frac{n_2+1}{2} - 1, n_2 - 1]$
1	1	0	1	1	1	$[\frac{n_2+1}{4}, \frac{n_2+1}{2} - 2]$, $[\frac{3(n_2+1)}{4}, n_2 - 1]$
1	1	1	0	1	1	$[0, \frac{n_2+1}{4} - 2]$, $[\frac{3(n_2+1)}{4}, n_2 - 1]$
1	1	1	1	0	1	$[\frac{n_2+1}{4}, \frac{n_2+1}{2} - 2]$, $[\frac{n_2+1}{2}, \frac{3(n_2+1)}{4} - 2]$
1	1	1	1	1	0	$[0, \frac{n_2+1}{4} - 2]$, $[\frac{n_2+1}{2}, \frac{3(n_2+1)}{4} - 2]$
1	1	0	0	1	1	$\{\frac{n_2+1}{4} - 1\}$, $[\frac{3(n_2+1)}{4}, n_2 - 1]$
1	1	0	1	0	1	$[\frac{n_2+1}{4}, \frac{n_2+1}{2} - 2]$, $\{\frac{3(n_2+1)}{4} - 1\}$
1	1	1	0	1	0	$[0, \frac{n_2+1}{4} - 2]$, $\{\frac{3(n_2+1)}{4} - 1\}$
1	1	1	1	0	0	$\{\frac{n_2+1}{4} - 1\}$, $[\frac{n_2+1}{2}, \frac{3(n_2+1)}{4} - 2]$
1	1	0	0	0	0	$\{\frac{n_2+1}{4} - 1\}$, $\{\frac{3(n_2+1)}{4} - 1\}$

Finding the Support of $y_i^{(0)}$. From the super support of $y_i^{(0)}$, we can determine $\mathrm{supp}(y_i^{(0)})$ using the fact that all indices of $y_i^{(0)}$ that are not in $\mathrm{ssupp}(y_i^{(0)})$ correspond to entries with value zero. As already discussed, we describe the proposed method for $\mathrm{HW}(y_i^{(0)}) \leq 2$ which can then be easily generalized to the case $\mathrm{HW}(y_i^{(0)}) > 2$.

Assume that $\mathrm{HW}(y_i^{(0)}) = 1$. We can find the support of $y_i^{(0)}$ by setting $\lceil \frac{n_2}{2} \rceil - 1$ entries in v_i to 1 for indices which are not in $\mathrm{ssupp}(y_i^{(0)})$. Keeping these entries fixed, we iterate through all vectors v_i with $|\mathrm{supp}(v_i) \cap \mathrm{ssupp}(y_i^{(0)})| = 1$. This procedure is depicted for $n_2 = 31$ and $\mathrm{ssupp}(y_i^{(0)}) = \{0, \ldots, 14\}$ in Fig. 3. Every time when the BCH decoder corrects an error, we know that $\mathrm{supp}(v_i) \cap \mathrm{ssupp}(y_i^{(0)}) \neq \mathrm{supp}(y_i^{(0)})$ and when the BCH decoder does not correct an error, we can conclude that $\mathrm{supp}(v_i) \cap \mathrm{ssupp}(y_i^{(0)}) = \mathrm{supp}(y_i^{(0)})$.

Fig. 3. Patterns to determine $\mathrm{supp}(y_i^{(0)})$ from $\mathrm{ssupp}(y_i^{(0)})$ for $n_2 = 31$ and $\mathrm{ssupp}(y_i^{(0)}) = \{0, \ldots, 14\}$.

For $\mathrm{HW}(y_i^{(0)}) = 2$, we fix $\lceil \frac{n_2}{2} \rceil - 2$ entries in v_i to 1 for indices which are not in $\mathrm{ssupp}(y_i^{(0)})$. In case Table 3 refers to one set as the super support of $y_i^{(0)}$, we brute-force all vectors v_i, where $|\mathrm{supp}(v_i) \cap \mathrm{ssupp}(y_i^{(0)})| = 2$. In case Table 3 refers to two sets, we iterate through all vectors v_i that have a non-empty intersection with both sets. As before, every time the BCH decoder corrects an error, we know that $\mathrm{supp}(v_i) \cap \mathrm{ssupp}(y_i^{(0)}) \neq \mathrm{supp}(y_i^{(0)})$ and when the BCH decoder does not correct an error, we state $\mathrm{supp}(v_i) \cap \mathrm{ssupp}(y_i^{(0)}) = \mathrm{supp}(y_i^{(0)})$.

3.3 Retrieving $y^{(1)}$ Using Linear Algebra

Due to fact that only the first $n_1 n_2$ positions of $v' \in \mathbb{F}_2^n$ are decoded in $\mathcal{C}$, we are so far not able to determine the support of the last $n - n_1 n_2$ positions of y for keys with $\mathrm{HW}(y^{(1)}) > 0$. In the following, we propose a method to obtain $\mathrm{supp}(y^{(1)})$ in these cases assuming that $\mathrm{supp}(y^{(0)})$ was successfully recovered.

Let $\mathcal{J} = \{j_0, \ldots, j_{t-1}\}$ denote the known support of $y^{(0)}$ and let $\mathcal{L} = \{l_0, \ldots, l_{w-t-1}\}$ be the support of $y^{(1)}$ that we want to determine. First, observe that $s = x + hy = x + H_{n+j_0}^\top + \ldots + H_{n+j_{t-1}}^\top + H_{n+l_0}^\top + \ldots + H_{n+l_{w-t-1}}^\top$, where H_i denotes the i-th column of $H = (1, \mathrm{rot}(h))$. Since s, h and $\mathcal{J}$ are known, we can compute $\tilde{s} = s + H_{n+j_0}^\top + \ldots + H_{n+j_{t-1}}^\top = x + H_{n+l_0}^\top + \ldots + H_{n+l_{w-t-1}}^\top$. Then, we repeatedly sample $w - t$ indices $\hat{l}_0, \ldots, \hat{l}_{w-t-1}$ from $\{0, \ldots, n - n_1 n_2 - 1\}$ and compute $\hat{x} := \tilde{s} + H_{n+\hat{l}_0}^\top + \ldots + H_{n+\hat{l}_{w-t-1}}^\top$ until $\mathrm{HW}(\hat{x}) = w$. In this case, $\hat{x} = x$ which means that $\{\hat{l}_0, \ldots, \hat{l}_{w-t-1}\} = \mathcal{L}$. We finally output $\mathcal{J} \cup \{\hat{l}_0, \ldots, \hat{l}_{w-t-1}\}$ as estimation of $\mathrm{supp}(y)$. The probability that $\{\hat{l}_0, \ldots, \hat{l}_{w-t-1}\} = \mathcal{L}$ is $\binom{n - n_1 n_2}{w-t}^{-1}$ and checking whether $\{\hat{l}_0, \ldots, \hat{l}_{w-t-1}\}$ is equal to $\mathcal{L}$ requires $w - t$ column additions which is in $O(n(w-t))$. This results in a complexity of $\mathcal{W}_\mathrm{L} = n(w-t)\binom{n - n_1 n_2}{w-t}$. Although the described method has an exponential complexity, it is easily solvable since $n - n_1 n_2$ is small for all parameter sets[3] and $w - t$ is close to zero with high probability. Assuming $w - t \leq 2$, the complexity is $2^{28.42}$, $2^{18.05}$ and $2^{21.47}$ for the parameter sets of HQC-128, HQC-192 and HQC-256.

3.4   Information Set Decoding

Due to errors during the power measurements or due to certain secret keys with $y_i^{(0)}$ of rather large Hamming weight, we might in some very rare cases not be able to determine the support of y but only a subset $\mathcal{P} = \{p_0, \ldots, p_{t-1}\} \subset \mathrm{supp}(y)$ of it. Then we can use $\mathcal{P}$ to reduce the complexity of information set decoding. To do so, we compute $s' = s + H_{n+p_0}^\top + \ldots + H_{n+p_{t-1}}^\top$. We observe that s' is a syndrome of the parity-check matrix H and an error (e_0', e_1'), where $e_0' \in \mathbb{F}_2^n$ has weight w and $e_1' \in \mathbb{F}_2^n$ has weight $w = w - t$. Thus, we can use the modification of Prange's algorithm as described in Sect. 2.4 which has a complexity of $\mathcal{W}_\mathrm{BCH} = n^3 \cdot \min_{k_1} \frac{\binom{n}{w}}{\binom{n-k_1}{w}} \frac{\binom{n}{w-t}}{\binom{k_1}{w-t}}$. We show the complexity of the modified Prange's algorithm for the parameters of HQC-128, HQC-192 and HQC-256 as a function of t in Fig. 4. It can be observed that if t is close to w, the complexity of the modified Prange's algorithm is far below the claimed security level.

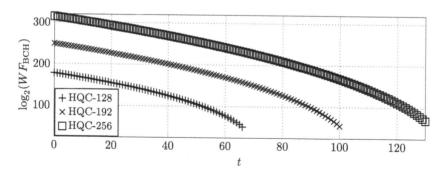

Fig. 4. Complexity $\mathcal{W}_\mathrm{BCH}$ for HQC-128, HQC-192 and HQC-256 as a function of t, where t is the number of non-zero positions in y that are correctly obtained by the proposed side-channel attack.

---

[3] The variable $n - n_1 n_2$ is equal to 123, 3 and 7 for HQC-128, HQC-192 and HQC-256, respectively.

4   Decoding Oracle Based on a Power Side-Channel

This section introduces a method to construct a decoding oracle through the power side-channel, which allows an attacker to identify whether the BCH decoder has to correct an error during the decoding step of the decryption of HQC. As explained in Sect. 3, this allows the attacker to retrieve the used secret key y regardless of the constant time implementation of the BCH decoder. First, we introduce the Welch's t-test, which is used to identify point of interest (POI) in the power measurements. Then the oracle itself is described, which is based on template matching through a sum of squared differences metric. Finally, we discuss our measurement setup and show attack results for the reference implementation of HQC.

4.1   Welch's *t*-test

The Test Vector Leakage Assessment (TVLA) [3] is an established tool to statistically evaluate a cryptographic implementation for existing and exploitable side-channel leakage. To achieve this goal, it uses Welch's t-test, which in essence evaluates whether two sets of data significantly differ from each other in the sense of their means being different. Given two sets S_0 and S_1 with their respective mean μ_0, μ_1 and variance s_0, s_1 the resulting *t-value* is calculated as $t = (\mu_0 - \mu_1)/(\sqrt{s_0^2/n_0 + s_1^2/n_1})$, where n denotes the respective cardinality of the set. Usually a threshold of $|t| > 4.5$ is defined, which states that there is a confidence of > 0.99999 that both sets can not be distinguished if the resulting t-value stays below this threshold. As the t-test can be individually performed for all the samples of a measurement trace, it acts as an efficient method for POI detection.

4.2   Construction of the Decoding Oracle

In [11] Ravi *et al.* mounted a successful attack against the NIST PQ candidates LAC [6] and Round5 [1], by utilizing a power side-channel that allows to distinguish whether the used error correction had to correct an error. This section introduces their attack methodology based on a POI-reduced template matching approach with respect to its application on HQC. The result of this attack methodology is an oracle $\mathcal{O}_{01}^{Dec}$ that returns 0 if no error had to be corrected by the BCH decoder and outputs 1 otherwise.

In order to initialize the oracle, templates for the two different classes are built using the ciphertext inputs shown in Table 4. We refer to Sect. 3.2 for an explanation on how these values are derived. Please note that an attacker does not need to know the used secret key y in order to construct the templates. This allows to directly build the templates on the device under attack, which significantly increases the strength of the attack. To start building the templates, a limited amount of N_t power traces for both classes, which will be denoted as T_0 and T_1, are recorded during the BCH decoding step of the function **Decode** in the decryption algorithm of HQC (c.f. Algorithm 3). In order to cope with environment changes during the measurement phase, e.g., DC offsets, the individual power traces t_i are normalized for both classes. This is done by subtracting the respective mean $\bar{t}_i$, such that $t'_i = t_i - \bar{t}_i \mathbf{1}$. Now, the t-test (c.f. Sect. 4.1) is used to identify measurement samples that can be used to distinguish between the two classes. Based on these t-test results and a chosen threshold value Th_{attack} both trace sets can be reduced to their respective POIs resulting in T'_0 and T'_1. Finally, the templates for both classes can be calculated as the mean over all traces in their respective set, resulting in t^0_m and t^1_m, respectively.

Table 4. Ciphertext input used for the initialization of the oracle.

$\mathcal{O}^{Dec}_{01}$	$u \in \mathbb{F}^n_2$	$v = (v_0, \ldots, v_{n1-1}) \in \mathbb{F}^{n_1 n_2}_2$ with $v_i \in \mathbb{F}^{n_2}_2$
0 (no error)	0	$(0, \ldots, 0)$
1 (error)	0	$(HW(v_0) = \lceil \frac{n_2}{2} \rceil, 0, \ldots, 0)$

In order to evaluate the oracle for a given ciphertext input (u, v) the corresponding power trace t_c has to be captured by the attacker. The classification process is performed by an evaluation of the sum of squared differences SSD_* to both templates. The trace t_c is classified as the class with the lowest SSD value. Note that t_c also has to be reduced to the previously found POI. If both the templates t^1_m, t^0_m and attack trace t_c are seen as a vector of their respective sample values, the evaluation can be written as

$$SSD_0 = ((t_c - \bar{t}_c \mathbf{1}) - t^0_m)^T \cdot ((t_c - \bar{t}_c \mathbf{1}) - t^0_m)$$
$$SSD_1 = ((t_c - \bar{t}_c \mathbf{1}) - t^1_m)^T \cdot ((t_c - \bar{t}_c \mathbf{1}) - t^1_m).$$

4.3   Oracle Evaluation

In order to evaluate the oracle we implemented the reference implementation of HQC-128 on our test platform consisting of an STM32F415RGT6 ARM Cortex-M4 microcontroller. The microcontroller is part of an CW308T-STM32F target board which is mounted on a CW308 UFO board running at a clock frequency of 10 MHz. The clock is provided by an external clock generator. We measured the power consumption through an integrated shunt resistor with a PicoScope 6402D USB-oscilloscope at a sampling rate of 156.25 MHz. A dedicated GPIO pin is used to provide a trigger signal to the oscilloscope indicating the duration of the function that is evaluated.

First we evaluated if both classes can be distinguished through the power side-channel using our setup. Therefore, we perform a t-test on 1000 measurements with a randomly chosen classes. As described in Sect. 2.3, there are three main steps during the BCH decoding, where each step could potentially be used for the distinction. In the original proposal of the attack methodology by Ravi *et al.*

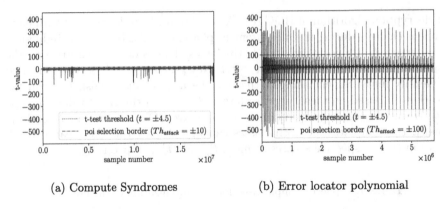

(a) Compute Syndromes   (b) Error locator polynomial

Fig. 5. T-test result using 1000 measurements for different functions of the BCH decoding during the HQC decryption. The computation of syndromes corresponds to the function `compute_syndromes()` and the error locator polynomial computation to the function `compute_elp()` of the reference implementation.

[11] the authors find the computation of syndromes a suitable operation during the decoding. The t-test results for this attack vector is shown in Fig. 5a.

It can be seen that there are some measurement samples with a t-value that indicates a sufficient amount of side-channel leakage in order to distinguish both classes. Nevertheless, we opted to additionally examine the computation of the error locator polynomial, as seen in Fig. 5b. The result shows a significantly higher t-value in addition with an execution time of only $\approx 33.3\%$ in comparison to the syndrome computation. Therefore, we use the computation of the error locator polynomial as our attack target.

In a second step, we prove the efficiency of the oracle by building the templates t_m^0 and t_m^1 using a total of 1000 template traces (500 for each class) using only the POI given by the attack threshold Th_{attack} depicted in Fig. 5b. The resulting templates are shown in Fig. 6. It can be clearly seen that there is a significant difference between both templates. After the initialization, we evaluated 20000 queries to the oracle given traces with a randomly chosen class. The oracle was able to correctly classify all measurements. In an effort to lower the required amount of traces for the initialization, we iteratively evaluated the classification results with a decreasing number of template traces. As a result, we were able to successfully classify all 20000 traces with exactly two template traces for each class. Please note that this includes the fact that the POI detection with the t-test also works with this low amount of traces.

Finally, we were able to successfully retrieve the complete secret key y of the reference implementation of HQC-128 using our measurement setup. In addition to the traces needed to initialize the oracle our complete attack, given a maximum $HW(y_i^{(0)}) = 1$, requires 1532 traces to find $\mathrm{ssupp}(y^{(0)})$ and 1005 traces for the final $\mathrm{supp}(y^{(0)})$. In case of a maximum $HW(y_i^{(0)}) = 2$ the amount of pattern increases to six and therefore 4596 traces are needed to find $\mathrm{ssupp}(y^{(0)})$. The

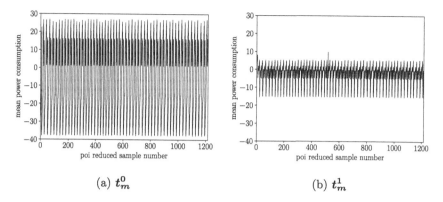

(a) t_m^0 (b) t_m^1

Fig. 6. Computed templates after the initialization step of the oracle using 500 traces for each class.

amount of traces to retrieve the final $\mathrm{supp}(\boldsymbol{y}^{(0)})$ is highly dependent on the result of $\mathrm{ssupp}(\boldsymbol{y}^{(0)})$ and therefore we only provide a worst case estimation, which is a total of 3976 traces.

5 Conclusion

In this paper we show the first power side-channel attack against the code-based post-quantum algorithm HQC in its Key Encapsulation Mechanism (KEM) version. We observe that the success of the attack significantly depends on the distribution of non-zero elements in the secret key under attack. Therefore, we additionally provide attack solutions for special types of keys through the use of linear algebra and in rare cases a modification of information set decoding. Using our measurement setup containing an ARM Cortex-M4 microcontroller, we are able to attack 93.2% of possible keys of the reference implementation of HQC-128 with less than 10000 measurement traces. Our attack threatens the security of the HQC KEM and makes the development of side-channel countermeasures for the used BCH decoder a high priority research task.

Acknowledgment. This work was supported by the German Research Foundation (DFG) under grant number SE2989/1-1 and by the European Research Council (ERC) under the European Union's Horizon 2020 research and innovation programme (grant agreement No 801434).

References

1. Baan, H., et al.: NIST Post-Quantum Cryptography Standardization Round 2 Submission: Round5. https://round5.org
2. Bernstein, D.J., Chou, T., Schwabe, P.: McBits: fast constant-time code-based cryptography. In: Bertoni, G., Coron, J.-S. (eds.) CHES 2013. LNCS, vol. 8086, pp. 250–272. Springer, Heidelberg (2013). https://doi.org/10.1007/978-3-642-40349-1_15

3. Goodwill, G., Jun, B., Jaffe, J., Rohatgi, P.: A testing methodology for side-channel resistance validation. In: NIST Non-Invasive Attack Testing Workshop, vol. 7, pp. 115–136 (2011)
4. Hofheinz, D., Hövelmanns, K., Kiltz, E.: A modular analysis of the Fujisaki-Okamoto transformation. In: Kalai, Y., Reyzin, L. (eds.) TCC 2017. LNCS, vol. 10677, pp. 341–371. Springer, Cham (2017). https://doi.org/10.1007/978-3-319-70500-2_12
5. Huguenin-Dumittan, L., Vaudenay, S.: Classical Misuse Attacks on NIST Round 2 PQC: The Power of Rank-Based Schemes. Cryptology ePrint Archive, Report 2020/409 (2020). https://eprint.iacr.org/2020/409
6. Lu, X., et al.: NIST Post-Quantum Cryptography Standardization Round 2 Submission: LAC: Lattice-based Cryptosystems. https://csrc.nist.gov/Projects/post-quantum-cryptography/round-2-submissions
7. Melchor, C.A., et al.: NIST Post-Quantum Cryptography Standardization Round 2 Submission: Hamming Quasi-Cyclic (HQC). http://pqc-hqc.org/
8. National Institute of Standards and Technology (NIST), U.S. Department of Commerce: Post-quantum cryptography standardization (2017)
9. Paiva, T.B., Terada, R.: A timing attack on the HQC encryption scheme. In: Paterson, K.G., Stebila, D. (eds.) SAC 2019. LNCS, vol. 11959, pp. 551–573. Springer, Cham (2020). https://doi.org/10.1007/978-3-030-38471-5_22
10. Prange, E.: The use of information sets in decoding cyclic codes. IEEE Trans. Inf. Theory 8(5), 5–9 (1962)
11. Ravi, P., Roy, S.S., Chattopadhyay, A., Bhasin, S.: Generic Side-channel attacks on CCA-secure lattice-based PKE and KEM schemes. Cryptology ePrint Archive, Report 2019/948 (2019). https://eprint.iacr.org/2019/948
12. Wafo-Tapa, G., Bettaieb, S., Bidoux, L., Gaborit, P., Marcatel, E.: A Practicable Timing Attack Against HQC and its Countermeasure. Cryptology ePrint Archive, Report 2019/909 (2019). https://eprint.iacr.org/2019/909

How Deep Learning Helps Compromising USIM

Martin Brisfors, Sebastian Forsmark, and Elena Dubrova$^{(\boxtimes)}$

Royal Institute of Technology (KTH), Stockholm, Sweden
{brisfors,sforsm,dubrova}@kth.se

Abstract. It is known that secret keys can be extracted from some USIM cards using Correlation Power Analysis (CPA). In this paper, we demonstrate a more advanced attack on USIMs, based on deep learning. We show that a Convolutional Neural Network (CNN) trained on one USIM can recover the key from another USIM using at most 20 traces (four traces on average). Previous CPA attacks on USIM cards required high-quality oscilloscopes for power trace acquisition, an order of magnitude more traces from the victim card, and expert-level skills from the attacker. Now the attack can be mounted with a $1000 budget and basic skills in side-channel analysis.

Keywords: USIM · MILENAGE · AES · Power analysis · Deep learning

1 Introduction

Today the Universal Subscriber Identity Module (USIM) card is perceived as an enabler for security, privacy, and trust in services and applications provided by the mobile communication networks. The USIM card is the only platform which is used to secure network access in Universal Mobile Telecommunications Service (UMTS) and Long-Term Evolution (LTE) cellular networks and it remains an essential part of New Radio (NG) cellular networks [23]. If the USIM's secret key is compromised, the attacker can decrypt the subscriber's communication, impersonate the subscriber, or impersonate the network.

SIM cards were introduced in 2G GSM systems in 1996 to address shortcomings discovered in previous analog systems and to meet emerging threats [14]. In particular, risk of fraud (making calls charged to other subscribers) was considered a major problem. The SIM enabled a subscriber's authentication using a pre-shared secret key stored in the SIM and, consequently, a correct charging.

However, the algorithm COMP-128, which implements a subscriber's authentication (A3) and session key generation (A8) functions defined by GSM standard [15], was soon broken. Originally confidential, the first version of COMP-128 was published in 1998 [18] and the second and the third in 2013 [24].

Supported by the research grant No 2018-04482 from the Swedish Research Council.

© Springer Nature Switzerland AG 2021

P.-Y. Liardet and N. Mentens (Eds.): CARDIS 2020, LNCS 12609, pp. 135–150, 2021.
https://doi.org/10.1007/978-3-030-68487-7_9

All three versions are based on a compression function which has a weakness in diffusion of the second round. This allows for a "narrow pipe" attack which can recover the secret key from the SIM from 131K challenge-response pairs [13]. An improved attack which can recover the key from 20K challenge-response pairs was presented at DEFCON 2004 [16].

To improve security, USIM cards were launched in 3G UMTS systems in 2001. In particular, procedures for mutual authentication of the subscriber and the core network based on the Authentication and Key Agreement (AKA) protocol were introduced. The mutual authentication was intended to mitigate threats of rogue radio base stations.

The main structure of a USIM-based access authentication remains intact in 4G and 5G. The 4G LTE standard uses the same mutual authentication scheme as UMTS. The latest 5G NG standard uses a hardened version, called 5G-AKA, as one of its mandatory authentication options [1,21].

The 3rd Generation Partnership Project (3GPP) recommends implementing the authentication and key generation functions of AKA using either MILE-NAGE based on AES [2], or TUAK based on SHA3 [3]. In this paper we focus on attacks on MILENAGE algorithm.

Previous Work. Implementations of MILENAGE in some commercial USIM cards are known to be vulnerable to Correlation Power Analysis (CPA) [10,17]. In [10], eight commercial USIM cards were analyzed. It was shown that it is possible to recover the secret key as well as other secret parameters required to clone the USIM card using 200 to 1000 power traces from the target USIM, depending on USIM's type. In [10], 9 commercial USIM cards were analyzed and one was found vulnerable. The secret key was recovered using 4000 power traces.

Our Contribution. We demonstrate the first attack on the implementation of MILENAGE in a commercial USIM card based on deep learning-based power analysis. The deep learning-based power analysis has three important advantages over CPA:

1. It requires an order of magnitude fewer traces from a victim USIM card.
2. It can bypass some countermeasures, e.g. jitter [7] and masking [12], and thus break some USIMs which cannot be broken by CPA.
3. It does not require expert-level skills in side-channel analysis (if a trained neural network and all scripts for the attack stage are available).

In addition, we believe that we are the first to break a commercial USIM using equipment with the total cost below $1000 (excluding PC). In a combination with (3), the latter makes the presented attack particularly threatening.

2   USIM Security

In this section, we describe key terms related to cellular networks and USIM cards, AKA protocol and MILENAGE algorithm.

We use the terms 2G, 3G, 4G and 5G to refer to the corresponding generations of the 3GPP defined systems. We typically use the terminology of 4G.

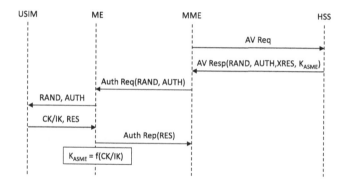

Fig. 1. The AKA protocol.

2.1   Network Structure

A mobile network consists of the following three essential types of entities:

- *Mobile Entity* (ME) equipped with a USIM.
- An authenticator in the serving network, called the *Mobility Management Entity* (MME).
- A database in the home network storing the subscriber credentials, called the *Home Subscriber Server* (HSS).

The USIM contains all necessary information about the subscription at the home network, including an *International Mobile Subscriber Identity* (IMSI). The USIM also stores a long-term key K which is pre-shared with the HSS. All cryptographic operations which involve K are carried out within the USIM.

The home network and the serving network are usually connected over a secure channel, such as IPsec or Transport Layer Security (TLS).

2.2   Authentication and Key Agreement Protocol

The 3GPP AKA is a challenge-response multi-party protocol based on symmetric key cryptography. The main steps are (see Fig. 1) [5]:

1. The MME initiates AKA by sending a request for an *Authentication Vector* (AV) associated with a particular subscriber in the HSS.
2. The HSS responds with an AV consisting of the 4-tuple (RAND, AUTN, XRES, K_{ASME}), where RAND is a random value, AUTN is a network authentication token, XRES is the expected response from the ME and K_{ASME} is the session key which is established in the ME and MME when the AKA run is completed. The AUTN, XRES and K_{ASME} are derived from the RAND and K. As an intermediate step in the derivation of K_{ASME}, the cipher key CK and integrity key IK are produced.
3. When the MME gets the AV, it initiates the authentication procedure with the ME by forwarding the RAND and AUTN.

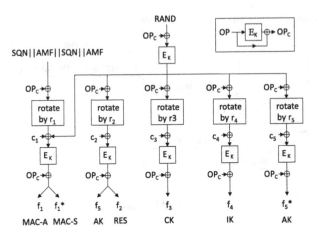

Fig. 2. The MILENAGE algorithm.

4. The ME sends the RAND and AUTN to the USIM, which verifies the authenticity and freshness of the AUTN parameter. If the verification succeeds, the USIM derives a response parameter RES and keys CK and IK from K, RAND and AUTN.
5. The USIM forwards the RES, CK and IK to the ME.
6. The ME derives K_{ASME} from the CK and IK and sends RES to the MME.
7. The MME verifies that RES is equal to XRES. If the verification is successful, MME accepts the authentication. Otherwise it rejects the authentication.

AKA uses 48-bit sequence numbers to prove the freshness of the RAND and AUTN parameters to the ME and USIM. The sequence number SQN is included in the AUTN parameter. If the sequence number is old, the ME or USIM rejects the authentication. AKA also includes a re-synchronization mechanism for sequence numbers.

The AKA protocol described above is a 4G AKA. Mutual authentication scheme of 3G AKA is the same. The 3G AKA and 4G AKA differ in the key agreement part. In 3G, the keys CK and IK are used to protect traffic, while in LTE they are used to derive a tree of keys. 2G systems can also use 3G AKA.

In 5G-AKA, the response RES computed in step 4 is processed one more time through a key derivation function (HMAC-SHA256) depending on RES, RAND, and CK || IK. The rest of the mutual authentication scheme is similar.

2.3   MILENAGE Algorithm

The 3GPP MILENAGE algorithm [2,4], implements seven security functions related to authentication and key agreement: $f_1, f_1^*, f_2, f_3, f_4, f_5, f_5^*$. The block diagram of the MILENAGE is shown in Fig. 2.

The functions f_1 and f_1^* compute a 64-bit, 128-bit or 256-bit network authentication code MAC-A and resynchronisation authentication code MAC-S, respectively. The function f_2 generates a 128-bit RES. The functions f_3 computes a

128-bit or 256-bit cipher key CK and integrity key IK, respectively. The functions f_5 and f_5^* generate a 48-bit anonymity key AK. AK is used to derive the sequence number SK.

The block denoted by E_K represents a 128-bit block cipher keyed with 128-bit or 256-bit key K. 3GPP recommends AES for implementing the block cipher.

The OP is an *Operator Variant Algorithm Configuration Field* defined by an operator and used for all subscribers. The OP_C is computed from OP and K as shown in the box at the top right corner of Fig. 2. There two alternative options for computing OP_C on the USIM which, in turn, determine where OP is stored:

- OP_C is computed off the USIM during the USIM pre-personalization process and stored on the USIM. In this case OP is not stored on the USIM.
- OP_C is computed on the USIM each time it is required in the algorithm. In this case OP is stored on the USIM.

A 128-bit random challenge RAND and a 16-bit Authentication Management Field AMF are controlled by the home network. A 48-bit sequence numbers SQN is a shared counter which is incremented with each successful authentication, to protect against replay attacks.

The parameters r_1, r_2, r_3, r_4, r_5 are integers in the range 0–127 which defines amounts by which intermediate variables are cyclically rotated. The parameters c_1, c_2, c_3, c_4, c_5 are 128-bit constants which are XORed with intermediate variables. Default values for $r_1 - r_5$ and $c_1 - c_5$ are set in the specification, however an operator may select different values for these constants to customize the algorithm further.

3   Attacking MILENAGE

3.1   Measurement Setup

Our measurement setup is shown in Fig. 3. It consists of the ChipWhisperer-Lite board, the CW308 UFO board and a custom smartcard reader for the ChipWhisperer called LEIA.

The ChipWhisperer is a hardware security evaluation toolkit based on a low-cost open hardware platform and an open source software [19]. It can be used to measure power consumption with a maximum sampling rate of 105 ms/sec.

The CW308 UFO board is a generic platform for evaluating multiple targets [9]. The target board is plugged into a dedicated U connector.

LEIA is the ISO7816 interface smart card reader compatible with the ChipWhisperer [11]. The reader is implemented on a STM32 microcontroller. It controls the clock and I/O lines to the smartcard under test and provides a trigger output to command the ChipWhisperer to start an acquisition. The reader has a resistor placed between the load and ground to enable voltage measuring.

The open source software [8] is run on a PC to control the hardware and execute the MILENAGE algorithm. The PC plays the role of MME. To initiate the authentication, the PC communicates with the USIM using the commands in Application Protocol Data Unit (APDU) language.

Fig. 3. Equipment for trace acquisition.

3.2 Attack Target

We used the commercial Sysmocom USIM cards sysmoSIM-SJS1 [25] as an attack target. These cards are compliant with 2G GSM, 3G UMTS and 4G LTE standards and can be used with any core network. The 2G SIM authentication algorithm is set to COMP128v1 and the 3G/UMTS authentication algorithm to MILENAGE [25]. All cards ship with a factory-default, card-individual random K and OP_C. However, the cards are fully re-programmable and the user can re-program K, OP or OP_C.

Sysmocom USIM cards were one of the target cards in the CPA attack presented in [10]. The CPA attack presented in [10] used 4000 power traces to recover the key from a Sysmocom USIM card.

3.3 Trace Acquisition

In order to find a time interval containing the attack points, we used a high-end LeCroy oscilloscope with the maximum sampling rate 10 GS/s and 1 GHz bandwidth per channel. If only low-cost equipment such as ChipWhisperer-Lite is available, the same result can be achieved by capturing at a lower sampling rate and shifting the offset until the distinct shape of AES encryption is found.

To capture a single trace, the following three steps are repeated in the script for trace acquisition:

1. Select a random RAND 16-byte value.
2. Call MILENAGE algorithm with the RAND as seed. This turns on a trigger signal which stays high until a response is received.
3. Capture and save the power trace as well as RAND.

Figure 4 shows a full power trace of USIM card for one call of MILENAGE. Figure 5 presents a zoomed interval of the trace in which seven AES encryptions can be clearly distinguished. Note that MILENAGE calls the encryption E_k only six times (see Fig. 2). However E_k is also used to compute OP_C (see the box at

Fig. 4. Power trace from a USIM card for one authentication call.

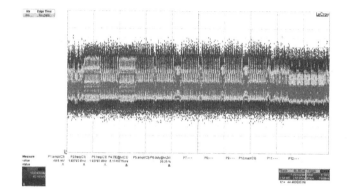

Fig. 5. Zoomed interval of the trace in Fig. 4 representing the MILENAGE execution.

the top right corner of Fig. 2). Even if OP_C is programmed into the USIM, it might by possible that the USIM performs the OP_C computation step anyway and then discards the result.

Since is was not clear whether the MILENAGE algorithm starts at the first or at the second AES encryption, we applied CPA to both time intervals. The CPA successfully recovered the key from 300 traces corresponding to the second AES encryption and failed on the first AES encryption. From this we concluded that the MILENAGE algorithm starts at the second AES encryption[1].

ChipWhisperer is well-known for its ability to perfectly synchronize traces. However, traces captured by ChipWhisperer in our experiments were desynchronized. Since ChipWhisperer controls LEIA and LEIA controls the USIM, when ChipWhisperer sends a command to the USIM to start MILENAGE, the command has to be forwarded by LEIA. The forwarding may cause de-synchronization.

Previous work on deep learning side-channel attacks on AES [22] has shown that desynchronized traces may be used directly if a CNN model is used for the attack. It is also possible to synchronize the traces before training and testing, regardless of the model's type. In our experiments we tried both approaches.

---

[1] In previous CPA attack on Sysmocom USIM cards [10] it was suggested that MILE-NAGE starts at the first AES encryption, but our results indicate otherwise.

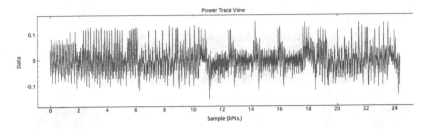

Fig. 6. Power trace representing the first round of AES (within 6KPt - 19KPt).

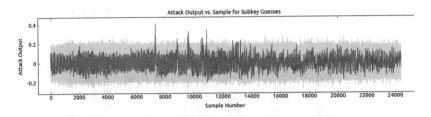

Fig. 7. Correlation results for the 10th byte of $OP_C \oplus K$.

3.4   Recovering Key from Profiling USIM by CPA

To train a deep learning model, we need a profiling USIM with known parameters K, OP_C, $r_1 - r_5$ and $c_1 - c_5$, The target USIMs in our experiments use default values for the constants $r_1 - r_5$ and $c_1 - c_5$[2]. They are also re-programmable, so we could simply re-write factory-default K and OP_C by new values. However, our focus is on extracting the factory-default K and OP_C in order to estimate the number of traces required for a successful CPA attack on this type of card. Below we describe our CPA attack based on the Hamming weight power model.

We can see from Fig. 2 that, at the first step of MILENAGE, $RAND \oplus OP_C$ is computed and then the result is encrypted. If AES-128 is used for implementing the encryption E_K, the 128-bit key K can be recovered as follows:

1. Use a USIM to execute MILENAGE for a large number of random challenges $RAND_0, \ldots, RAND_{n-1}$ and capture the resulting power traces $T = \{T_0, \ldots, T_{n-1}\}$ as described in Sect. 3.3.
2. First, recover $OP_C \oplus K$ by a CPA with the S-box output in the first round of AES as the attack point.
3. Second, recover the first round key, RK_1 by a CPA with the S-box output in the second round of AES as the attack point.
4. Using the key expansion algorithm of AES-128, deduce K from RK_1.
5. Compute OP_C as $OP_C = (OP_C \oplus K) \oplus K$.

---

[2] If a USIM uses non-default values for $r_1 - r_5$ and $c_1 - c_5$, they can be derived using the technique presented in [17].

A similar two-step strategy for recovering K and OP_C was used in the CPA attacks on MILENAGE presented in [10,17]. Next we describe the process of recovering $OP_C \oplus K$ in more details.

Figure 6 shows a power trace representing the execution of the first round of AES. The four operations SUBBYTES(), SHIFTROWS(), MIXCOLUMNS() and ADDROUNDKEY() are executed approximately between the points 6KPt and 19KPt.

Let $RAND_{j,k}$ denote the kth byte of $RAND_j$, $k \in \{0, \ldots, 15\}$, $j \in \{0, \ldots, n-1\}$. For each $RAND_j$ and each possible value $v \in \{0, \ldots, 255\}$ of the kth byte of $OP_C \oplus K$, the power estimate $x_{j,v}$ for the trace $T_j \in T$ and the guess v is calculated as the Hamming weight of the S-box output in the first round:

$$x_{j,v} = HW(\text{S-box}[RAND_{j,k} \oplus v]).$$

Let $y_{j,i}$ denote the data point i in the trace $T_j \in T$, for $j \in \{0, \ldots, n-1\}$, $i \in \{0, \ldots, m-1\}$, where m is the number of data points in the trace. For the trace in Fig. 6, $m = 24.4K$ (buffer size of ChipWhisperer-Lite).

To check how well the HW model and measured traces correlate for each guess v and data point i, Pearson correlation coefficients, $r_{v,i}$, for the data sets $\{x_{1,v}, \ldots, x_{n,v}\}$ and $\{y_{1,i}, \ldots, y_{n,i}\}$ are computed:

$$r_{v,i} = \frac{\sum_{j=0}^{n-1}(x_{j,v} - \bar{x}_v)(y_{j,i} - \bar{y}_i)}{\sqrt{\sum_{j=0}^{n-1}(x_{j,v} - \bar{x}_v)^2 \sum_{j=0}^{n-1}(y_{j,i} - \bar{y}_i)^2}},$$

where n is the sample size, and $\bar{x}_v = \frac{1}{n}\sum_{j=0}^{n-1} x_{j,v}$ and $\bar{y}_i = \frac{1}{n}\sum_{j=0}^{n-1} y_{j,i}$ are the sample means.

In our experiments, the maximum correlation coefficients for different bytes of $OP_C \oplus K$ ranged in the interval 0.2758–0.4208. Figure 7 shows correlation results for the 10th byte of $OP_C \oplus K$. One can clearly see distinct peaks.

Once all bytes of $OP_C \oplus K$ are recovered, we can estimate the number of traces required for a successful attack using the Partial Guessing Entropy (PGE) [20]. When the PGEs of all bytes reach zero, the $OP_C \oplus K$ is recovered. From Fig. 8, we can see that about 300 traces are required to recover the key in this attack.

The process of recovering RK_1 by a CPA with the S-box output in the second round AES as an attack point is similar. The power estimate $x_{j,v}$ for the trace $T_j \in T$, for $j \in \{0, \ldots, n-1\}$, and each RK_1 subkey guess $v \in \{0, \ldots, 255\}$ is calculated as the Hamming weight of the S-box output in the second round for the input $state_{j,k} \oplus v$, where $state_{j,k}$ is the kth byte of the AES state $state_j$ after SHIFTROWS() and MIXCOLUMNS() in the first round for the challenge $RAND_j$. Note that RK_1 can only be recovered after all bytes of $OP_C \oplus K$ are recovered because only then can SHIFTROWS() and MIXCOLUMNS() be fully evaluated. This is necessary for determining the input to the second round.

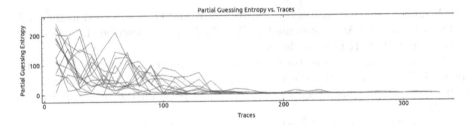

Fig. 8. Partial guessing entropy vs. number of traces.

3.5   Profiling Stage

At the profiling stage, the models $\text{CNN}_{1,k}$ and $\text{CNN}_{2,k}$ for recovering the bytes of $\text{OP}_C \oplus \text{K}$ and RK_1, respectively, are trained for all $k \in \{0, \ldots, 15\}$ as follows:

1. Identify the start of MILENAGE execution in the trace of the profiling USIM (see Fig. 4 and 5). Set the offset for capture so that traces include the computation of S-box in the first round of AES.
2. Use the profiling USIM to execute MILENAGE for a large number n_p of random challenges $\text{RAND}_0, \ldots, \text{RAND}_{n_p-1}$ and capture the resulting set of traces $\boldsymbol{T}_{p,1} = \{T_0, \ldots, T_{n_p-1}\}$. Let m be the number of data points in each trace $T_j \in \boldsymbol{T}_{p,1}$.
3. For each $k \in \{0, \ldots, 15\}$:
   - Assign to each trace $T_j \in \boldsymbol{T}_{p,1}$ a label $l_k(T_j)$ equal to the value of the S-box output in the first round during the evaluation of the kth byte of $\text{RAND}_j \oplus (\text{OP}_C \oplus \text{K})$:

$$l_k(T_j) = \text{S-box}[\text{RAND}_{j,k} \oplus (\text{OP}_C \oplus \text{K})_k],$$

   where $(\text{OP}_C \oplus \text{K})_k$ is the kth byte of $\text{OP}_C \oplus \text{K}$ and $\text{RAND}_{j,k}$ is the kth byte of the challenge RAND_j used to generate T_j. $\text{OP}_C \oplus \text{K}$ and $\text{RAND}_{j,k}$ is assumed to be known during profiling.
   - Use the labeled set of traces $\boldsymbol{T}_{p,1}$ to train a model $\text{CNN}_{1,k} : \mathbb{R}^m \to \mathbb{I}^{256}$, $\mathbb{I} := \{x \in \mathbb{R} \mid 0 \leq x \leq 1\}$, which takes as input a trace $T_j \in \mathbb{R}^m$ and produces as output a score vector $S_{j,k} = \text{CNN}_{1,k}(T_j) \in \mathbb{I}^{256}$ in which the value of the ith element, $s_{j,k,i}$, is the probability that the S-box output in the first round is equal to $i \in \{0, \ldots, 255\}$ when the kth byte of $\text{RAND}_j \oplus (\text{OP}_C \oplus \text{K})$ is processed:

$$s_{j,k,i} = \Pr(\text{S-box}[\text{RAND}_{j,k} \oplus (\text{OP}_C \oplus \text{K})_k] = i).$$

   The training strategy is described in Sect. 4.1.
4. Once all bytes of $\text{OP}_C \oplus \text{K}$ are recovered, use the profiling USIM to capture a large set of power traces $\boldsymbol{T}_{p,2}$ including the interval corresponding to the execution of S-box in the second round of AES.
5. For each $k \in \{0, \ldots, 15\}$:

– Assign to each trace $T_j \in \boldsymbol{T}_{p,2}$ a label $l_k(T_j)$ equal to the value of the S-box output in the second round during the evaluation of the kth byte of $state_j \oplus RK_1$:

$$l_k(T_j) = \text{S-box}[state_{j,k} \oplus RK_{1,k}],$$

where $RK_{1,k}$ is the kth subkey of the RK_1 and $state_{j,k}$ is the kth byte of $state_j$ after SHIFTROWS() and MIXCOLUMNS() in the first round for the challenge $RAND_j$. The value of $state_k$ is known for any $RAND_j$ once all bytes of $OP_C \oplus K$ are recovered.

– Use the labeled set of traces $\boldsymbol{T}_{p,2}$ to train a model $CNN_{2,k} : \mathbb{R}^m \to \mathbb{I}^{256}$ which takes as input a trace $T_j \in \mathbb{R}^m$ and produces as output a score vector $S_{j,k} = CNN_{2,k}(T_j) \in \mathbb{I}^{256}$ in which the value of the ith element, $s_{j,k,i}$, is the probability of that the S-box output in the second round is equal to $i \in \{0, \dots, 255\}$ when the kth byte of $state_j \oplus RK_1$ is processed:

$$s_{j,k,i} = \Pr(\text{S-box}[state_{j,k} \oplus RK_{1,k}] = i).$$

The training strategy is described in Sect. 4.1.

3.6   Attack Stage

At the attack stage, the trained models $CNN_{1,k}$ and $CNN_{2,k}$ are used to recover the kth byte of $OP_C \oplus K$ and RK_1, respectively, for all $k \in \{0, \dots, 15\}$.

To recover the bytes of $OP_C \oplus K$:

1. Identify the start of MILENAGE execution in the trace of the victim USIM (see Fig. 4 and 5). Set the offset for capture so that traces include the computation of S-box in the first round of AES.
2. Use the victim USIM to execute MILENAGE for a small number n_a of random challenges $RAND_0, \dots, RAND_{n_a-1}$ and capture the resulting set of traces $\boldsymbol{T}_{a,1} = \{T_0, \dots, T_{n_a-1}\}$, with m data points in each trace where m is the input size of $CNN_{1,k}$.
3. For each $k \in \{0, \dots, 15\}$, use the model $CNN_{1,k}$ to classify the traces of an ordered set $\boldsymbol{T}_{a,1}$. For each $j \in \{0, \dots, n_a - 1\}$, the trace $T_j \in \boldsymbol{T}_{a,1}$ is classified as

$$\tilde{l} = \operatorname*{arg\,max}_{i \in \{0, \dots, 255\}} \left(\prod_{l=0}^{j} s_{l,k,i} \right),$$

where $s_{l,k,i}$ is the ith element of the score vector $S_{l,k} = CNN_{1,k}(T_l)$ of a trace $T_l \in \boldsymbol{T}_{a,1}$ which precedes T_j in $\boldsymbol{T}_{a,1}$. Once $\tilde{l} = l_k(T_j)$, the classification is successful. The kth byte of $OP_C \oplus K$ is then recovered as

$$(OP_C \oplus K)_k = \text{S-box}^{-1}(l_k(T_j)) \oplus RAND_{j,k}.$$

where $RAND_{j,k}$ is the kth byte of $RAND_j$ used to generate the trace T_j.

The subkeys of the round key RK_1 are recovered similarly using the models $CNN_{2,k}$, $k \in \{0, \ldots, 15\}$, except that the offset for capture is selected so that traces of the set $\boldsymbol{T}_{a,2} = \{T_0, \ldots, T_{n_a-1}\}$ include the computation of S-box in the second round of AES. Once a trace $T_j \in \boldsymbol{T}_{a,2}$ is successfully classified as $\tilde{l} = l_k(T_j)$ for some $j \in \{0, \ldots, n_p - 1\}$, the kth byte of RK_1 is recovered as

$$RK_{1,k} = \text{S-box}^{-1}(l_k(T_j)) \oplus state_{j,k},$$

where $state_{j,k}$ is the kth byte of $state_j$ after SHIFTROWS() and MIXCOLUMNS() in the first round for the challenge $RAND_j$.

Finally, K is derived from RK_1 using the key expansion algorithm of AES.

4   Experimental Results

In the experiments, we used two identical USIMs of type described in Sect. 3.2. One card was used for profiling and another - for attack. In the section, we refer to these cards as $USIM_p$ and $USIM_a$, respectively.

Using the equipment and the method described in Sects. 3.1 and 3.3, we captured two large sets of traces of size $n_p = 35.5K$ from $USIM_p$ - one for the first round, $\boldsymbol{T}_{p,1}$, and another the second round of AES, $\boldsymbol{T}_{p,2}$. Similarly, we captured two smaller sets of traces, $\boldsymbol{T}_{a,1}$ and $\boldsymbol{T}_{a,2}$, of size $n_a = 6K$ from $USIM_a$. Each trace in these four sets contains $m = 24.4K$ data points.

4.1   Training Process

Initially, we tried three strategies: (1) Training an MLP model on synchronized traces; (2) Training a CNN model on synchronized traces; (3) Training a CNN model on de-synchronized traces.

Early testing showed that both MLP and CNN models trained on traces from $USIM_p$ can recover subkeys from $USIM_a$. It was also possible to recover the key using a CNN model trained on de-synchronized traces. However, the CNN model trained on synchronized traces has shown significantly better results than the other two, so we focused on it.

We used 70% of traces from $USIM_p$ for training and 30% for validation. We searched for the best options for learning rate, number of epochs, and number of layers. A lot of different sizes of filter kernels were tried for the convolution layers, and different input sizes were tested.

After many experiments, we settled for the model with the architecture shown in Table 1. The model was trained for 100 epochs using batch size 100. The RMSprop optimizer with a learning rate of 0.0001 and no learning rate decay was used. No dropout was used. We found it is best to train on the entire buffer of ChipWhisperer, which contains 24.4K data points. For this reason, the input layer size of the model in Table 1 is 24.4K. The first kernel is quite large because the execution of S-box operation takes a large number of data points (approx. 900). The shape of a power trace suggests that a single S-box operation is performed on four bytes at a time, i.e. this USIM uses a 32-bit microcontroller.

Table 1. Architecture of the best CNN model.

Layer type	Output shape	Parameter #
Input (Dense)	(None, 24400, 1)	0
Conv1D 1	(None, 24400, 8)	7208
AveragePooling1 1	(None, 3050, 8)	0
Conv1D 2	(None, 3050, 16)	1296
AveragePooling1 2	(None, 305, 16)	0
Conv1D 3	(None, 305, 32)	5152
AveragePooling1 3	(None, 61, 32)	0
Conv1D 4	(None, 61, 64)	18496
AveragePooling1 4	(None, 6, 64)	0
Conv1D 5	(None, 4, 128)	24704
AveragePooling1 5	(None, 1, 128)	0
Flatten	(None, 128)	0
Dense 1	(None, 300)	38700
Output (Dense)	(None, 256)	77056

Total Parameters: 172,612

To train the model $CNN_{1,k}$ which classifies the kth byte of $OP_C \oplus K$, each trace $T_j \in \boldsymbol{T}_{p,1}$ is assigned a label equal to the value of the S-box output for the input $RAND_{j,k} \oplus (OP_C \oplus K)_k$, where $RAND_{j,k}$ is the kth byte of the challenge $RAND_j$ used to generate T_j, for all $k \in \{0, \ldots, 15\}$ and $j \in \{0, \ldots, n_p - 1\}$.

To train the model $CNN_{2,k}$ which classifies the kth subkey of RK_1, each trace $T_j \in \boldsymbol{T}_{p,2}$ is assigned a label equal to the value of the S-box output for the input $state_{j,k} \oplus RK_{1,k}$, where $state_{j,k}$ is the kth byte of $state_j$ after SHIFTROWS() and MIXCOLUMNS() in the first round, for all $k \in \{0, \ldots, 15\}$ and $j \in \{0, \ldots, n_p - 1\}$.

We would like to mention that it might possible to train a *single* neural network capable of recovering any byte of $OP_C \oplus K$ (or RK_1). Such a possibility has been already demonstrated for an 8-bit microcontroller implementation of AES-128 [6]. The MLP model presented in [6] can recover all subkeys from the target device different from the profiling device. The MLP was trained on a union of 16 sets of power traces $\boldsymbol{T}_k = \{T_{k,1}, \ldots, T_{k,n}\}$, $k \in \{0, \ldots, 15\}$, such that the trace $T_{k,j} \in \boldsymbol{T}_k$, $j \in \{0, \ldots, n-1\}$, contains data points in which S-box evaluates the kth byte of P $\oplus$ K, where P is the plaintext. However, taking into account that our USIM implementation of AES-128 is based on a 32-bit microcontroller, we have chosen to train the networks separately for each byte position.

4.2 Testing Results

For any $k \in \{0, 1, \ldots, 15\}$, the $CNN_{1,k}$ with the architecture shown in Table 1 trained on traces $\boldsymbol{T}_{p,1}$ from $USIM_p$ successfully recovers the kth byte of $OP_C \oplus$

K from at most 10 traces $T_{a,1}$ of $USIM_a$. The byte number does not seem to matter. As an example, Fig. 9(a) and (b) show the worst and the average ranks of models $CNN_{1,0}$ and $CNN_{1,5}$. One can see that the plots are similar. For $k = 0$, the average number of traces is 2.24. For $k = 5$, it is 2.5.

Similarly, for any $k \in \{0, 1, \ldots, 15\}$, the $CNN_{2,k}$ with the architecture shown in Table 1 trained on traces $T_{p,2}$ from $USIM_p$ successfully recovers the kth subkey of RK_1 from at most 20 traces $T_{a,2}$ of $USIM_a$ (see Fig. 9(c)). The average number of traces for $k = 0$ in the second round is 4.09.

We believe that the results for the first and second rounds are different because we tuned the model architecture in Table 1 for the first round. Since we trained on the entire buffer of ChipWhisperer, traces of the first round include the computation of $RAND \oplus (OP_C \oplus K)$ in the initial round. By selecting the segments of traces more carefully and making the model's input size equal to exact size of rounds, it might be possible to get more similar results.

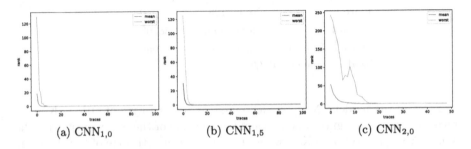

(a) $CNN_{1,0}$ (b) $CNN_{1,5}$ (c) $CNN_{2,0}$

Fig. 9. Average and worst ranks for 6K traces from $USIM_a$.

We also tested the models' abilities to attack other byte positions. Unsurprisingly, the $CNN_{1,0}$ could not recover the 5th byte of $OP_C \oplus K$ and vice versa, the $CNN_{1,5}$ could not recover the 0th byte of $OP_C \oplus K$. More surprising was that the $CNN_{1,0}$ showed no noticeable ability to recover the 0th subkey of RK_1. Previous work has shown that some deep learning models can do that [6]. We suppose that this is a drawback of training on the entire buffer, 24.4K data points, instead of the part of the trace corresponding to the S-box operation only, as in [6].

On the positive side, our current methodology yields highly specialized models with excellent classification accuracy. Recall that we need 300 traces from the USIM to recover the key by CPA (see Fig. 8). So, the presented models require an order of magnitude fewer traces from the victim USIM to recover the key.

5   Conclusion

We demonstrated a profiled deep learning attack on a commercial USIM card which requires less than 20 traces to recover the key (four traces on average).

Given the huge investments in deep learning, deep learning techniques are likely to become more efficient in the future. More efficient techniques may reduce the number of traces required recover the key from a USIM to a single trace. This may have serious consequences for the security of services and applications provided by mobile communication networks unless appropriate countermeasures are designed.

Acknowledgements. The authors are deeply grateful to Christophe Devine at ANSSI for providing us with re-programmable USIM cards and David Elbaze at ANSSI for helping us debug our problems with the LEIA platform. We also want to thank Huanyu Wang at KTH for helping with getting LEIA manufactured.

References

1. 3GPP TS 33.501: Security architecture and procedures for 5G system. http://www.3gpp.org/DynaReport/33501.htm
2. 3GPP TS 35.206: MILENAGE algorithm set: Algorithm specification. http://www.3gpp.org/DynaReport/35206.htm
3. 3GPP TS 35.231: Specification of the TUAK algorithm set. http://www.3gpp.org/DynaReport/35231.htm
4. 3GPP TS 55.205: GSM-MILENAGE algorithms: Functions a3 and a8. http://www.3gpp.org/DynaReport/55205.htm
5. Arkko, J., Norrman, K., Näslund, M., Sahlin, B.: A USIM compatible 5G AKA protocol with perfect forward secrecy. In: 2015 IEEE Trustcom/BigDataSE/ISPA, vol. 1, pp. 1205–1209, August 2015
6. Brisfors, M., Forsmark, S.: Deep-learning side-channel attacks on AES. B.Sc. thesis, KTH, TRITA-EECS-EX-2019:110 (2019)
7. Cagli, E., Dumas, C., Prouff, E.: Convolutional neural networks with data augmentation against jitter-based countermeasures. In: CHES, pp. 45–68 (2017)
8. Cryptography for mobile network - C implementation and Python bindings. https://github.com/mitshell/CryptoMobile
9. CW308 UFO Target. https://wiki.newae.com/CW308_UFO_Target
10. Devine, C., Pedro, M.S., Thillard, A.: A practical guide to differential power analysis of USIM cards. In: SSTIC (2018)
11. El-Baze, D., Renard, M., Trebuchet, P., Benadjila, R.: LEIA: the lab embedded ISO7816 analyzer a custom smartcard reader for the ChipWhisperer. In: SSTIC (2019)
12. Gilmore, R., Hanley, N., O'Neill, M.: Neural network based attack on a masked implementation of AES. In: HOST, pp. 106–111 (2015)
13. Goldberg, W.: GSM cloning. www.isaac.cs.berkeley.edu/isaac/gsm.html
14. GSM World: Brief history of GSM & the GSMA. http://gsmworld.com/about-us/history.htm
15. GSMA: SG.03 rules for the management and the distribution of the GSM example algorithm A3/A8 (COMP 128, COMP 128–2, and COMP128-3) used for authentication and cipher key generation v3.6
16. Hulton, D.: 3GPP 5G security (2018). http://www.dachb0den.com/projects/scard/smartcards.ppt
17. Liu, J., et al.: Small tweaks do not help: differential power analysis of MILENAGE implementations in 3G/4G USIM cards. In: ESORICS, pp. 468–480 (2015)

18. Briceno, M., Goldberg, I., Wagner, D.: An implementation of the GSM A3/A8 algorithm (specifically COMP128). http://www.iol.ie/~kooltek/a3a8.txt
19. NewAE Technology: Chipwhisperer. https://newae.com/tools/chipwhisperer
20. Pahlevanzadeh, H., Dofe, J., Yu, Q.: Assessing CPA resistance of AES with different fault tolerance mechanisms. In: ASP-DAC, pp. 661–666, January 2016
21. Prasad, A.R., Zugenmaier, A., Escott, A., Soveri, M.C.: 3GPP 5G security. https://www.3gpp.org/news-events/1975-sec_5g
22. Prouff, E., Strullu, R., Benadjila, R., Cagli, E., Canovas, C.: Study of deep learning techniques for side-channel analysis and introduction to ASCAD database. IACR Cryptol. ePrint Arch. **2018**, 053 (2018)
23. SIMalliance: (2018). https://simalliance.org/wp-content/uploads/2018/11/What-is-a-3GPP-R15-5G-SIM-card-20-11-2018-FINAL-1.pdf
24. Tamas, J.: Secrets of the SIM. http://www.hackingprojects.net/2013/04/secrets-of-sim.html
25. Welte, H.: SysmoUSIM-SJS1 user manual (2016)

Differential Analysis and Fingerprinting of ZombieLoads on Block Ciphers

Till Schlüter[1,2,3(✉)] and Kerstin Lemke-Rust[2]

[1] CISPA Helmholtz Center for Information Security, Saarbrücken, Germany
till.schlueter@cispa.de
[2] Bonn-Rhein-Sieg University of Applied Sciences, Sankt Augustin, Germany
till.schlueter@smail.inf.h-brs.de, kerstin.lemke-rust@h-brs.de
[3] Saarbrücken Graduate School of Computer Science, Saarbrücken, Germany

Abstract. Microarchitectural Data Sampling (MDS) [16,18] enables to observe in-flight data that has recently been loaded or stored in shared short-time buffers on a physical CPU core. In-flight data sampled from line-fill buffers (LFBs) are also known as "ZombieLoads" [16]. We present a new method that links the analysis of ZombieLoads to Differential Power Analysis (DPA) techniques and provides an alternative way to derive the secret key of block ciphers. This method compares observed ZombieLoads with predicted intermediate values that occur during cryptographic computations depending on a key hypothesis and known data. We validate this approach using an Advanced Encryption Standard (AES) software implementation. Further, we provide a novel technique of *cache line fingerprinting* that reduces the superposition of ZombieLoads from different cache lines in the data sets resulting from an MDS attack. Thereby, this technique is helpful to reveal static secret data such as AES round keys which is shown in practice on an AES implementation.

Keywords: ZombieLoad · Side channel attack · Microarchitectural Data Sampling (MDS) · Differential analysis · DPA · Block cipher · AES · Cache line fingerprinting

1 Introduction

Many attacks targeting optimization mechanisms of modern CPUs have been published in recent years. A subset of those, Microarchitectural Data Sampling (MDS) attacks, are applicable to the majority of Intel CPUs sold in the last decade [5], affecting a significant number of personal computers and servers worldwide. ZombieLoad [16] is one representative from this class. It allows an attacker to observe data from memory lines that have recently been loaded or stored at the time of the attack on the same physical core. The *domino attack* uses this primitive to recover the secret key from an AES implementation [16].

In this paper, we investigate further methods to extract secret keys from block cipher implementations using ZombieLoad primitives. First, we present

© Springer Nature Switzerland AG 2021
P.-Y. Liardet and N. Mentens (Eds.): CARDIS 2020, LNCS 12609, pp. 151–165, 2021.
https://doi.org/10.1007/978-3-030-68487-7_10

a new differential technique by considering that ZombieLoads can also stem from intermediate computational results of a block cipher. We recover the key by linking ZombieLoads with analysis techniques originating from Differential Power Analysis (DPA): we predict expected intermediate results and use a statistical analysis to determine the key. Because of this, protecting the secret key, for example by transferring it as rarely as possible or in obfuscated form, might not be sufficient to protect cryptographic implementations from MDS leakage. Second, we provide cache line fingerprinting as a useful tool to reliably associate ZombieLoads to their original static byte sequence within a memory line.

This paper is structured as follows: We give an introduction into transient execution and cache leakage, MDS attacks with focus on ZombieLoad, and DPA in Sect. 2. Next, we make the following contributions: In Sect. 3, we transfer the idea of analyzing intermediate results of a cryptographic algorithm from DPA into the domain of MDS post-processing. We present the general analysis procedure as well as a case study to an AES implementation. In Sect. 4, we further introduce an independent tool called *cache line fingerprinting* that makes it easier to assign leaked bytes to their originating cache lines. We show that this tool is suitable to leak AES round keys in an exemplary implementation.

2   Preliminaries

2.1   Transient Execution and Cache Leakage

The publication of Spectre and Meltdown [8,9] introduced a new class of side-channel attacks that use effects of microarchitectural optimization techniques of modern CPUs to leak data across privilege boundaries. These attacks make use of specially crafted *transient instructions*, i.e., instructions that are erroneously executed due to false predictions or out-of-order processing. Following this observation, many further transient execution attacks targeting different microarchitectural structures have been published in recent years [3].

Transient execution attacks often influence microarchitectural structures like caches in a targeted manner to encode information into them: An attacker process allocates a so-called *probe array* in memory and ensures that it is not cached. The size of the probe array is often set to $256 \cdot p$ bytes, where p is the page size in bytes, e.g., $p = 4096$. This array is suitable to encode the value v of a single byte into the cache by transiently accessing index $v \cdot p$. When an element of the probe array is accessed by a transient instruction, the memory line containing this array element is loaded into the cache and remains cached even when the CPU detects the erroneous execution and discards all speculative results [9].

Depending on the microarchitectural implementation, some security checks are not yet performed during transient execution. Thus, an attacker can use transient instructions to perform unauthorized load requests to otherwise inaccessible memory regions and extract them using the cache side-channel [9].

2.2   Microarchitectural Data Sampling (MDS) and ZombieLoad

Microarchitectural data sampling attacks extract in-flight data of concurrent processes, e.g., values that are loaded from or stored to memory in close temporal proximity to the attack. MDS attacks published to date target different microarchitectural structures to extract data from. They focus on store buffers [2], fill buffers [16,18], or structures concerned with bus snooping [4]. Further improvements include targeted attacks on attacker-specified memory regions [17] and attacks that overcome the common precondition that victim and attacker share the same physical CPU core [14].

In this paper, we mostly build upon the findings of the ZombieLoad publication [16]. ZombieLoad allows to observe values loaded from (or stored in) memory at the time of the attack across logical cores. It presumably leaks values that are present in line-fill buffers (LFBs), an intermediate stage between the L1 cache and higher-level caches. LFBs are shared among all processes executed on the same physical CPU core, including processes that are concurrently executed on the same physical but different logical core. On vulnerable CPUs, memory load operations are not canceled immediately when a fault (e.g., a page fault) occurs. Instead, the load may speculatively be answered with a value from an LFB. Until the fault is handled and the result of the load request is discarded, the CPU may execute additional transient instructions that operate on stale values from an LFB and leak them through a cache-based side-channel. Leaking data may stem from concurrent user-space applications, the kernel, SGX enclaves, hypervisors or virtual machines running on sibling cores [16].

Attack Variants. In this paper, we use ZombieLoad variants 1 and 2. Variant 1 is closely related to the Meltdown attack, abusing transient instructions after a page fault. Variant 2, also known as TSX Asynchronous Abort (TAA), makes use of insufficient transient error handling in the transactional memory implementation when a memory conflict occurs. Both variants are well suited for attacks among user space processes on Linux systems [16].

Further ZombieLoad variants use properties of SGX, unchangeable memory regions or page-table walks [16]. A similar approach to leak data from LFBs is Rogue In-Flight Data Load (RIDL) [18] which uses page faults that occur due to demand paging.

Domino Attack. The domino attack is a ZombieLoad case study to leak the key from an AES implementation [16]. The 16-byte key has to be observed multiple times and is extracted byte-by-byte. First, the attacker samples bytes from varying positions in arbitrary LFB entries. To find bytes chains that frequently appear together (and therefore are key candidates), so-called *domino bytes*, combinations of two neighboring bytes, are leaked as well. Domino bytes are leaked through the same side-channel as data bytes, but in separate ZombieLoad iterations. Finally, the attacker searches the sampled data for chains of 16 consecutive bytes that are backed by both bytes from LFB entries and domino bytes to find AES key candidates [16].

2.3 Differential Power Analysis and Its Application to White-Box Implementations

DPA [7,10] exploits the fact that processing an algorithm on a hardware platform causes (noisy) physical side-channel leakage such as data-dependent power consumption over time. If a cryptographic algorithm is considered, the side-channel leakage can include information about secret cryptographic keys.

A DPA attacker samples the power consumption of a circuit over time and thereby obtains a high number of noisy sampled data per execution of an algorithm, i.e., a DPA trace. As DPA is a statistical attack, many repetitions of algorithm execution are carried out using varying known input (or output) data to the cryptographic implementation. For analysis, the attacker predicts the intermediate state of the cryptographic implementation and thereby derives the expected power consumption in a hypothetical model dependent on known input (or output) data and a key hypothesis using a divide-and-conquer approach. If the model is suited and leaks exist, the predicted values show a high degree of correlation with the measured samples for the correct key. The model is typically applied to internal intermediate state values that occur at the beginning (or the end) of the cryptographic computation.

Adaptations of this attack on a white-box software implementation used Dynamic Binary Instrumentation (DBI) tools to record traces of memory transactions that are comparable to noise-free DPA traces and can be analyzed in a similar way [1].

3   Differential Analysis of ZombieLoads

3.1 System and Attacker Model

System Model. A victim process runs a block cipher that repeatedly encrypts or decrypts a given input with a fixed key. The input varies periodically. We assume that the block cipher computations are performed in software on a CPU that is vulnerable to an MDS attack.

Attacker Model. An attacker program runs concurrently to the victim process on the sibling core and constantly collects samples using an MDS attack, e.g., ZombieLoad. We assume that the attacker knows the inputs or outputs (plaintexts or ciphertexts) as well as the used block cipher. The attacker has the capability to freely choose the byte index within the LFB entry from which the next sample is leaked. Assuming that the LFB consists of N_b bytes, the attacker maintains N_b sampling pools for each known plaintext (or ciphertext). Let N be the number of different plaintexts (or ciphertexts), each sampling pool is indexed with the pair (i, j) with $0 \leq i < N_b$ and $0 \leq j < N$.

3.2 Attack Procedure

The differential attack is divided into two phases, sampling and analysis. These can optionally be preceded by a profiling phase.

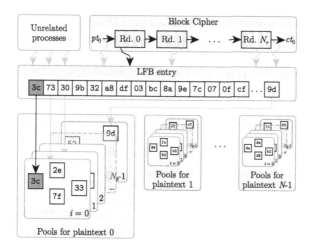

Fig. 1. Sampling process for differential analysis

Sampling. Figure 1 illustrates the data flow during sampling. While the victim process executes the block cipher, the attacker collects samples from varying byte indices i and sorts each of them into the according sampling pool indexed with the pair (i, j) of LFB byte index (i) and a reference to the plaintext that was encrypted during sampling (j). In practice, the observed samples may stem from observable intermediate results of block cipher operations in one of N_r rounds, from the processed plaintext or ciphertext or from unrelated processes which contribute additional noise. The sampling process has three distinctive properties: First, a very low sampling rate, i.e., the sampling frequency is small compared to the frequency of block ciphering operations, second, asynchronous sampling, i.e., a synchronization with the ciphering process is hard for the attacker's process, and third, random sampling, i.e., the origin and outcome of the next sampling process is unknown.

Analysis. In the analysis phase, a divide-and-conquer key hypothesis test similar to DPA [7, 10] is executed. The attacker targets each key byte individually. For each key byte, the attacker computes the intermediate values that are expected to leak for each of the 256 possible values. For the correct key byte hypotheses, the expected intermediate values appear in the corresponding sampling pools.

Profiling (Optional). The exact analysis algorithm clearly depends on the leakage pattern of the victim application and the used block cipher. The attacker can either guess which intermediate values leak during computation or use an identical implementation to the victim process to characterize the probability distribution of relevant observables in the sampling pools. We refer to the latter option as *profiling*. To profile an implementation, we set it up to process a fixed known input with a fixed known key repeatedly while ZombieLoad samples are collected. All intermediate values that potentially occur can easily be computed off-line or extracted from a running process using a debugger. We search the extracted samples for the computed intermediate values. Those values that occur in the correct sampling pools are candidates for attack vectors in the analysis phase.

3.3   Case Study: Practical Application to an AES Implementation

To show that our attack is indeed practical, we picked a byte-oriented AES implementation called *aes-min*[1] as a target to tailor an exemplary differential attack. All AES functions are implemented closely to the specification [13] in C and without optimizations in terms of side-channel resistance. *aes-min* is meant to be used on embedded devices with limited resources [11] but can also be compiled for general-purpose CPUs.

Table 1. CPUs under investigation.

CPU	Microarchitecture	Microcode	Environment	TSX	AES-NI
i3-2120	Sandy Bridge	0x28	Lab	✗	✗
i7-2620M	Sandy Bridge	0x1a	Lab	✗	✓
i5-4300M	Haswell	0x1c	Lab	✗	✓
Xeon E3-1270v6	Kaby Lake	0xb4	Cloud	✓	✓
i7-8650U	Kaby Lake R	0x96	Lab	✓	✓

Testing Environment. We used the CPUs from Table 1 running Debian 9 and gcc 6.3.0-18 for our experiments. We distinguish between lab CPUs running an uniform operating system image with LXDE user interface, and Cloud CPUs, which were rented as dedicated machines from a hosting provider running a pre-installed Debian 9 image without graphical user interface. Relevant mitigations including Kernel Address Space Layout Randomization (KASLR), Kernel Page-Table Isolation (KPTI), or clearing vulnerable CPU buffers were disabled on all systems[2]. We used a signal handler to handle the fault triggered by ZombieLoad attack variant 1 architecturally, as TSX is not supported by some of our systems.

Profiling *aes-min*. We executed the profiling step on the i7-2620M CPU using ZombieLoad variant 1. We computed the AES state after each operation off-line and used these values to assign the recorded samples to their originating state with high probability. Figure 2 shows that we observed leakage from the AES state after every operation in every round, as well as plaintext (0/input) and ciphertext (10/output). About 59% of the samples could not be assigned to any

---

[1] https://github.com/cmcqueen/aes-min/tree/728e156091/.
[2] Kernel parameters: `nokaslr nopti mds=off tsx_async_abort=off`.

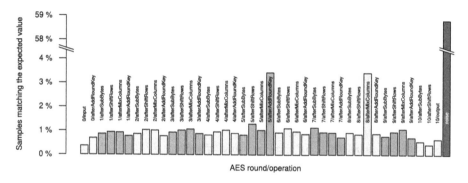

Fig. 2. Empirical assignment of samples to AES operations for *aes-min* on i7-2620M.

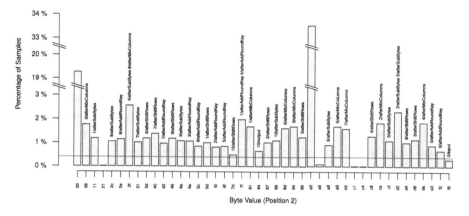

Fig. 3. Empirical distribution of samples at byte position 2 for *aes-min* on i7-2620M.

of the AES states and are therefore considered noise. There are two states that appear to leak more samples than the other. These states contain the byte value 00, which is generally overrepresented because it is the fallback value for failed ZombieLoad attempts.

Figure 3 shows all the byte values that occurred during an *aes-min* encryption for a specific byte position. We observed that noise is limited to seven values on average for most byte positions. Many of the 256 possible values do not appear at all. The red line in Fig. 3 shows the expectancy value for the assumption that all recorded samples distributed equally over the 256 possible values. Most noise values stay below the red line while bytes that occur in intermediate states stay above. This value could therefore be used as a threshold to filter out noise.

Analysis Algorithm for *aes-min*. Our analysis algorithm in Fig. 4 conducts the key hypothesis test: the attack targets each byte of the key on its own (line 2) and also considers the samples recorded for each plaintext independently (line 3). All further steps are conducted only with those samples that match these properties, i.e., which were sorted into the same sampling pool.

Require: p: Array containing the plaintexts used during the attack.
   SP: Matrix of sampling pools after measurement.
Ensure: k^*: Array containing the best key hypothesis for each index.
 1: $\mathbf{C} = 0$
 2: **for** $idx = 0$ **to** 15 **do**
 3:    **for** $pt = 0$ **to** $\mathrm{length}(p) - 1$ **do**
 4:       **for** $hyp = 0$ **to** 255 **do**
 5:          $afterARK = p\,[pt]\,[idx] \oplus hyp$
 6:          $afterSB = \texttt{SubBytes}(afterARK)$
 7:          **if** $afterARK \in SP\,[idx]\,[pt]$ **and** $afterSB \in SP\,[idx]\,[pt]$ **then**
 8:             $c_{idx,hyp} \mathrel{+}= 1$
 9:          **end if**
10:       **end for**
11:    **end for**
12:    $k^*_{idx} = \underset{hyp}{\mathrm{argmax}}\ c_{idx,hyp}$
13: **end for**

Fig. 4. Differential analysis algorithm for *aes-min* (pseudo code)

We compute the first steps of an AES encryption for a known plaintext byte. Remember that the AES encryption starts with `AddRoundKey` followed by a `SubBytes` operation [13]. Since the correct key byte is unknown, we simply perform these calculations for all 256 possible values (line 4-6). For the correct key byte hypothesis, we expect that both intermediate results appear at least once in the curent sampling pool (line 7). If this is the case, we record the observation in a result matrix $\mathbf{C} = (c_{idx,hyp})$, $0 \leq idx < 16, 0 \leq hyp < 256$. $\mathbf{C}$ is initialized to zero (line 1). Each element $c_{idx,hyp}$ represents a counter that is increased when all expected intermediate values for key hypothesis hyp at index idx occur in the current sampling pool (line 8). The underlying idea for key recovery is that the counters for the correct key hypotheses increase faster than for any other hypotheses the more different plaintexts are analyzed. If leakage exists, the most probable 16-byte key hypothesis can finally be extracted from $\mathbf{C}$: the column index hyp of the maximum value in each row idx specifies the most probable key byte at index idx (line 12).

Success Rates for *aes-min*. Figure 2 shows that we identified 41 intermediate AES observables that appear in ZombieLoads during *aes-min* encryptions. We simplify that each observable AES intermediate result appears in the samples and additional noise is neglected. Considerng the algorithm of Fig. 4, false positives for wrong key hypotheses can be produced by `AddRoundKey` and `SubBytes` operations in the subsequent nine AES rounds, any pair of the 21 remaining observable AES operations (plaintext byte, ten `ShiftRows`, nine `MixColumns` and one `AddRoundKey` which yields the ciphertext byte), or combinations thereof. They are sieved out by considering multiple plaintexts.

We performed 200,000 noise-free simulations of this leakage pattern for a single byte and received approximately 13.01 competing key hypotheses on average after the first plaintext, including the correct one. We further simulated 200,000 noise-free attacks on the full AES key to determine how many plaintexts are required to find it. We consider the key found as soon as the most probable key byte hypothesis matches the correct key byte for all 16 positions. Using the outputs of AddRoundKey *and* SubBytes as shown in Fig. 4, line 7, two plaintexts were enough to leak the full key in very rare cases (0.02%). After three plaintexts, 69% of the attacks were successful, 98% succeeded after four plaintexts and eight plaintexts were required at most. If we only used the value after AddRoundKey *or* SubBytes in line 7, three plaintexts would be sufficient for very rare cases (0.03%), 25% of the attacks succeeded after four plaintexts, 83% after five, 97% after six, and all after considering eleven plaintexts.

Table 2. Experimental results for the differential attack on different CPUs ($n = 10$ repetitions).

	CPU	Variant	No. of samples	Samples/ plaintext	Avg. duration (s)	Avg. key bytes	Full key recoveries
(1)	i3-2120	1	30,000	500	3.4	14.7	1/10 (10%)
			100,000	1,000	10.0	16.0	10/10 (100%)
	i7-2620M	1	60,000	8,000	6.2	14.9	1/10 (10%)
			200,000	4,000	53.7	16.0	10/10 (100%)
	i5-4300M	1	20,000	1,000	8.0	13.2	1/10 (10%)
			200,000	4,000	65.4	16.0	10/10 (100%)
(2)	E3-1270v6	1	3,000	500	732.7	0	0/10 (0%)
	i7-8650U	1	3,000	500	1,033.4	0	0/10 (0%)
(3)	E3-1270v6	2	800,000	300	405.1	11.7	0/10 (0%)
	i7-8650U	2	600,000	1,000	122.3	14.8	4/10 (40%)
			800,000	300	197.2	15.8	8/10 (80%)

Experimental Results for *aes-min*. We implemented[3] a wrapper program around *aes-min* that takes a 16 byte plaintext, which is repeatedly encrypted with a hard coded key until the process is shut down. It performs approx. 298,000 encryptions per second on the 9-year-old i3-2120 and approx. 528,000 on the most recent of our CPUs (i7-8650U). This victim process is started by the attacker who also chooses the plaintext. ZombieLoad samples are collected while the process is running and stored in the corresponding sampling pools. The plaintext is changed in predefined intervals by stopping the victim process and starting it again with a different plaintext. While this approach technically implements a chosen-plaintext scenario, it should be noted that it is not strictly necessary for an attacker to choose the plaintext freely. The attack is also applicable in a known-plaintext scenario where each plaintext is repeatedly encrypted during a time frame known to the attacker. After collecting a sufficient number of samples, we stop the victim program and execute the analysis algorithm from Fig. 4.

---

[3] The source code of all implementations used in this paper can be found at https://github.com/tillschlueter/zombieload-on-block-ciphers.

We executed the attack based on ZombieLoad variant 1 first. We set the number of samples to collect to 3,000, 10,000, 20,000, 30,000, 60,000, 100,000, or 200,000, while changing the plaintext every 500, 1,000, 4,000, or 8,000 samples. For each parameter combination, we repeated the attack 10 times. A subset of the results is listed in Table 2, section (1). For each CPU, we list results for two parameter sets: first, for the smallest number of samples and plaintexts required to recover the full AES key in 1 out of 10 tries in our experiments, and second, for the smallest parameters required to recover the key in 10 out of 10 tries. The average attack duration for the first parameter set is between 3.4 to 8.0 s, while it varies between 10.0 and 65.4 s for the second parameter set. The number of plaintexts used ranges from 8 to 100.

The attack was unsuccessful for the Kaby Lake CPUs in our test field, as shown in section (2) of Table 2: We observed many unrelated samples with value 0x00 at those positions where we expected AES intermediates. Filtering out these values led to very low average sampling rates (<10 B/s) in this attack scenario, and the resulting samples were still unrelated to the targeted intermediate values. Because both affected CPUs support TSX, we tried using ZombieLoad variant 2 instead. To overcome low sampling rates with variant 2, we allocated the probe array on a single 2 MB page. This allows us to load the address translation into the Translation Lookaside Buffer (TLB) in advance, ensuring that no costly page table walk has to be performed during transient execution. With variant 2, we received samples containing the targeted intermediate values, as well as many unrelated samples, leading to many false positives in the analysis phase. To counter this effect, we collected more samples (200,000, 400,000, 600,000, or 800,000) and changed plaintexts more frequently (after 300, 500, or 1,000 samples). In this way we could find up to 11.7 key bytes on average on the Xeon E3-1270v6 CPU, while full key recovery was possible on the i7-8650U (see Table 2(3)). For the latter CPU, we list the parameter set with the smallest number of samples and plaintexts required for full key recovery and the parameter set that led to the most successful attacks in our experimental setup (8/10 tries).

We conclude that type and quantity of leakage strongly depends on the specific environment and the microarchitecture, and that implementations that leak fewer values in one setting may behave differently in others.

4   Cache Line Fingerprinting

In this section, we propose a new fingerprinting technique to extract constant chains of consecutive bytes (like cryptographic keys) from frequently observed cache lines. As Wampler et al. [19] demonstrated in a Spectre scenario, it is sometimes possible to access the probe array multiple times from within a single transient execution window. This approach also works in the context of MDS attacks [12,15]. Instead of using the additional capacity to extract multiple bytes from the same LFB entry, we propose to transfer an additional byte that identifies the LFB entry from which the data value was sampled with high probability. We call this byte a *cache line fingerprint*.

4.1   Attack Procedure

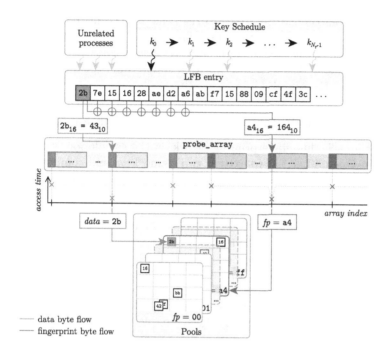

Fig. 5. Storage of leaked bytes in pools. For each byte, the appropriate pool is selected based on the fingerprint of the originating LFB entry.

An overview of the cache line fingerprinting method is given in Fig. 5. During transient execution, the probe array is accessed twice. To prevent collisions of these accesses, the length of the probe array is doubled to $4096 \cdot 512$ bytes. As in previous attacks, the first access is used to encode a data byte from the LFB into the first half of the probe array. Then we make use of the fact that the whole LFB entry is accessible during transient execution and generate a fingerprint using a function that maps from a subset of the LFB entry content to a single byte. We achieved good results with a fingerprint function that computes the logical XOR operation on the first eight bytes. This function covers a sufficiently large subset of the LFB entry to identify it and is yet fast to compute. The fingerprint byte is encoded into the second half of the probe array. Finally, the attacker program iterates over the extended probe array and recovers a pair $(data,\ fp)$ containing a data byte and a fingerprint byte.

Again, we store the recovered bytes in multiple pools as shown in Fig. 5. We set up one pool for each possible fingerprint value, i.e., 256 pools for an 8-bit fingerprint. Each data byte $data$ is stored in the pool that is indexed with the fingerprint value fp. Within the pool, data bytes are further separated by their position in the LFB entry.

When the same cache line is observed again in a later ZombieLoad iteration, the generated fingerprint will be identical. This property allows to assign bytes from several ZombieLoad iterations to the same fingerprint pool and therefore to the same cache line – apart from collisions, i.e., when two or more cache lines are mapped to the same fingerprint. If necessary, collisions could be further reduced by changing the fingerprint function or determining expected probability distributions for the samples in a fingerprint pool.

4.2   Practical Application to an AES Implementation

We mount a cache line fingerprinting attack on the calculation of the AES key schedule in OpenSSL 1.1.0l to extract two round keys and compute the initial key. This method enables us to automatically identify AES (round) keys in the leaked sample set and even works if the initial key is subject to increased noise while some round keys are less affected.

A victim process uses the EVP_* functions in OpenSSL's *libcrypto* to repeatedly compute the AES key schedule and encrypt a message while an attacker program concurrently performs ZombieLoads with cache line fingerprinting on a sibling core. For AES128, 11 round keys (k_0, k_1, ..., k_{10}) are computed. The first round key k_0 is equal to the initial key.

The attack is divided into sample collection and analysis phase. During sample collection, the attacker program collects samples continuously and sorts them into pools based on their fingerprints. After a predefined number of samples was collected, the analysis phase begins. The attacker checks for each pool whether it contains a continuous chain of 16 bytes starting at a 16 byte offset. Each of these chains can be seen as an AES round key candidate. If multiple colliding byte values were recorded for any index within a pool, the attacker may choose the value based on the frequency of occurrence.

If the attack was successful, at least one round key is among the detected chains. For each chain, the attacker should first check whether the chain itself is the AES key k_0. Otherwise, the inverted key schedule yields 10 key candidates per chain, including k_0 if the observed chain is a valid round key. If two or more round keys leaked, the attacker can also find the AES key k_0 without knowing any plaintext-ciphertext pair for verification. Let k_{r_1} and k_{r_2} be two different AES round keys among the extracted chains. We pick any of the recorded chains and assume it is round key k_{r_1}. We calculate the set of potential previous round keys using the inverted AES key schedule. If k_{r_2} is among the calculated round keys, we know we probably picked a correct round key and can calculate k_0.

We executed the attack on the CPUs in our testing environment that support AES-NI (see Table 1). We noticed that the transient execution window of ZombieLoad variant 2 is too small to compute even the simple XOR-based fingerprint, so we confined to variant 1 in all cases.

The attack was successful on both CPUs listed in section (1) of Table 3. We tried sample sizes from 60,000 to 120,000 samples and observed the highest success probability after recording 100,000 samples on both devices. The attack is still susceptible to noise, which explains the relatively low rate of successful

Table 3. Experimental results for the cache line fingerprinting attack on different CPUs ($n = 10$ repetitions).

	CPU	No. of samples	Avg. duration (s)	Full key recoveries
(1)	i7-2620M	100,000	12.1	9/10 (90%)
	i5-4300M	100,000	11.3	3/10 (30%)
(2)	E3-1270v6	100,000	10.9	0/10 (0%)
	i7-8650U	100,000	12.1	0/10 (0%)

full key recoveries: it fails as soon as one byte of a round key is misdetected. Again, we noticed strong differences in leakage patterns and quantity depending on the microarchitecture: On both CPUs listed in section (2) of Table 3, the attack was infeasible due to too much noise from parallel activity.

4.3   Discussion

Comparison to the Domino Attack. In the domino attack [16], values from all observed cache lines overlap in the entire sample set; the only distinctive property of recorded samples is the index inside the LFB entry. The domino attack deals with a set of frequency distributions where each distribution reflects all values observed at a given index. All samples in our improved attack have two distinctive properties: index and fingerprint. This leads to 256 sets of frequency distributions, one set per fingerprint pool. In each set, data from different cache lines only superimpose where the fingerprint collides. Another advantage of cache line fingerprinting is the direct association of the fingerprint with the data value, while the domino attack samples data bytes and domino bytes at different points in time and with no inherent connection between them. It is noted that cache line fingerprinting shares the limitation with the domino attack that only constant values that appear repeatedly can be extracted from cache lines. Clearly, if the first eight bytes of a cache line change, the fingerprint likely changes as well.

Comparison to RIDL's Mask-Sub-Rotate. Van Schaik et al. [18] propose Mask-Sub-Rotate (MSR), a technique that may look similar to ours at first sight. Both approaches access the full cache line during transient execution. While MSR leaks sequences identified by some sub-sequence, our technique extracts all frequent constant sequences, without knowing any identifying marker sequence. Furthermore, we leak two bytes per iteration (value and fingerprint), while MSR leaks either a single byte value (if the cache line begins with the identifying sequence) or nothing (otherwise).

5   Mitigations

Both the differential attack as well as cache line fingerprinting require that ZombieLoads can be collected. For general countermeasures to prevent ZombieLoad leakage we refer to [16]. Considering that disabling both HyperThreading and TSX is necessary to fully mitigate ZombieLoad on vulnerable CPUs [6], we assume that mitigations are still incomplete on many real-world systems.

As a software mitigation, the presented differential attack can be prevented similarly to the secret sharing approach in [16] by masking the entire cryptographic implementation [10]. Masking flattens the statistical distributions in the sampling pools towards a uniform distribution which thereby prevents the described leakage of the differential attack. Second-order attacks are assessed to be difficult as the leakage frequency of ZombieLoads is much smaller than the execution frequency of AES, however, it should be ensured that mask and masked data are never stored in the same cache line to make it harder for an attacker to target the mask. A limited countermeasure to cache line fingerprinting could be to only mask the key storage. As cache line fingerprinting depends on static cache data, a regularly refreshed masking of the key storage, e.g., after a certain number of AES executions, counteracts this attack assumption.

6   Conclusion

In this paper, we showed that sampled intermediate results of cryptographic implementations can be used for key recovery in an MDS scenario. This differential attack can succeed with very few known plaintexts or ciphertexts and does not require the key bytes to be directly observable via MDS. Exploitable leakage was observed with the implementation *aes-min* and the AES key was successfully recovered in less than four seconds on an i3-2120 CPU. While the actual leakage pattern strongly depends on the specific implementation, environment, and CPU, we want to raise awareness that intermediate values can be used to recover secret data in MDS contexts as well and should be considered as a potential threat. This is especially true for algorithms other than AES without special hardware-support which rely even more on software-based computations that are potentially susceptible to leakage. As second main contribution, we proposed the use of cache line fingerprinting in order to pin ZombieLoad samples to a cache line with high probability. This allows to extract constant byte sequences more efficiently for key recovery.

Acknowledgments. We would like to thank our anonymous reviewers and our shepherd Daniel Gruss for their valuable feedback. We also thank Michael Schwarz for sharing his knowledge on the subtleties of implementing microarchitectural attacks.

References

1. Bos, J.W., Hubain, C., Michiels, W., Teuwen, P.: Differential computation analysis: hiding your white-box designs is not enough. In: Gierlichs, B., Poschmann, A.Y. (eds.) CHES 2016. LNCS, vol. 9813, pp. 215–236. Springer, Heidelberg (2016). https://doi.org/10.1007/978-3-662-53140-2_11

2. Canella, C., et al.: Fallout: leaking data on meltdown-resistant CPUs. In: Proceedings of the 2019 ACM SIGSAC Conference on Computer and Communications Security, CCS 2019, pp. 769–784. ACM, New York (2019)
3. Canella, C., et al.: A systematic evaluation of transient execution attacks and defenses, May 2019. https://arxiv.org/pdf/1811.05441v3
4. Intel Corp.: Deep dive: snoop-assisted L1 data sampling (2020). https://software.intel.com/security-software-guidance/deep-dives/deep-dive-snoop-assisted-l1-data-sampling
5. Intel Corp.: Processors affected: microarchitectural data sampling (2020). https://software.intel.com/security-software-guidance/insights/processors-affected-microarchitectural-data-sampling
6. Kernel Development Community: Hardware vulnerabilities - The Linux Kernel documentation (2020). https://www.kernel.org/doc/html/v5.8/admin-guide/hw-vuln/index.html. See MDS and TAA subsections
7. Kocher, P., Jaffe, J., Jun, B.: Differential power analysis. In: Wiener, M. (ed.) CRYPTO 1999. LNCS, vol. 1666, pp. 388–397. Springer, Heidelberg (1999). https://doi.org/10.1007/3-540-48405-1_25
8. Kocher, P., et al.: Spectre attacks: exploiting speculative execution. In: 40th IEEE Symposium on Security and Privacy (S&P 2019), San Francisco (2019)
9. Lipp, M., et al.: Meltdown: reading kernel memory from user space. In: 27th USENIX Security Symposium (USENIX Security 18). USENIX Association, Baltimore, August 2018
10. Mangard, S., Oswald, E., Popp, T.: Power Analysis Attacks. Springer, Boston, MA (2007). https://doi.org/10.1007/978-0-387-38162-6
11. McQueen, C.: aes-min, December 2018. https://github.com/cmcqueen/aes-min/blob/728e156091/README.md
12. Moghimi, D., Lipp, M., Sunar, B., Schwarz, M.: Medusa: microarchitectural data leakage via automated attack synthesis. In: 29th USENIX Security Symposium (USENIX Security 20). USENIX Association, Boston, August 2020
13. National Institute of Standards and Technology: Specification for the Advanced Encryption Standard (AES), November 2001. https://nvlpubs.nist.gov/nistpubs/FIPS/NIST.FIPS.197.pdf. FIPS 197
14. Ragab, H., Milburn, A., Razavi, K., Bos, H., Giuffrida, C.: CrossTalk: speculative data leaks across cores are real (2020). https://download.vusec.net/papers/crosstalk_sp21.pdf
15. Schlüter, T.: ZombieLoad-Angriff auf den Advanced Encryption Standard. Master's thesis, Bonn-Rhein-Sieg University of Applied Sciences, January 2020
16. Schwarz, M., et al.: ZombieLoad: cross-privilege-boundary data sampling. In: Proceedings of the 2019 ACM SIGSAC Conference on Computer and Communications Security, CCS 2019, pp. 753–768. ACM, New York (2019)
17. van Schaik, S., Minkin, M., Kwong, A., Genkin, D., Yarom, Y.: CacheOut: leaking data on Intel CPUs via Cache Evictions (2020). https://arxiv.org/pdf/2006.13353v1.pdf
18. van Schaik, S., et al.: RIDL: rogue in-flight data load. In: 40th IEEE Symposium on Security and Privacy (S&P 2019). San Francisco (2019)
19. Wampler, J., Martiny, I., Wustrow, E.: ExSpectre: hiding malware in speculative execution. In: Proceedings 2019 Network and Distributed System Security Symposium. Internet Society, San Diego (2019)

Low-Cost Body Biasing Injection (BBI) Attacks on WLCSP Devices

Colin O'Flynn[✉]

Dalhousie University, Halifax, Canada
colin@oflynn.com

Abstract. Body Biasing Injection (BBI) uses a voltage applied with a physical probe onto the backside of the integrated circuit die Compared to other techniques such as electromagnetic fault injection (EMFI) or Laser Fault Injection (LFI), this technique appears less popular in academic literature based on published results. It is hypothesized being due to (1) moderate cost of equipment, and (2) effort required in device preperation.

This work demonstrates that BBI (and indeed many other backside attacks) can be trivially performed on Wafer-Level Chip-Scale Packaging (WLCSP), which inherently expose the die backside. A low-cost ($15) design for the BBI tool is introduced, and validated with faults introduced on a STM32F415OG against code flow, RSA, and some initial results on various hardware block attacks are discussed.

Keywords: Fault injection · Glitch attacks · Body biasing injection

1 Introduction

Fault injection attacks allow an attacker to modify the operation of a device under test. This can include simple control-flow attacks allowing bypass of secure boot and other security checks, or differential fault analysis attacks that allow recovery of secret cryptographic material [7,10]. These faults are introduced by various methods [4] – the least equipment-intensive manipulated the external clock or voltage supply, but many other methods including optical via flash tubes or lasers [18,20,23], electromagnetic faults [18], X-Rays [2], and body biasing injection (BBI) [11,12].

The popularity of various techniques depend on both the deployed countermeasures (i.e., what is required to bypass devices in practice), along with the complexity and cost of the techniques. Originally voltage and clock fault injection were popular due to their low-cost of implementation, but the well-tested countermeasures, along with changes such as more devices running from internal oscillators, has pushed new injection techniques such as laser fault injection

An extended version of this paper with additional figures and details is available from https://eprint.iacr.org.

© Springer Nature Switzerland AG 2021
P.-Y. Liardet and N. Mentens (Eds.): CARDIS 2020, LNCS 12609, pp. 166–180, 2021.
https://doi.org/10.1007/978-3-030-68487-7_11

and EM fault injection (EMFI). EMFI has the advantage of requiring almost no changes to the target device in many cases - devices can even be attacked without opening the target [15].

The popularity of EMFI has resulted in several commercial tools (Riscure EM-FI, NewAE Technology ChipSHOUTER, Langer EM Pulse Injector, etc.), along with several open-source tools and implementation papers [1,3,9].

Considerable less has been published on practical attacks using BBI, that is beyond the seminal work on the topic [12] and related follow-up [6,22]. The authors of this paper aim to bring BBI to a wider audience by addressing two issues which have complicated the use of BBI in practice, and demonstrate some additional attacks that BBI can accomplish, including the potential for permanent damage or modification of non-volatile memory.

The first complication with BBI is that it may require a level of device preparation beyond the capabilities of a low-cost laboratory. The second is that BBI requires a fault injection tool to generate the high-voltage pulse, which was previously demonstrated with moderate-cost high-voltage injection tools.

To address the first point, we primarily rely on the usage of a particular package type called Wafer-Level Chip-Scale Package (WLCSP). This package type inherently exposes the backside of the die, at most requiring a small amount of mechanical or chemical preparation that can easily be performed. To address the second point, we have released an open-source tool that can be built for approximately $15, assuming an existing adjustable power supply and pulse generation platform. Even including all supporting tools besides a computer, a practical platform can be build for between $100-$1000 depending on the effort the attacker wishes to put into development. Additional equipment for characterization used in this paper cost up to $10 000, but these tools are not required for application of the work.

To demonstrate the practicality of the attack, fault injection attacks are performed on a popular microcontroller (STM32F415) available in WLCSP. These attacks start with a simple glitch parameterization code (loop), then perform a classic attack on RSA code from MBED-TLS, before finally attempting fault attacks on the hardware AES engine.

In addition, a new result is demonstrated that non-volatile memory can have their contents disrupted by the BBI method, although the specific method remains under investigation.

This work will demonstrate that not all device packages are not created equal. The simple choice of a small WLCSP results in a relatively trivial application of the BBI attack, and may also be beneficial for other attacks such as EMFI, Laser Fault Injection (LFI), and EM side-channel analysis.

The authors have made available not only the design of the tooling used in this paper, but the capture and analysis software scripts (in the form of Python code in Jupyter notebooks), along with various raw datasets. It is hoped this effort helps to jump-start interest in BBI, by providing a starting point for others to replicate and extend these results. See https://github.com/newaetech/chipjabber-basicbbi for these tools.

1.1   Contributions

This paper contributes to the research area the following items:

- An open-source and simple design for a BBI tool.
- Methods for characterizing a BBI setup.
- Demonstrating that BBI on WLCSP devices is trivial to perform.
- Characterization of several fault attacks on the STM32F415 device.
- Initial results on memory damage/corruption with BBI.
- Replication of the RSA-CRT fault attack from the seminal BBI paper [12].

1.2   Body Biasing Injection

Forward Body Biasing Injection (FBBI or just BBI) relies on a 'connection' between the die backside and internal transistors and nets on the integrated circuit. By inserting pertubations onto the backside (die substrate), there will be some coupling of these perturbations to the internal sensitive nets [12]. Any such perturbations on the internal power rails and nets are known to cause faults in a general sense, no matter where or how they are injected [24].

BBI attacks can also take advantage of the semiconductor physics of this interconnection. Thus the positive or negative pulses will result in differing amounts of energy injected into the CMOS logic elements [6]. As BBI is known to also have some spatial dimension in that the location of the probe connection affects the result [12], it appears there are many parameters we can tweak with BBI to achieve a desired result.

1.3   Wafer-Level Chip-Scale Packaging

As consumer devices continue to shrink, the usage of the smallest possible device packaging, called Wafer-Level Chip-Scale Packaging (WLCSP) has increased. This package has effectively the sawn chip wafer placed onto a minimal carrier built in the same process, with solder balls attached to this carrier. An example of the WLCSP device under investigation in this paper is given in Fig. 1.

Fig. 1. STM32F415 in WLCSP with low-cost carrier PCB. C5 is a 0603 capacitor footprint for scale.

This package is easily identifiable as the underside often has identifiable chip structures, and the top-side is normally reflective as simply presents the backside of the silicon wafer. Early packages of this type had problems with light causing resets for example [5], and thus a thin coating may also be applied to the package to block light (and allow more visible package markings). For devices with this thin coating, we found it can be easily removed by physically scraping the coating off with a sharp knife. If devices are removed from a board, they can also be soaked in acetone for 24 h which seemed to remove the coating without damaging the device.

Many devices are available in this package - this includes standard microcontrollers, along with secure devices such as the NXP SLM 78[1], A71CH[2], etc.

WLCSP and Physical Attacks. Intuitively, we expect the WLCSP to be useful for a range of physical attacks. Most obviously are anything where backside attacks are in-scope, including for example backside LFI [23] and photon emission analysis [17]. Some thinning may yet be required, but this may be easier since the device is designed to be handled, and can be soldered onto a carrier board for example. Other attacks such as lateral LFI (LLFI) that relies on an exposed die edge should be applicable to WLCSP packages with minimal effort [16].

Using small electromagnetic probes for both side-channel analysis [21] and fault injection may require the probe to be closer to the die than a normal TQFP or similar packaging technologies allow. Previously the target was partially decapsulated, but with WLCSP you get closer to the die (via the backside) with minimal effort. It may also be possible to access the front-side, depending on the layout of balls and how the device can be physically manipulated. On many devices visible micro-vias allow access to the interface signals even if the normal balls are removed.

Building WLCSP Targets. If the attacker wishes to build a target board, there may be a perceived complexity (and cost) for WLCSP designs. In practice we found that for our targets we did not require the expensive "via-in-pad" services. Instead we use a 4 mil trace/space PCB service (which is available even from many low-cost providers), and avoided placing some pads to provide space to break out signals from internal balls, as can be seen in Fig. 1. For full details see the target PCB layout described next. During assembly, the devices are soldered using a "flux-only" process, which avoids the need for very fine stencils and careful alignment.

2   STM32F415 Target

The primary target device investigated is a STM32F415OG, which is a microcontroller from ST Micro. Previous work on EMFI has used the similar STM32F411

---

[1] https://www.eetimes.com/infineon-claims-first-industrial-grade-wlcsp-esim-chip.

[2] https://www.nxp.com/products/security-and-authentication/authentication/plug-and-trust-the-fast-easy-way-to-deploy-secure-iot-connections:A71CH.

in TQFP packaging for characterizing an EMFI tool [3]. A very similar device (STM32F215) in the TQFP package is used in the Trezor bitcoin wallet, for which fault attacks have been demonstrated against in practice [15].

A close-up of the WLCSP STM32F415OG device was shown in Fig. 1, and the full PCB can be seen as part of Fig. 3. The full details (including schematic, board files, etc.) of the target are available[3]. The top covering of the WLCSP package can be scraped off once the device is soldered down, or a more gentle removal is done by soaking the device in acetone before soldering the device. Note the STM32F415OG appears to be easily killed by optical flashes once the covering is removed – future work may look at WLCSP and optical injection, and we had briefly experimented with a Xenon flash. Exposing the topside[4] to such a flash causes the device to enter a CMOS latch-up state, but does not recover from this state with a power cycle (i.e., the device is dead and gets very hot).

This follows previously reported publications, showing that optical (or laser) fault injection has a high chance of causing a latch-up effect [19].

To support the target, we are using the ChipWhisperer CW308 UFO base-board that board provides power and reset signals to the target device. This base-board also provides diode clamping on the output lines running back to our control platform (ChipWhisperer-Lite), as during this attack we will be presenting high voltages that could escape on the I/O lines.

3   Low-Cost BBI Probe

The low-cost BBI probe uses a transformer coupling to generate the required voltage pulse, which is then coupled into the target device. A schematic of the probe is given in Fig. 2, and a photo of a prototype is seen in Fig. 3. The 4.7 uF ceramic capacitors C1 and C2 are charged by a variable power supply limited to 100 mA current – if the power supply does not have current limiting a series resistor or **must** be inserted inline. The logic-level MOSFET allows any normal drive circuitry (FPGA, microcontroller, or bench pulse generator), with gate resistor R1 to limit overswing, and a pull-down resistor R2 to ensure the MOSFET is normally off when disconnected.

The heart of the circuit is transformer X1 which is (poorly) custom-wound. The primary winding is 6 turns of 26 AWG magnet wire, wound on a ferrite rod, part number 3061990871 from Fair-Rite Corporation. The secondary winding is 60 turns of 30 AWG magnet wire, wound directly on-top of the primary winding in several layers. The transformer construction is fairly insensitive to variations in parameters, and the winding ratio was chosen somewhat arbitrary with the expected objective of achieving around 300V output with a standard 30V DC power supply. A low number of primary turns was required to allow rapid pulse

---

[3] https://github.com/newaetech/chipwhisperer-target-cw308t/tree/master/ CW308T_STM32F4_CSP.

[4] We will use 'topside' to refer to the top WLCSP package surface for clarify, which is the backside of the IC wafer.

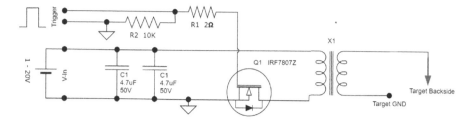

Fig. 2. The BBI injection device relies on transformer X1 to produce a higher voltage from a simple capacitor based circuit.

transients, as higher primary turns would typically increase the inductance, and thus limit the slew rate and thus pulse duration.

The probe tip used here is Harwin part number P25-0123. Various sizes of probe tips are easily available, including smaller tips and different materials. More details of the construction are available in the accompanying public GIT repository at https://github.com/newaetech/chipjabber-basicbbi.

Fig. 3. The BBI setup includes the low-cost probe, the target board, a ChipWhisperer-Lite for triggering, and various probes for characterizing results.

3.1 Power Supply

The probe assumes the existence of a power supply. The injection parameter can be controlled by the drive signal (i.e., pulse duration), as well as the voltage of the probe. In practice both may need to be varied to achieve the desired results.

In these experiments a Rigol DP832 power supply is used ($500), which includes a simple USB interface for computer control. This power supply is overkill for the requirements however - there is almost no current required during operation, and a simple linear regulator built with a LM317 would be sufficient in practical scenarios ($10).

3.2   Pulse Generation

Any fault injection circuit requires a pulse generator. A ChipWhisperer-Lite ($250) is used herein, but for a lower-cost attack a simple FPGA board or micro-controller could also be used ($50).

3.3   Characterization Setup

In order to characterize the BBI tool and WLCSP combination, we place the probe on the topside of the prepared WLCSP target, and will then measure injection characteristics for various settings. The physical measurement equipment setup is shown in Fig. 4.

As previously reported, the backside connection had a fairly large resistance. Measuring with a multimeter showed a resistance of $220\,K\Omega$ from the backside of the die to the ground net. To better understand the voltage and current relationship (that is, assuming it is not a simple resistive connection) we will now characterize our probe on the die backside.

For this characterization, the target device is held in reset to avoid code execution. Before every injection we power cycle the device, to ensure no effects such as CMOS latch-up are present. We have chosen a relatively large 680 nS pulse width for our tests, which was based on some initial characterization (to be discussed in Sect. 4).

Fig. 4. A closer view of the BBI probe touching the WLCSP topside (i.e., die backside), with the CT6 current probe for measuring injection current, and an oscilloscope probe for measuring injection voltage.

Current Measurement. The current measurement is performed with a Tektronix CT6 current probe. This probe has a 2 GHz bandwidth, and the injection needle passes directly through the CT6 probe. Thus the CT6 probe is as close as practical to the actual target device, to ensure the most accurate measurement possible.

The CT6 probe is terminated by enabling the 50 Ω input option of the Pico-Scope 6403D, and thus our measurement chain should closely match the claimed calibrated scaling factor.

Voltage Measurement. The voltage measurement is performed with a 100 MHz bandwidth, 100:1 oscilloscope probe (the higher voltages of the target exceeds the limits of the normal 10:1 probe for our oscilloscope). This probe is connected to the injection needle directly, just above the current measurement probe CT6.

3.4 Pulse Examples

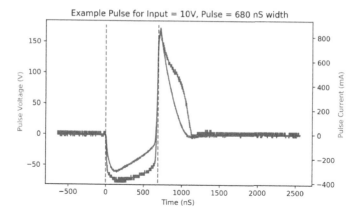

Fig. 5. Example of the pulse output generated by the circuit. The vertical lines show a 680 nS time offset showing the negative/positive spikes on each edge.

As an example of the injected pulse is shown in Fig. 5. The close alignment of voltage and current suggests that the load does not contain substantial capacitive or inductive components. Note the large positive voltage is generated by the turn-off of the MOSFET at the falling edge of the input pulse at time 680 μS.

The absolute peak of the voltage and current is used to generate a graph of the output voltage and current for a given drive voltage. This is shown in Fig. 6, and will be discussed next.

3.5   Input Voltage vs. Outputs

It can be seen that fairly high voltages and currents are generated for low input voltages. Notably this suggests that a successful attack may be possible even with lower-cost power supplies. The actual impedance during the pulse is much lower than the DC resistance measured with the DMM (of 220 KΩ). It can be seen from Fig. 6 graph the effective impedance appears closer to 250 Ω, based on the voltage and current peaks.

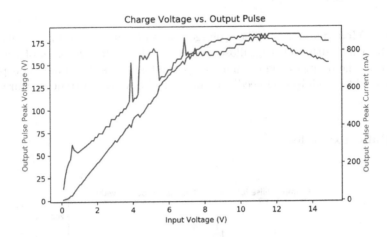

Fig. 6. Peak pulse voltage and current injected into WLCSP device based on changing charge (input) voltage.

4   Fault Attack Results

Three main fault injection attempts are performed. Starting with some basic characterization of the target, we then demonstrate a classic fault attack on RSA-CRT, before performing some initial work on characterizing the AES hardware accelerator.

The initial characterization is done with a simple "double-loop", which is widely used in previous work [8] (also see Listing 1 in [13]). This code runs an inner and outer loop, and counts the total iterations through both loops. The objective of this glitch is to corrupt the total loop counter variable. This corruption is detectable under a wide variety of conditions. If the glitch causes a loop exit, instruction skip, register corruption, or memory corruption it will result in an incorrect final loop value but not a device reset.

The results can be seen in Fig. 7 with the device running at the default speed for the ChipWhisperer Hardware Abstraction Layer (HAL) build system (7.37 MHz), and a higher 40 MHz speed in Fig. 8 as a comparison. The width of the glitch insertion is linked to the device clock cycle (the same clock is used for both during our test), hence at the higher 40 MHz speed the number of cycles faulted is higher for the same width of an injected pulse.

4.1 RSA-CRT Fault

The seminal work on fault attacks demonstrated how an incorrect calculation during a signing operation on many implementations of the RSA algorithm (using RSA-CRT) allowed immediate recovery of the secret key [7]. This attack is summarized also in the seminal BBI work [12], as the same attack is applied therein.

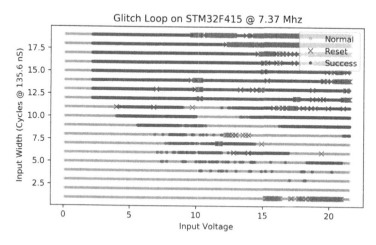

Fig. 7. The double-loop code running at 7.37 MHz, showing a wide variety of settings with highly successful fault injections.

For our target we used MBED-TLS, which provides a suitable RSA implementation. The current codebase includes a signature verification step before returning the signature, specifically to check for a faulty signature and prevent the attack in [7]. Thus executing this attack requires either (1) a double fault, or (2) modification to the source code ('cheating') to remove the check. As it appears the previous BBI work [12] did not require a double-fault, we present results using the latter option to better compare our test setup.

Based on Fig. 7 we fixed the voltage setting to 5.0V and a width of 10 cycles. As in [12] we estimated the total RSA time, and inserted a glitch approximately 65% of the way into the operation, which is expected to be in one of the vulnerable operations. We swept the glitch through various times in the area, and recorded the data in Table 1.

For a returned invalid signature, we check if the attack successfully recovers part of the known secret key value (in this case p or q, which allows recovery of all other secrets) and mark it as 'exploitable', otherwise it is some unknown invalid result. It can be seen that 54% of injection attempts result in an exploitable invalid signature, meaning that even adding the complexity of double-fault should still leave a reasonably high success rate.

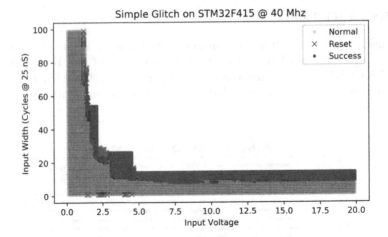

Fig. 8. The double-loop code running at 40 MHz. Due to the larger search space, an optimized search decreases the width at higher voltages, and thus some areas are not searched.

4.2 Hardware AES Faults

Several DFA attacks on AES have been previously presented, and we wished to examine the AES engine for a known vulnerability [10]. We presented a constant cipher-text for the majority of this work, along with an easily identifiable constant key (00 01 02 03 04 05 06 07 08 09 0a 0b 0c 0d 0e 0f).

As the leakage for the STM32F415 hardware AES engine is known [14], we used a CPA attack to confirm the last-round of the AES cipher is around clock cycle 270 from our trigger. We thus swept our attack at clock cycles 250 to 280 from a known trigger. The width of the glitch would cover approximately 5 clock cycles of the target device. To begin with, we characterized the responses into three main categories:

– Normal (correct response).
– Reset or no response.
– Incorrect Response (possible fault).

Table 1. RSA-CRT fault attack.

RSA signing result	Occurrence
Exploitable (p or q)	54.2 %
Device Reset	28.0 %
Normal	11.9 %
Invalid	5.9 %

Readers are directed to the extended version of this paper on IACR E-Print for more details of the AES fault attack, including a figure showing the location of faults with time. Briefly, we can summarize the results as that the fault injection causes several clear-text return of parts of the encryption key. In additional, several faulty ciphertexts are returned. What was not clear is if the ciphertexts are a fault in the AES engine itself, or simply faulty operations on the control instructions using the AES engine.

5   Permanent and Quasi-Permanent Faults

During our work, several additional results were observed. While they are not yet well characterized, they are worth reporting as an area of future study.

The first was some devices appear to have entered a permanent CMOS latch-up state. One device for example was observed that programming was rarely successful - this device would still respond to commands as the built-in boot-loader could read memory, and would execute a flash erase or program without reporting an error. It was assumed some internal short developed, and this short allowed enough voltage for the core to execute, but could not write memory cells[5].

With the probe from Fig. 2, we observed various effects on the non-volatile memory as well. With an empty device (i.e., flash is in 0xFF state), we performed a sweep of a fault where we set a 28V input voltage and $6.8\mu S$ pulse width, and physically moved the probe across the device during insertion of 5000 pulses. After each campaign of 5000 pulses we read the FLASH memory state, and observed that between 50–2048 bytes of the FLASH memory from the start of flash were now 0x00. The 00 bytes were consecutive, and the number of 00s were related to the delay between injection pulses. A higher delay between pulses meant more 00 bytes. Thus we hypothesize that one of the fault injections triggered the flash program hardware, and was the interrupted by another fault injection. Where security information is stored in flash memory, such program triggering could be a useful attack vector.

A second effect seen was apparent damage to sections of flash memory. On another test device we noticed that the flash area with offset 0x40000 − 7FFFF would no longer read as the erased state of all 1 bits, but instead would randomly read about 20% of bits as 0. On each read the location of the erroneous bits would change. We could successfully *program* that area to be all 0 without error (all bits now read as 0). Calling erase would return the area again to only partially functioning, with approximately 20% of bits reading transiently as 0 instead of 1. The damaged area represents exactly half of the flash on the chip, whereas the other half of the flash on the chip continued to function normally as both erase and program worked without error. We hypothesize that some damage was done to transistors connecting the erase voltage to half of the flash array in this case, and they were no longer at a valid 1 level after erase.

---

[5] The device would also immediately get very hot...

These preliminary results do not appear to offer any sort of localized precision such as X-Ray attacks promise related to modification of non-volatile memory [2]. Yet this demonstrates that BBI offers new possibilities, and more effort is required to better understand the nuances of this fault injection technique.

6   Scanning of X-Y Location

In order to understand the affect of the probe position on the results, we used an XYZ table to scan the probe across the chip surface. In previous sections, a low-cost table vise is used to demonstrate that finding a good position can be done without a XYZ table. In this section, we determine the sensitivity to spatial position, which was again covered in previous work [12].

More details of the scanner setup are in the extended version of this paper, available on IACR E-Print. The result of scanning at 0.2 mm steps are shown in Fig. 9, showing the number of resets and successful glitches, based on the double-loop from Sect. 4. The voltage input for this scan was limited to 0.5 V–10.0 V, as we found larger voltages beyond 10.0V increased the chance of damage to the device (either temporarily flash erasure, or permanent damage).

Note the "threshold" of where resets and successes is not consistent over the chip surface either, see the extended version of this paper for details.

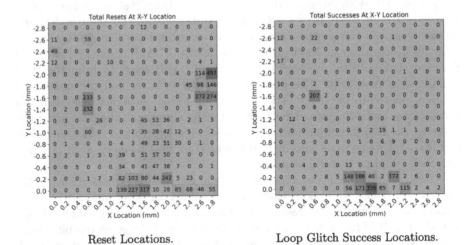

Reset Locations.   Loop Glitch Success Locations.

Fig. 9. Scanning WLCSP surface at 0.2mm steps to determine spatial position sensitivity, from a total of 4180 attempts at each location.

7   Conclusions

Forward Body Biasing Injection (FBBI or just BBI) is a relatively new fault injection method, first introduced in [12]. It remains less explored in academic publications compared to other methods such as electromagnetic fault injection (EMFI) and laser fault injection (LFI). This work demonstrates that BBI can be accomplished with very simple equipment, and in fact it is even easier to build a BBI injection setup than with EMFI, as no high-voltage source is required.

This technique is particularly effective with WLCSP devices, which naturally expose the die backside. Thus the complication of exposing the die backside can be skipped for these devices. The BBI technique with the simple transformer-based probe allows faults on microcontrollers with high repeatability, as demonstrated on several target programs. In addition, it appears there may be some physical effects that cause permanent faults on the target device, which is an area requiring more study.

Finally, the WLCSP is likely to remain interesting for other attack methods. Several attacks depend on, or are improved by, the quasi-exposed die that the WLCSP presents. This knowledge should be considered both by security researchers who do not have access to decapsulation equipment, and designers of secure systems when specifying devices.

References

1. Abdellatif, K., Hériveaux, O.: SiliconToaster: a cheap and programmable EM injector for extracting secrets. In: Proceedings of 2020 Workshop on Fault Diagnosis and Tolerance in Cryptography (2020)
2. Anceau, S., Bleuet, P., Clédière, J., Maingault, L., Rainard, J., Tucoulou, R.: Nanofocused X-ray beam to reprogram secure circuits. In: Fischer, W., Homma, N. (eds.) CHES 2017. LNCS, vol. 10529, pp. 175–188. Springer, Cham (2017). https://doi.org/10.1007/978-3-319-66787-4_9
3. Balasch, J., Arumí, D., Manich, S.: Design and validation of a platform for electromagnetic fault injection. In: 2017 32nd Conference on Design of Circuits and Integrated Systems (DCIS), pp. 1–6, November 2017
4. Bar-El, H., Choukri, H., Naccache, D., Tunstall, M., Whelan, C.: The sorcerer's apprentice guide to fault attacks. Proc. IEEE **94**(2), 370–382 (2006)
5. Benchoff, B.: Photonic Reset Of The Raspberry Pi 2, February 2015. https://hackaday.com/2015/02/08/photonic-reset-of-the-raspberry-pi-2/, library Catalog: hackaday.com
6. Beringuier-Boher, N., Lacruche, M., El-Baze, D., Dutertre, J.M., Rigaud, J.B., Maurine, P.: Body biasing injection attacks in practice. In: Proceedings of the Third Workshop on Cryptography and Security in Computing System, CS2 2016, pp. 49–54. Association for Computing Machinery, Prague, Czech Republic, January 2016
7. Boneh, D., DeMillo, R.A., Lipton, R.J.: On the importance of checking cryptographic protocols for faults. In: Fumy, W. (ed.) EUROCRYPT 1997. LNCS, vol. 1233, pp. 37–51. Springer, Heidelberg (1997). https://doi.org/10.1007/3-540-69053-0_4
8. Carpi, R.B., Picek, S., Batina, L., Menarini, F., Jakobovic, D., Golub, M.: Glitch it if you can: parameter search strategies for successful fault injection. In: Francillon, A., Rohatgi, P. (eds.) CARDIS 2013. LNCS, vol. 8419, pp. 236–252. Springer, Cham (2014). https://doi.org/10.1007/978-3-319-08302-5_16

9. Cui, A., Housley, R.: BADFET: defeating modern secure boot using second-order pulsed electromagnetic fault injection. In: Proceedings of 11th USENIX Workshop on Offensive Technologies (WOOT 2017) (2017)
10. Dusart, P., Letourneux, G., Vivolo, O.: Differential fault analysis on A.E.S. In: Zhou, J., Yung, M., Han, Y. (eds.) ACNS 2003. LNCS, vol. 2846, pp. 293–306. Springer, Heidelberg (2003). https://doi.org/10.1007/978-3-540-45203-4_23
11. Maurine, P.: Techniques for EM fault injection: equipments and experimental results. In: 2012 Workshop on Fault Diagnosis and Tolerance in Cryptography, pp. 3–4, September 2012
12. Maurine, P., Tobich, K., Ordas, T., Liardet, P.Y.: Yet another fault injection technique: by forward body biasing injection, September 2012. https://hal-lirmm.ccsd.cnrs.fr/lirmm-00762035
13. O'Flynn, C.: Fault injection using crowbars on embedded systems. Technical report 810 (2016). http://eprint.iacr.org/2016/810
14. O'Flynn, C.: I, For One, Welcome Our New Power Analysis Overlords An Introduction to ChipWhisperer-Lint (2018)
15. O'Flynn, C.: MIn()imum failure: EMFI attacks against USB stacks. In: Proceedings of the 13th USENIX Conference on Offensive Technologies, WOOT 2019, p. 15. USENIX Association, Santa Clara, CA, USA, August 2019
16. Rodriguez, J., Baldomero, A., Montilla, V., Mujal, J.: LLFI: Lateral laser fault injection attack. In: 2019 Workshop on Fault Diagnosis and Tolerance in Cryptography (FDTC), pp. 41–47, August 2019
17. Schlösser, A., Nedospasov, D., Krämer, J., Orlic, S., Seifert, J.-P.: Simple photonic emission analysis of AES. In: Prouff, E., Schaumont, P. (eds.) CHES 2012. LNCS, vol. 7428, pp. 41–57. Springer, Heidelberg (2012). https://doi.org/10.1007/978-3-642-33027-8_3
18. Schmidt, J.M., Hutter, M.: Optical and EM fault-attacks on CRT-based RSA: concrete results. In: Proceedings of Austrochip 2007, 15th Austrian Workshop on Microelectronics (2007)
19. Selmke, B., Zinnecker, K., Koppermann, P., Miller, K., Heyszl, J., Sigl, G.: Locked out by latch-up? an empirical study on laser fault injection into arm cortex-M processors. In: 2018 Workshop on Fault Diagnosis and Tolerance in Cryptography (FDTC), pp. 7–14, September 2018
20. Skorobogatov, S.P., Anderson, R.J.: Optical fault induction attacks. In: Kaliski, B.S., Koç, K., Paar, C. (eds.) CHES 2002. LNCS, vol. 2523, pp. 2–12. Springer, Heidelberg (2003). https://doi.org/10.1007/3-540-36400-5_2
21. Specht, R., Heyszl, J., Kleinsteuber, M., Sigl, G.: Improving non-profiled attacks on exponentiations based on clustering and extracting leakage from multi-channel high-resolution EM measurements. In: Mangard, S., Poschmann, A.Y. (eds.) COSADE 2014. LNCS, vol. 9064, pp. 3–19. Springer, Cham (2015). https://doi.org/10.1007/978-3-319-21476-4_1
22. Tobich, K., Maurine, P., Liardet, P.Y., Lisart, M., Ordas, T.: Voltage spikes on the substrate to obtain timing faults. In: 2013 Euromicro Conference on Digital System Design, pp. 483–486, September 2013
23. van Woudenberg, J.G., Witteman, M.F., Menarini, F.: Practical Optical Fault Injection on Secure Microcontrollers. In: 2011 Workshop on Fault Diagnosis and Tolerance in Cryptography. pp. 91–99, September 2011
24. Zussa, L., Dutertre, J.M., Clediere, J., Robisson, B.: Analysis of the fault injection mechanism related to negative and positive power supply glitches using an on-chip voltmeter. In: 2014 IEEE International Symposium on Hardware-Oriented Security and Trust (HOST), pp. 130–135, May 2014

Let's Tessellate: Tiling for Security Against Advanced Probe and Fault Adversaries

Siemen Dhooghe$^{(\boxtimes)}$ and Svetla Nikova

imec-COSIC, KU Leuven, Leuven, Belgium
{siemen.dhooghe,svetla.nikova}@esat.kuleuven.be

Abstract. The wire probe-and-fault models are currently the most used models to provide arguments for side-channel and fault security. However, several practical attacks are not yet covered by these models. This work extends the wire fault model to include more advanced faults such as *area faults* and *permanent faults*. Moreover, we show the tile probe-and-fault adversary model from CRYPTO 2018's CAPA envelops the extended wire fault model along with known extensions to the probing model such as *glitches, transitions*, and *couplings*. In other words, tiled (*tessellated*) designs offer security guarantees even against advanced probe and fault adversaries.

As tiled models use multi-party computation techniques, countermeasures are typically expensive for software/hardware. This work investigates a tiled countermeasure based on the ISW methodology which is shown to perform significantly better than CAPA for practical parameters.

Keywords: Masking · Non-interference · Probing security · SIFA

1 Introduction

Symmetric primitives such as block ciphers are designed to resist black-box adversaries. These adversaries can view and choose the primitive's input and output. While the black-box model aims on high security guarantees, in practice, the adversary is often capable of more than choosing inputs and outputs. Since the primitive is implemented, either in hardware or in software, the adversary can observe leakage from operations or tamper with its execution. The former capability describes side-channel analysis where a typical side-channel is found in the power consumption of the device. As this consumption is correlated to the processed data, its observation allows for data-extraction as first described by Kocher *et al.* [20]. A second attack vector is found with an active adversary which tampers with the device to force incorrect outputs. While such outputs by themselves typically break cryptographic assumptions, they can additionally be used for data-extraction as explained by Biham and Shamir [6].

© Springer Nature Switzerland AG 2021
P.-Y. Liardet and N. Mentens (Eds.): CARDIS 2020, LNCS 12609, pp. 181–195, 2021.
https://doi.org/10.1007/978-3-030-68487-7_12

In order to provide cryptographic arguments of security against passive and active attacks, adversary and security models are needed. The most well-known model for passive security is the probing model introduced by Ishai, Sahai and Wagner (ISW) [19]. The described probing adversary is capable of reading the exact values on a number of circuit wires, where the minimal number of observed wires needed to uncover a sensitive variable is defined as the order of probing security. Probing security can be reduced to the noisy leakage model as shown by Duc *et al.* [14] where the assumptions lie in the presence of sufficient noise and independent wire leakage. The probing model is extended by Barthe *et al.* [1] to capture composable security called the non-interference model in which several secure countermeasures have been made, e.g., [3–5, 8, 10, 15, 17, 24]. Active adversaries are usually considered as the malicious variant of the probing model where the adversary can choose and fault up to a threshold number of circuit wires. The active (combined) security model is also extended to a composable security model called NINA [12]. Lately more advanced fault attacks such as Dobraunig *et al.*'s Statistical Ineffective Fault Attacks (SIFA) [13], which combine Clavier's ineffective faults [9] and Fuhr *et al.*'s statistical fault analysis [16], have appeared breaking both side-channel as fault resistant implementations. These attacks call for cryptographic arguments to show the security of countermeasures and for the design of new countermeasures.

While the probing and wire fault models are a good step forward to allow for cryptographic arguments of security, the adversaries' capabilities do not always closely resemble practical attacks. Concerning the probing model, there are several effects such as glitches, transition leakage, and couplings which invalidate the probing model's assumption of independent wire leakage. When these effects occur, the adversary can mount side-channel attacks at a lower cost than estimated by the probing security of the implementation, e.g., see the work by Moos *et al.* [21]. As a reaction to these effects, Faust *et al.* [15] proposed extensions of the probing model (called the robust probing model) such that hardware effects can be captured. The authors also describe how to protect smaller components in the primitive's circuit against these effects using the non-interference models. In 2011, Prouff and Roche [22] proposed to use Multi-Party Computation (MPC) techniques to passively secure implementations against hardware effects. However, both works only properly discussed the effect of glitches. Concerning the wire fault model, no extensions to the model are currently proposed. The work proposed by Reparaz *et al.* [23] (CAPA) considers an MPC model where an implementation is split in parts (tiles). The authors consider a new adversary model dubbed the tile probe-and-fault model where adversaries can read or fault tiles. This adversarial formalisation allows the capture of more topological and temporal effects in the circuit while still allowing for the design of countermeasures. The countermeasures, however, are based on MPC methods which are optimised to reduce communication costs rather than area and randomness costs. Instead there is a need for MPC methods which optimise for software/hardware costs.

1.1 Contributions

This paper provides extensions to the wire fault adversary to better capture the effect of realistic fault attacks. More specifically, the work puts forward two extensions: *area-extended faults*, which target an area around a wire; and *permanent faults*, which target a wire and allows the adversary to control it throughout the entire operation. Both extensions allow to better quantify the security of countermeasures against realistic attacks.

We put forward the stand-alone multi-party security model as one which covers many potential attacks jointly. It is shown that the model captures the effects of area-extended faults as well as faults targeting a specific resource throughout the computation. Moreover, to the best of our knowledge, the model is currently the only one capable of capturing *all* the physical effects described by Faust et al. [15]. Finally, recent introduced attacks such as Statistical Ineffective Fault Attacks (SIFA) and combined attacks, combining both side-channel analysis and fault analysis, are also covered by the model.

To show the feasibility of the tile model, this paper provides a multiplier secured in the stand-alone model. This multiplier is based on the well-known ISW methodology [19] showing that one can create multi-party protocols which are optimised for computational costs as opposed to communication costs. We compare the new multiplier to the one provided by Reparaz *et al.* [23] (CAPA) and we show that it performs significantly better with respect to elementary operations and randomness for practical parameters.

2 Preliminaries

This section introduces masking and share-duplication methods together with the known circuit and tile models including their adversaries and composable security models.

2.1 Masking and Redundancy

Using masking each variable x in the algorithm is split into shares x_i such that $x = \sum_i x_i$ over a finite field $\mathbb{F}_{2^m}$. To defend against fault attacks redundancy is added to the shares by duplicating them. Checking whether all duplicates are equal, creates an error detection mechanism checking whether a fault was injected in the computation. Combining duplication with masking gives the following sharing of a secret x:

$$\left(x_1^1, ..., x_1^{k+1}, x_2^1, ..., x_{d+1}^{k+1}\right),$$

such that $\sum_{i=1}^{d+1} x_i^\ell = x$ for all $\ell \in [k+1]$ and $x_i^1 = ... = x_i^{k+1}$ for all $i \in [d+1]$. The above sharing has a passive threshold d meaning that no d shares give information on the secret x and an active threshold k meaning that any faults on at most k shares could be detected in the vector.

2.2   The Circuit Model

This section introduces the circuit model and gadgets as defined by Ishai, Sahai and Wagner [19]. Consider algorithms in an arithmetic circuit form, a directed acyclic graph whose nodes are operations over $\mathbb{F}_{2^m}$ and whose edges are wires. Additionally, consider probabilistic circuits which have nodes with no input and uniform random elements over $\mathbb{F}_{2^m}$ as output, where the random elements are independent and identically distributed, and the correctness of the circuit does not depend on them. In order to resist fault attacks, consider nodes with no output capable of aborting the computation. This abort signal works as a broadcast making all wires in the circuit read $\perp$ when the signal is sent out.[1] Finally, a gadget is a probabilistic circuit with shared inputs/outputs and, if needed, the capability to abort the computation.

Consider passive, active, or combined adversaries as those which interact with a circuit by placing probes, faults, or both respectively. The adversary's strength is determined by which and how many wires in the circuit it can probe or fault. For example, the capability of an active attacker can vary from faulting a single wire (e.g., using a laser) or targeting several wires at once; attackers can trigger a fault once or multiple times (even in a single cycle). The fault may effect the value on the wire in one cycle or during multiple cycles or even for the total protocol execution.

After the adversary has chosen which wires to probe and fault, the circuit reacts by setting or toggling the values on the faulted wires (as specified by the adversary) and returning the values on the probed wires. The state of the abort signal (true or false) is returned as well. Following the notation by Duc et al. [14], for $t = 0, ..., \ell$, a (d, k)-threshold-probe-and-faulting adversary on $\mathbb{F}_{2^m}^\ell$ is a machine $\mathcal{A}$ that plays the following game against an oracle $\mathcal{O}$:

1. $\mathcal{A}$ specifies a set $\mathcal{I} = \{i_1, ..., i_{|\mathcal{I}|}\}$ of cardinality at most d and a set of tuples $\mathcal{J} = \{(j_1, h_1), ..., (j_{|\mathcal{J}|}, h_{|\mathcal{J}|})\}$ of cardinality at most k,
2. $\mathcal{O}$ computes an arbitrary sequence $(x_1, ..., x_\ell) \in \mathbb{F}_{2^m}^\ell$ with $(x_{j_1}, ..., x_{j_{|\mathcal{J}|}})$ faulted (bit-flip or stuck-at) according to $(h_{j_1}, ..., h_{j_{|\mathcal{I}|}})$.
3. $\mathcal{A}$ receives $(x_{i_1}, ..., x_{i_{|\mathcal{I}|}})$ with the abort state $\perp$.

Security consists of both a privacy and a correctness aspect. The number of probe and faults an adversary needs to place to break the scheme determines the order of security.

Definition 1. (Order of Combined Security [12]). *A circuit is (d, k)-order combined secure if the following holds against a (d, k)-threshold-probe-and-faulting adversary.*

1. *Privacy: The probed d-tuple with the state of the abort can be simulated from scratch.*
2. *Correctness: The circuit either aborts $\perp$ or gives a correct output.*

---

[1] On hardware this functionality is replaced by a specialised mechanism such as a cascading gadget from the work by Ishai et al. [18].

Composable security follows simulation based arguments. For specific definitions and examples, we refer the reader to the following works [3,8,12]. In short, a simulation based proof for a particular gadget works as follows. The adversary (distinguisher) is either interacting with the actual gadget or with a simulator. This simulator is given only a few of the input shares. The distinguisher's goal is to determine whether it is interacting with the simulator or with the actual gadget. A failure to do so implies that the adversary can know at most the shares given to the simulator.

Non-interference. Typically it is impossible to prove the security of a large circuit. Instead, one proves the composable security of several smaller gadgets. The composable notion for probing security has been studied by Barthe *et al.* [1], where the notion of Strong Non-Interference (SNI) is defined.

Definition 2 (d-Strong Non-Interferent (d-SNI) [1]). *A gadget G is d-SNI if for any set of d_1 probes on its intermediate variables and every set of d_2 probes on its output shares such that $d_1 + d_2 \leqslant d$, the totality of the probes can be simulated by only d_1 shares of each input.*

When this notion is combined with a sharing scheme of passive threshold d it provides d^{th}-order probing security.

Non-accumulation. The composable security model for active attacks has been considered by Dhooghe and Nikova [12]. This notions demands that a wire fault affects only one output share of the gadget.

Definition 3 (k-Strong Non-Accumulative (k-SNA) [12]). *A gadget G is k-SNA if for any set of k_1 errors on each input and every set of k_2 errors on the intermediate variables, with $k_1 + k_2 \leqslant k$, the gadget either aborts or gives an output with at most k_2 errors.*

The Strong NINA notion, forming the combined SNI and SNA notions, considers composable security against a combined adversary.

2.3   The Tile Model

The tile probe-and-fault model, as introduced by Reparaz *et al.* [23], captures implementations which are segmented into several areas called tiles. This tile model is linked to Multi-Party Computation (MPC) where each tile would represent a party. A tile is defined as follows.

Definition 4 (Tile). *A tile is a set of hardware resources (wiring, logic, and potential RNGs) dividing the platform where the tiles are interconnected by wires.*

The redefinition of the circuit model then captures how to represent algorithms in a tiled construction.

Definition 5 (Tiled Circuit). *A tiled circuit is a directed acyclic graph where each node is a resource with a tag indicating which tile it belongs to and which clock cycles activate it.*

The tiled methodology also considers a passive adversary as one capable of observing segments of the tiled circuit.

Definition 6 (Transient Tile Probe). *A transient tile probe observes all resources of a tile which were used for computation during a single clock cycle.*

A transient tile fault on the other hand allows the adversary to fault all computation in a tile.

Definition 7 (Transient Tile Fault). *A tile fault faults (bit-flip or stuck-at) all resources of a tile during a single clock cycle.*

Finally, (d, k)-order combined security considers the circuits correctness and privacy when up to d tiles are corrupted, at most k of which being faulted.

Stand-alone Security. Composable security for the tiled methodology follows standard definitions from the field of multi-party computation. More specifically, in this work it is sufficient to consider stand-alone security with abort in the static model. Since sequential operations represent different samples on a power trace, this security model is sufficient.[2] It is formally shown by Canetti [7] that proving security under the stand-alone definitions for secure multi-party computation suffices for obtaining security under sequential general composition. In the extended version an overview of a proof of stand-alone security is given in case of either passive or combined corruptions [11].

3   The Tile Probing Model Against Advanced Probing Attacks

This section considers known physical effects which affect the probing security of an implementation and invalidate the separate wire leakage assumption. These effects were already discussed considering the circuit model in the work by Faust *et al.* [15]. However, this section adopts their arguments and discusses the physical effects in the tile probing model instead. In short, the tile model efficiently captures these extensions and the stand-alone security model gives composable security even when faced with the discussed physical effects.

3.1   Glitches

Glitches in the platform can cause one wire to contain information which is different from what is described in the algorithm. As a result, glitches can cause a wire to release unwanted information to the adversary and to reduce the order of probing security.

When requiring that the wires interconnecting the tiles are separated by registers, placed in the outgoing tile, glitches are prevented to propagate information from one tile to another. Because of this separation, and since a transient tile

---

[2] A connection between the security of parallel operations and the probing security of sequential operations is discussed in the work by Barthe *et al.* [2].

probe already views the effect of all possible glitches inside a tile, stand-alone security is sufficient to prove composability of tiled operations even in the presence of glitches.

3.2 Transitions

The power consumption of a device based on CMOS technology is correlated to the number of bit flips in the computation. Due to this effect, an attacker can observe the transition from old to new values in memory cells.

To capture transition effects one can adapt a tile probe to observe a tile's resources for two cycles assuming that the tile's state is refreshed each cycle. However, the more natural solution is found by extending the probe to see all computations made over the entire run of the protocol. To that end, the following extended tile probe is defined.

Definition 8 (Permanent Tile Probe). *A permanent tile probe observes all resources of a tile during the entire run of the protocol.*

As stand-alone security has already been proven to provide composable security in the MPC setting where the adversary views the state of a party throughout the entire operation, this model is sufficient for composable security of tiled operations even in presence of transition leakage.

3.3 Coupling Effects

Coupling effect cause adjacent wires to have dependent leakage which allows the attacker to view leakage from bundles of wires.

In the tile model, all resources from the same tile are required to be bundled together such that the tiles form a connected set of resources. By assuming that different tiles exhibit separate leakage (as was done by Reparaz *et al.* [23]), coupling effects do not carry information from one tile to another and making a tile probe capture coupling effects. Thus, the coupling security of a circuit is reduced to the assumption that the tiles leak independently. Additionally, the stand-alone model is again sufficient for composable security.

4   Passive Tiled Methodology

This section discusses the transformation of the ISW methodology from Ishai *et al.* into a tiled structure which is proven secure in the stand-alone model. The reader is referred to the work by Ishai *et al.* [19] for the original methodology, the DOM methodology by Groß *et al.* [17] for a hardware variant, and the work by Faust *et al.* [15] for a glitch secure version. This work's adaptation solely induces an overhead in the used randomness compared to the original model. This increase is needed as the $(d + 1)$-shared variant of the ISW method is not stand-alone secure and vulnerable against a permanent tile probing adversary.

The tiled methodology makes use of $(d + 1)^2$ tiles consisting of $d + 1$ main tiles T_i for $i \in [d + 1]$ and $d(d + 1)$ auxiliary tiles denoted by $T_{i,j}$ for $i, j \in [d + 1]$ and $i \neq j$. These $d + 1$ main tiles are equipped with RNGs.[3] We only consider the multiplication operation.

The shared multiplication is depicted for $d = 1$ in Fig. 1. The operation starts with the main tiles T_i holding the ith share of the variables a and b. These variables are sent to the auxiliary tiles $T_{i,j}$ which calculate the cross products giving a share $a_i b_j$. The cross products are then refreshed with $d(d + 1)$ extra random values generated by the RNGs of the main tiles. After refreshing the masks on the cross products, the auxiliary tiles send their cross products back to the main tiles. In the extended version we give the pseudo-code for higher-orders and prove its stand-alone security [11].

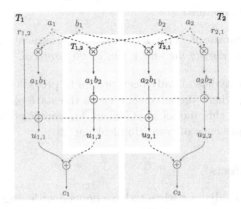

Fig. 1. The passive secure tiled multiplier with $d = 1$, where dashed lines denote values taken from registers.

This multiplication, and the other basic operations, provide d^{th}-order passive security in the stand-alone model. As a result, the methodology is secure in case of transition leakage. In order to additionally secure against glitches, registers are required to be placed on the wires interconnecting the tiles. To secure against coupling, the resource placement should also be enforced by the designer and the resources belonging to the same tile should be grouped together.

5   Extending the Wire and Tile Fault Models

This section discusses extensions of the wire fault adversary such that the model is closer to realistic fault effects. Additionally, the composable security for the circuit model using non-accumulation is discussed. Finally, this section shows that the tile model easily captures these advanced fault attacks and that the stand-alone security model allows for composable security.

---

[3] The $d + 1$ RNGs can be replaced by a dth-order tiled secure RNG if this is available.

5.1 Area Faults

Typically laser or EM pulses are capable of affecting entire areas in an implementation instead of a single wire. For this fault to be useful for a cryptographic attack, this area is assumed to be limited.

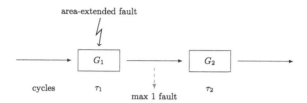

Fig. 2. The effect of an area-extended fault on two sequential gadgets G_1, G_2 where both gadgets are 1-SNA considering area-extended faults. The first gadget G_1 runs the first τ_1 cycles followed by τ_2 cycles of gadget G_2. At most 1 output of G_1 can be faulted.

Wire Fault Model. To protect against area-wide faults, one considers a topological circuit where each pair of wires has the label of their distance and whether they are coupled or not. Area-extended faults are defined as faults which affect all wires within a certain distance of each other.

Definition 9 (Area-Extended Fault). *For any set of adjacent wires $W = (w_1, ..., w_k)$, area-extended faults can be modelled with c-extended wire faults so that faulting one wire w_i allows the adversary to fault c wires adjacent to w_i.*

The non-accumulation definitions can be adapted to consider area-extended faults as opposed to normal wire faults. Using this extension, noting that area faults affect only parallel running gadgets, k-SNA security is sufficient for composable security against k area-extended faults. A visual representation is given in Fig. 2.

Tile Fault Model. Considering the tile model, by requiring that all resources belonging to the same tile are bundled together and assuming that an area-extended fault only affects one tile (which was also assumed in the work by Reparaz *et al.* [23]), area-extended faults are modelled by tile faults. This reduces the area fault security for a complex circuit to the assumption that the fault targets one tile. As a result, the stand-alone model with combined corruptions is sufficient for composable security considering area-extended faults.

5.2 Permanent Faults

Consider fault injections which target specific resources in the platform and fault them throughout the entire operation (think of faulting the output of an RNG to zero due to a dedicated laser).

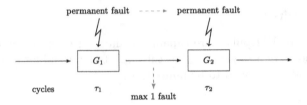

Fig. 3. The effect of a permanent wire fault on two sequential gadgets G_1, G_2 where both gadgets are 1-SNA considering permanent wire faults. The first gadget G_1 runs the first τ_1 cycles followed by τ_2 cycles of gadget G_2. In case G_1 and G_2 share the same faulted resource, it is possible for G_2 to receive a faulted input while also being affected by the permanent fault.

Wire Fault Model. Permanent wire faults are defined as those which target a certain hardware resource faulting it for the entire operation. Circuits are now viewed with cycles to model that resources are used more than once in the computation.

Definition 10 (Permanent Wire Fault). *For any wire w, faults on all values passing through w can be modelled with r-extended faults so that faulting one wire allows the adversary to fault all r values passing through that wire.*

Consider the extension of the non-accumulation model considering permanent wire faults. In this case, however, an overhead on the security is required meaning that each gadget is required to be $2k$-SNA to secure against k permanent wire faults. Requiring that each gadget is $2k$-SNA is sufficient since each gadget gives back at most k faulty shares and each gadget is faulted at most k times. A visual representation is given in Fig. 3.

Tile Fault Model. To model adversaries controlling resources for a longer period in a tiled structure, tile faults are considered as those which affect a tile during the entire operation. Thus, analogous to the definition of a permanent tile probe, we define a permanent tile fault.

Definition 11 (Permanent Tile Fault). *A permanent tile fault faults all resources of a tile during the entire run of the protocol.*

It is clear that a permanent tile fault is stronger than a permanent wire fault as the tile fault affects more than one resource in the circuit. Due to the stand-alone model capturing the security in MPC protocols where adversaries corrupt a party for the entire duration of the computation, this model is sufficient for composable security considering the permanent faults.

6   Combined Tiled Methodology

This section details a combined secure transformation of the ISW methodology into a tiled structure. Security with abort is considered where each tile keeps a copy of the abort flag. The used sharing is a duplicated Boolean sharing where each value is shared in $d+1$ masks and each mask is duplicated $k+1$ times. This countermeasure protects against a combined adversary which corrupts up to d tiles where up to k of them are faulted. There are a total of $(k+1)(d+1)^2$ tiles where $(k+1)(d+1)$ are main tiles T_i^t and $(k+1)d(d+1)$ are auxiliary tiles $T_{i,j}^t$. The tiles T_i^1 have RNGs, and $T_{i,j}^t$ hold abort states such that when $T_{i,j}^t$ aborts the other tiles halt as well. We only consider the multiplication operation.

The multiplication operation is the combined secure variant of the method given in Sect. 4. A depiction of the multiplication for $d, k = 1$ is given in Fig. 4. The multiplication operates by sending all each duplicate share from the main tiles T_i^t to the auxiliary tiles $T_{i,j}^t$ and $T_{j,i}^t$. These auxiliary tiles then perform an error check on the received duplicates. Randomness is then sampled in the main tiles and sent to the auxiliary tiles to refresh the cross products. In case no errors are found, the auxiliary tiles $T_{i,j}^t$ send their cross product back to the main tiles. Last, the main tiles add the received cross products to obtain a share of the multiplication. The pseudo-code for higher-orders and a proof of stand-alone security considering combined corruptions is given in the extended version [11].

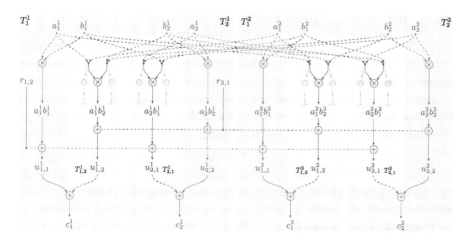

Fig. 4. The combined secure tiled multiplier over $\mathbb{F}_{2^m}$ with $d = 1$ and $k = 1$, where dashed lines denote values taken from registers. The auxiliary tiles $T_{i,j}^t$ receive all duplicate shares a_i^ℓ and b_j^ℓ for $\ell \in \{1, 2\}$ and check their integrity.

This methodology is proven to be stand-alone secure considering combined corruptions. By requiring registers to be present on the wires connecting the tiles and enforcing the placement of the tiles, the methodology provides security in face of transitions, glitches, and coupling effects. Additionally, the methodology also captures security against area-extended and permanent faults including the effects of combined passive and active attacks, and statistical ineffective faults as introduced by Dobraunig et al. [13].

7   A Note on the ε-Faulting Adversary

The authors of CAPA [23] introduce two types of adversaries: the tile probe-and-fault adversary and the ε-faulting adversary. The latter is defined as follows: "We consider an ε-faulting adversary which is able to insert a random-value fault in any variable belonging to any party. The ε-faulting adversary may inject the random-value fault according to some distribution (for example, flip each bit with certain probability), but he cannot set all intermediates to a chosen fixed value.". The attentive reader observes this adversary is not discussed in this work. The reason is that the ε-faulting adversary's definition can lead to various interpretations. In addition, the corresponding details from the protection scheme are vaguely described which leads to a possible contest of CAPA's security bound. To recall, CAPA claims that an ε-faulting adversary can break its scheme with probability $|\mathbb{F}|^{-m}$, where m is the number of used tags.

Since the adversary may inject random-value faults in any variable belonging to any party, consider an adversary which targets $d + 2$ bits in the scheme. The distribution of the fault is taken as a uniform bit-flip, i.e., there is a 50% probability of the fault leaving the bit unaltered otherwise it is flipped. The attack works as follows: first the adversary targets a bit in a variable of its choosing. With high probability this fault will cause the $d + 1$ abort flags to be raised. With the remaining $d + 1$ bit-flips the adversary flips these abort flags. This results in the fault to remain undetected with high probability. The total success probability of this attack is $(1 - \mathbb{F}^{-m}) \cdot (1/2)^{d+2}$ which, in case m or $|\mathbb{F}|$ is large, is higher than $|\mathbb{F}|^{-m}$.

Another example is to attack the constants which are duplicated over the different tiles. The ε-faulting adversary targets, for example, the first bit of each duplicated constant. The success probability of this attack is 2^{-d-1}, which can be far higher than $|\mathbb{F}|^{-m}$.

The problem we highlight here stems from the vaguely defined ε-faulting adversary, namely whether it relates to the ability of the attacker to choose which bits to fault, or to the way it modifies the values, or to both.

8   Efficiency Measures

This section provides efficiency measures of the introduced countermeasures. The efficiency of the proposed secure multiplications is measured in terms of the number of elementary operations, namely additions and multiplications. Additionally, the number of random elements is counted. For simplicity, the cost of the equality operator "Eq" is overestimated to $3(n-1)$ field additions, where the operator is given n arguments. The shared multipliers are then compared with the countermeasure by Reparaz et al. [23] (CAPA). The results are depicted in Table 1. To get a better view of these numbers, in Table 2, the comparison is made using practical parameters. Following the examples given in CAPA, $(1, 1)$ and $(2, 2)$-order combined protection is considered. We observe that this work's combined secure multiplication requires significantly fewer elementary operations and randomness.

Table 1. Comparison of the multiplication gadget from CAPA (both offline and online phase) and this work's multipliers in the number of field additions, multiplications, and number of random elements. Denoting d the passive protection order, k the active protection order and m the number of tags for CAPA.

Alg.	×	+	Rand
Sect. 4 (pass. sec.)	$(d+1)^2$	$3d(d+1)$	$d(d+1)$
Sect. 6 (comb. sec.)	$(k+1)(d+1)^2$	$9(k+1)d(d+1)$	$d(d+1)$
CAPA	$(d+1)((6m+2)(d+1)+5m+3)$	$(d+1)(14dm+6d+13m+6)$	$(d+1)(d(1+3m)+4)$

Table 2. Comparison of CAPA and this work's multipliers for practical parameters. The scheme of CAPA has a $|\mathbb{F}|^{-m}$ probability of a fault breaking its security, while this work's multiplier always guarantees security.

Alg.	$d,k,m=1$			$d,k,m=2$		
	×	+	Rand.	×	+	Rand.
Sect. 6	8	36	2	27	162	6
CAPA	48	78	16	165	300	54

The implementation of this work's tiled methodology would make for interesting future work, both for its security evaluation as performance measurements.

9   Conclusion

We extended the wire fault model considering faults which affect entire areas of the implementation and faults which target specific resources. We connected the extended probe-and-fault models with the tile model showing that the latter model envelops our extensions. Moreover, while the stand-alone security model achieves protection with the minimal number of shares, the non-interference and non-accumulation models will require an overhead.

This transition from a regular circuit to a tiled circuit, first, allows for the capture of temporal attacks which include passive attacks such as transition leakages, and active attacks such as permanent faults. Second, by bundling all resources from the same tile, the designer can better defend implementations against topological effects such as coupling effects or area-wide faults. This translation to label and bundle resources is thus a general transformation technique to protect implementations against more advanced attacks.

On the practise side, we provided tiled variants of the ISW countermeasure and showed that our tiled multiplication improves over the CAPA multiplication. Developing more efficient algorithms secure against advanced probe-and-fault attacks would develop interesting future work.

Acknowledgements. We thank François-Xavier Standaert and Gaëtan Cassiers for the interesting discussions. Siemen Dhooghe is supported by a PhD Fellowship from the Research Foundation – Flanders (FWO). Svetla Nikova was partially supported by the Bulgarian National Science Fund, Contract No. 12/8

References

1. Barthe, G., et al.: Strong non-interference and type-directed higher-order masking. In: Weippl, E.R., Katzenbeisser, S., Kruegel, C., Myers, A.C., Halevi, S. (eds.) ACM CCS 2016, pp. 116–129. ACM Press, October 2016. https://doi.org/10.1145/2976749.2978427

2. Barthe, G., Dupressoir, F., Faust, S., Grégoire, B., Standaert, F.-X., Strub, P.-Y.: Parallel implementations of masking schemes and the bounded moment leakage model. In: Coron, J.-S., Nielsen, J.B. (eds.) EUROCRYPT 2017. LNCS, vol. 10210, pp. 535–566. Springer, Cham (2017). https://doi.org/10.1007/978-3-319-56620-7_19

3. Belaïd, S., Benhamouda, F., Passelègue, A., Prouff, E., Thillard, A., Vergnaud, D.: Randomness complexity of private circuits for multiplication. In: Fischlin, M., Coron, J.-S. (eds.) EUROCRYPT 2016. LNCS, vol. 9666, pp. 616–648. Springer, Heidelberg (2016). https://doi.org/10.1007/978-3-662-49896-5_22

4. Belaïd, S., Benhamouda, F., Passelègue, A., Prouff, E., Thillard, A., Vergnaud, D.: Private multiplication over finite fields. In: Katz, J., Shacham, H. (eds.) CRYPTO 2017. LNCS, vol. 10403, pp. 397–426. Springer, Cham (2017). https://doi.org/10.1007/978-3-319-63697-9_14

5. Belaïd, S., Goudarzi, D., Rivain, M.: Tight private circuits: achieving probing security with the least refreshing. In: Peyrin, T., Galbraith, S. (eds.) ASIACRYPT 2018. LNCS, vol. 11273, pp. 343–372. Springer, Cham (2018). https://doi.org/10.1007/978-3-030-03329-3_12

6. Biham, E., Shamir, A.: Differential fault analysis of secret key cryptosystems. In: Kaliski, B.S. (ed.) CRYPTO 1997. LNCS, vol. 1294, pp. 513–525. Springer, Heidelberg (1997). https://doi.org/10.1007/BFb0052259

7. Canetti, R.: Security and composition of multiparty cryptographic protocols. J. Cryptology **13**(1), 143–202 (2000). https://doi.org/10.1007/s001459910006

8. Cassiers, G., Standaert, F.X.: Towards globally optimized masking: from low randomness to low noise rate. IACR TCHES **2019**(2), 162–198 (2019). https://doi.org/10.13154/tches.v2019.i2.162-198, https://tches.iacr.org/index.php/TCHES/article/view/7389

9. Clavier, C.: Secret external encodings do not prevent transient fault analysis. In: Paillier, P., Verbauwhede, I. (eds.) CHES 2007. LNCS, vol. 4727, pp. 181–194. Springer, Heidelberg (2007). https://doi.org/10.1007/978-3-540-74735-2_13

10. Coron, J.-S.: High-order conversion from boolean to arithmetic masking. In: Fischer, W., Homma, N. (eds.) CHES 2017. LNCS, vol. 10529, pp. 93–114. Springer, Cham (2017). https://doi.org/10.1007/978-3-319-66787-4_5

11. Dhooghe, S., Nikova, S.: Let's tessellate: tiling for security against advanced probe and fault adversaries. IACR Cryptol. ePrint Arch. 2020, 1146 (2020). https://eprint.iacr.org/2020/1146

12. Dhooghe, S., Nikova, S.: My gadget just cares for me - how NINA can prove security against combined attacks. In: Jarecki, S. (ed.) CT-RSA 2020. LNCS, vol. 12006, pp. 35–55. Springer, Cham (2020). https://doi.org/10.1007/978-3-030-40186-3_3

13. Dobraunig, C., Eichlseder, M., Korak, T., Mangard, S., Mendel, F., Primas, R.: SIFA: exploiting ineffective fault inductions on symmetric cryptography. IACR TCHES **2018**(3), 547–572 (2018). https://doi.org/10.13154/tches.v2018.i3.547-572, https://tches.iacr.org/index.php/TCHES/article/view/7286

14. Duc, A., Dziembowski, S., Faust, S.: Unifying leakage models: from probing attacks to noisy leakage. In: Nguyen, P.Q., Oswald, E. (eds.) EUROCRYPT 2014. LNCS, vol. 8441, pp. 423–440. Springer, Heidelberg (2014). https://doi.org/10.1007/978-3-642-55220-5_24

15. Faust, S., Grosso, V., Pozo, S.M.D., Paglialonga, C., Standaert, F.X.: Composable masking schemes in the presence of physical defaults & the robust probing model. IACR TCHES **2018**(3), 89–120 (2018). https://doi.org/10.13154/tches.v2018.i3.89-120, https://tches.iacr.org/index.php/TCHES/article/view/7270

16. Fuhr, T., Jaulmes, É., Lomné, V., Thillard, A.: Fault attacks on AES with faulty ciphertexts only. In: 2013 Workshop on Fault Diagnosis and Tolerance in Cryptography, Los Alamitos, CA, USA, August 20, 2013, pp. 108–118 (2013). https://doi.org/10.1109/FDTC.2013.18, https://doi.org/10.1109/FDTC.2013.18

17. Groß, H., Mangard, S., Korak, T.: Domain-oriented masking: Compact masked hardware implementations with arbitrary protection order. In: Proceedings of the ACM Workshop on Theory of Implementation Security, TIS@CCS 2016 Vienna, Austria, October 2016, p. 3 (2016). https://doi.org/10.1145/2996366.2996426

18. Ishai, Y., Prabhakaran, M., Sahai, A., Wagner, D.: Private circuits II: keeping secrets in tamperable circuits. In: Vaudenay, S. (ed.) EUROCRYPT 2006. LNCS, vol. 4004, pp. 308–327. Springer, Heidelberg (2006). https://doi.org/10.1007/11761679_19

19. Ishai, Y., Sahai, A., Wagner, D.: Private circuits: securing hardware against probing attacks. In: Boneh, D. (ed.) CRYPTO 2003. LNCS, vol. 2729, pp. 463–481. Springer, Heidelberg (2003). https://doi.org/10.1007/978-3-540-45146-4_27

20. Aumann, Y., Rabin, M.O.: Information theoretically secure communication in the limited storage space model. In: Wiener, M. (ed.) CRYPTO 1999. LNCS, vol. 1666, pp. 65–79. Springer, Heidelberg (1999). https://doi.org/10.1007/3-540-48405-1_5

21. Moos, T., Moradi, A., Schneider, T., Standaert, F.X.: Glitch-resistant masking revisited. IACR TCHES **2019**(2), 256–292 (2019). https://doi.org/10.13154/tches.v2019.i2.256-292, https://tches.iacr.org/index.php/TCHES/article/view/7392

22. Prouff, E., Roche, T.: Higher-order glitches free implementation of the AES using secure multi-party computation protocols. In: Preneel, B., Takagi, T. (eds.) CHES 2011. LNCS, vol. 6917, pp. 63–78. Springer, Heidelberg (2011). https://doi.org/10.1007/978-3-642-23951-9_5

23. Reparaz, O., De Meyer, L., Bilgin, B., Arribas, V., Nikova, S., Nikov, V., Smart, N.: CAPA: the spirit of beaver against physical attacks. In: Shacham, H., Boldyreva, A. (eds.) CRYPTO 2018. LNCS, vol. 10991, pp. 121–151. Springer, Cham (2018). https://doi.org/10.1007/978-3-319-96884-1_5

24. Ueno, R., Homma, N., Sugawara, Y., Nogami, Y., Aoki, T.: Highly efficient $GF(2^8)$ inversion circuit based on redundant GF arithmetic and its application to AES design. In: Güneysu, T., Handschuh, H. (eds.) CHES 2015. LNCS, vol. 9293, pp. 63–80. Springer, Heidelberg (2015). https://doi.org/10.1007/978-3-662-48324-4_4

Author Index

Printed in the United States
By Bookmasters